MW01027939

The Dream Is Freedom

The Dream Is Freedom

Pauli Murray and
American Democratic Faith

SARAH AZARANSKY

OXFORD
UNIVERSITY PRESS

OXFORD
UNIVERSITY PRESS

Oxford University Press, Inc., publishes works that further
Oxford University's objective of excellence
in research, scholarship, and education.

Oxford   New York
Auckland   Cape Town   Dar es Salaam   Hong Kong   Karachi
Kuala Lumpur   Madrid   Melbourne   Mexico City   Nairobi
New Delhi   Shanghai   Taipei   Toronto

With offices in
Argentina   Austria   Brazil   Chile   Czech Republic   France   Greece
Guatemala   Hungary   Italy   Japan   Poland   Portugal   Singapore
South Korea   Switzerland   Thailand   Turkey   Ukraine   Vietnam

Copyright © 2011 by Oxford University Press, Inc.

Published by Oxford University Press, Inc.
198 Madison Avenue, New York, New York 10016

www.oup.com

Oxford is a registered trademark of Oxford University Press

All rights reserved. No part of this publication may be reproduced,
stored in a retrieval system, or transmitted, in any form or by any means,
electronic, mechanical, photocopying, recording, or otherwise,
without the prior permission of Oxford University Press.

Library of Congress Cataloging-in-Publication Data
Azaransky, Sarah.
The dream is freedom : Pauli Murray and American democratic faith/
Sarah Azaransky.
p.   cm.
Includes bibliographical references and index.
ISBN 978-0-19-974481-7
1. Murray, Pauli, 1910–1985.   2. Murray, Pauli, 1910–1985—Political and social views.   3. Murray
Pauli, 1910–1985—Religion.   4. Democracy—Religious aspects—Christianity—History—20th
century.   5. African American intellectuals—Biography.   6. African American poets—Biography.
7. African American lawyers—Biography.   8. African American women civil rights workers—
Biography.   9. African American feminists—Biography.   10. Episcopal Church—Clergy—
Biography.   I. Title.
E185.97.M95A93 2011
973'.0496073092—dc22
[B] 2010023213

1 3 5 7 9 8 6 4 2
Printed in the United States of America
on acid-free paper

ACKNOWLEDGMENTS

I am indebted to many people for their support and guidance as I worked on this project, but I owe the topic to Heather Booth and Taylor Branch. I interpret the serendipity of Heather and Taylor suggesting that I write about Pauli Murray as a kind of blessing. I hope that what follows adequately expresses my gratitude.

The project received early support in the form of dissertation fellowships from the University of Virginia Graduate School of Arts and Sciences and from UVA's Department of Religious Studies. A dissertation grant from the Arthur and Elizabeth Schlesinger Library on the History of Women in America provided funding for travel and research.

Carmen Mitchell, Sarah Hutcheons, and Lynda Leahy at the Schlesinger Library and JoEllen ElBashir, the curator of manuscripts at the Moorland Spingarn Research Center at Howard University, provided assistance in navigating their respective archives. Thanks also to archivists at the Southern Oral History Program at the University of North Carolina, Chapel Hill.

One of the joys of writing this book has been discovering how Murray's work is meaningful to so many different people. Thank you to everyone who has shared stories and reflections about Murray, particularly Patricia Hill Collins, Barbara Lau, and the Reverend Dr. Victoria R. Sirota.

Camaraderie of close friends has buoyed me between bouts of writing. A special thanks to Jenny McBride for her unfailing support and good-humor during graduate school and beyond and to Julie Falk for years of friendship, and all its attendant support, encouragement, and advice.

Writing about Murray has offered extraordinary opportunities to engage with a number of different disciplines and methodologies and challenged critical genealogies I had received. Thank you to fellow graduate students in the department of Religious Studies at the University of Virginia and to my students at the University of San Diego, who have helped me to muddle through what it means to be a Sarah among twenty-first century descendents of Ishmael and Isaac. Also essential to the development of this project was the guidance and encouragement of Stephen White and Paul Jones. Corey Walker read the first pages I wrote about Pauli Murray helped me to identify her as democratic thinker. I greatly appreciate the time and energy that Chuck Mathewes invested by reading multiple drafts and always commenting in critical, insightful, and encouraging ways. Thanks to Charles Marsh for his careful readings and for his continued interest in and support of the larger intellectual project of which this work is a part.

I am also grateful for the collegiality of the faculty of the Department of Theology and Religious Studies at the University of San Diego, particularly of writing group members Susie Babka, Jeannie Constantinou, Mary Doak, Emily Reimer-Barry, Lekshe Tsomo, and Karen Teel. Karen deserves special thanks. This book's completion is due in no small part to the promise of earning checkmarks from Karen at our Friday writing meetings. Karen's encouragement kept me working toward smaller deadlines and focused on finishing the book. My editor, Cynthia Read, doled out advice and good cheer at crucial junctures. The anonymous readers at Oxford University Press offered important challenges that have strengthened the book's arguments.

Most importantly I want to thank my husband, Kevin Keenan, and our children, Finn Keenan and Lucy Azaransky. Finn may never understand how much he has enlivened my work, but I hope that the book reflects some sense of the curiosity and wonderment he models for me daily. Lucy arrival in the book's final stages was a joyful distraction and incentive to finish the project. Kevin's unfailing support and excitement about Pauli Murray has energized me and, at crucial moments, kept me going. But I am most grateful for Kevin's inspiring example of how to do what it is I have been writing about. Thank you, Kevin, for showing me every day how to live democratic convictions with integrity and hope.

Permission for quotations from *Dark Testament and Other Poems, Song in a Weary Throat: An American Pilgrimage,* and from Pauli Murray's papers was granted by the literary estate of Pauli Murray. Permission for access and use of Pauli Murray's papers was given by The Arthur and Elizabeth Schlesinger Library on The History of Women in America at Harvard University.

CONTENTS

The Dream Is Freedom

Introduction

On August 28, 1963, Pauli Murray—author, activist, lawyer, and later Episcopal priest—was among the hundreds of thousands of Americans who joined the March on Washington. Murray, a seventh-generation Episcopalian, marched with a delegation from her New York City church. Then, also a lawyer and a committed civil libertarian, she reversed course to meet up with her local American Civil Liberties Union (ACLU) affiliate and marched under its banner. In a later interview, she called the March "the nearest thing I've seen to judgment day. You know our romantic notions about judgment day? Well, these were great throngs, you know, it was like the great gettin' up morning."[1]

That Murray understood her libertarian and religious commitments as interrelated ways to participate among the great throngs offers a telling glimpse into Murray's political and religious practice and thought. Throughout her careers as a writer, lawyer, professor, and trailblazing civil rights and feminist activist, Pauli Murray wrote passionately about American democratic faith and the possibilities of racial reconciliation. She insisted on the interrelation of all human rights, even as many civil rights and feminist leaders of the time ignored her. When, late in her life, she became an Episcopal priest, her sermons focused on the particularity of African American women's experiences while proclaiming a universal message of salvation.

The Dream Is Freedom traces the development of Murray's democratic and theological criticism from the 1930s to the 1980s. Ranging from Murray's theologically rich democratic criticism of the 1930s to her democratically inflected sermons of the 1980s, this study proclaims Murray to be a significant twentieth-century African American intellectual who grounded her calls for democratic transformation in Christian concepts of reconciliation and of the coming kingdom. While investigating her remarkable career and contributions to major political, social, and theological debates of her time, this book demonstrates how Murray articulated a theologically grounded democratic criticism that employs theological norms to interrogate democratic practices and democratic norms to interrogate religious practices. In so doing, the book reveals Murray as not only an important figure in civil rights and women's liberation but also as an innovative democratic theorist, who addressed how democracy can recognize difference, signaled the role of history and memory in shaping democratic character, and modeled a democratic disposition of critical hope. The first detailed account of Pauli Murray's democratic thought, *The Dream Is Freedom* contributes to a small, but growing collection of scholarship about Murray.[2]

Pauli Murray (1910–1985) was witness to and actively participated in the great social movements of the twentieth century. An activist on the vanguard of the Black Freedom movement who organized sits-ins and integrated an inter-state bus in the 1940s, she became a lawyer who was instrumental in expanding equal protection provisions for African American women. Through the 1940s and 1950s, her professional and personal relationships included major figures in the ongoing struggle for civil rights for all Americans, including Eleanor Roosevelt and Thurgood Marshall. As an author, she published political essays, poetry, short stories, and a family memoir that offered prophetic hope in the face of brutal history. In the 1960s, she moved to the newly independent Ghana to teach con-stitutional law and, upon her return to the US, earned a doctorate in law at Yale University, writing a genre-bending dissertation about the history of American race relations and later becoming a professor in one of the nation's first American Studies programs. In the 1970s, Murray entered seminary and called for African American women to develop a critique of emerging black and feminist theol-ogies. Becoming one of the first women and the first African American woman Episcopal priest in 1977, she developed a vision of the kingdom of God as a place where people will be reconciled in their differences.

A straightforward, if extraordinary, catalog of Murray's professional achieve-ments can overlook fascinating aspects of her personality. In the 1930s, she was enthralled by emerging scholarship of the time about sexuality and hoped that it would provide categories to describe her own experiences as a male-identified woman who loved other women. She experimented with cross-dressing and petitioned doctors to perform exploratory surgery to find latent male organs that she was convinced she had. People who knew Murray in a professional capacity often described her as prickly, stubborn, and even combative, but her private journals and letters depict a playful, witty woman who called her annual letter to friends and family the "Pixie Encyclicals."

The Dream Is Freedom examines not only Murray's substantial body of pub-lished writings but also a significant archival collection of her personal letters, journals, and unpublished manuscripts. Throughout her published and unpub-lished writings, I discerned three themes repeatedly at work—identity, history, and the distance between the promise and fulfillment of American democracy, what I call a democratic eschatology. These themes form a kind of nervous system for Murray's democratic thought. Throughout fifty years of writing, they are the categories to which Murray returned again and again to make sense of who we are (identity), our becoming who we are (history), and to look ahead to who we might become (democratic eschatology).

The chapters that follow trace the development of these three central themes that together demonstrate her prescient insistence on the interrelation of all human rights. Long before the era of identity politics and postmodern criticism, Murray consistently characterized identity as by its very nature unstable and complex, even as she employed it strategically in her politics and writing. The book traces Murray's lifelong engagement with questions about the ways in which multiple dimensions of identity intersect, from her earliest writing about sexual and racial identity to a theological account of reconciliation that posits identity differences as integral to human wholeness. History is another critical category, which Murray develops in her family memoir, *Proud Shoes*, in which she presents her family's experiences as exemplary of the Ishmaelite character of America's past and present, and in her dissertation where she argues that before it can live up to its founding promises, America must forge and embrace a new kind of American history that recognizes its multiple origins. What I term Murray's democratic eschatology is a third central theme that pervades her work. From her days as a young activist and law student trying to sort through the contradictions between the democratic claims of America's foreign policy and the domestic realities of African Americans to her later period as a veteran of the feminist and Black Freedom movements who sees the distance the nation must still travel, Murray repeatedly described American democracy using an eschatological register of promise and fulfillment. Whereas promises of the nation's founding documents—of "we the people" and "liberty and justice for all"—have yet to be fulfilled, Murray counsels democratic faith and emphasizes strategic coalition building to make more justice available for more Americans.

The book addresses Murray's work, writing, and activism against a biographical background. Murray's life story is critical to understanding her democratic thought because she often referred to her identity and her family's history as paradigmatic of the nation. She grounded her democratic thought, therefore, in the story of an African American woman who was the granddaughter of enslaved people and of slave owners. Though proceeding chronologically through the decades of Murray's professional life, this book is not a biography. Rather it has the specific aim of demonstrating how Pauli Murray's political and religious writing outline a vision of American democracy a partially present and yet to come.

Chapter 1 examines Murray's coming of age politically in Harlem in the 1930s and 1940s. By examining her poetry, short stories, and political essays, the chapter traces Murray's emerging concerns around race, gender, and sexuality and the historic disfranchisement of black Americans. It shows how the themes of identity, history, and democratic eschatology emerge in Murray's early writing.

Chapter 2 covers Murray's career and writings as a young lawyer in the late 1940s through the 1950s. It explores Murray's development of a new kind of American history and an account of black American identity as integral to her democratic thought. In response to McCarthyist insinuations that she is disloyal, she published a family memoir that portrayed her multiracial family and the history of violence against which it was formed. In the late 1950s, Murray left the United States for Ghana in search for a sense of home, but ultimately concluded that her racial identity and history made her irrevocably American.

Chapter 3 describes landmark legal arguments Murray made about equal protection in the 1960s. Using the category of "Jane Crow," Murray demanded that the law be responsive to the synthetic nature of identity. In so doing, Murray placed African American women's experiences at the center of democratic consideration. Despite her attempts to build coalitions, she found herself increasingly at odds with leaders of the feminist and Black Freedom movements.

Chapter 4 discusses her transition in the 1970s and 1980s from a career focused on the law to one devoted primarily to what she called "moral and spiritual problems." It offers a systematic reading of the themes of salvation, suffering, and the coming kingdom that animated Murray's sermons and places Murray's theological program in conversation with contemporary womanist and black feminist scholars.

Chapter 5 concludes that Pauli Murray's critical attentions to identity, history, and her articulation of a democratic eschatology provide readers with resources for contemporary discussions of Christianity and American democracy. The chapter considers Murray's project in conversation with the work of Jean Bethke Elshtain and Cornel West, two contemporary theorists who aim to inform democratic theory with Christian theological imagination and commitments.

The book focuses on Murray's writing and work from the 1930s to the 1980s, but a consideration of Murray's childhood is important for contextualizing later developments. Anna Pauline Murray was born in Baltimore, Maryland, on November 20, 1910. Her mother, Agnes, had been raised by a family of teachers in North Carolina and, along with her sisters, had attended St. Augustine's College in Raleigh, the alma mater of Anna Julia Cooper, where she became a nurse. Her father, Will, was a school principal and graduate of Howard University. Members of a growing middle class, they belonged to a prominent black Episcopal church and were active in settlement house work.

Murray's home life unraveled while she was still a toddler. Murray was the fourth of six children born in quick succession. In the midst of tending to six young children, Agnes nursed her husband from the brink of death from typhoid fever. Although he survived, Will's personality was changed, and he suffered from severe mood swings and bouts of depression. The pressure of raising her children largely by herself and fearing that her husband might be violent put a great strain on Agnes. When Pauli was only 3 years old, her mother died of a massive cerebral hemorrhage. (In her autobiography, Murray noted neighborhood rumors that her mother had committed suicide.) As Will was unable to care for his six children, they were sent to live with relatives. Within three years, he was committed to a state psychiatric hospital, where he was murdered by a guard ten years later. Though Murray had only fragmentary memories of her parents, she grew up hearing about her parents' personalities and began to recognize in herself the high-spiritedness, wry sense of humor, and quick temper often ascribed to her mother. Stories about her father's relentless efforts to improve his education and excel at his profession modeled perseverance in the face of white racism that would shape her life's work.

The year before her death, Agnes had written to her sister Pauline asking her to look after young Pauline, her namesake, should anything happen to Agnes. After her mother's death, Murray was thus sent to Durham, North Carolina, to live with her mother's family. When the rest of Murray's brothers and sisters remained with her father's family in Baltimore, Murray was raised in the home of her maternal grandparents and two aunts.

While she did not often reflect on her parents' influences, one cannot help but read into her later accounts of the lonely status of being a minority within a minority, the sense of isolation that must have followed her parents' deaths. Her loneliness was no doubt compounded by the fact that she was raised, although in an indisputably loving household, as an only child among adults and at a great distance from siblings. While Murray rarely identified herself as an orphan, her early experiences of being alone and without an immediate family were partially replicated later when she did not find a home in the social movements to which she devoted her energy and vision. But growing up in her grandparents' home also provided the foundation for her democratic vision: her grandparents' multiracial ancestries not only witnessed how white violence and exploitation shaped American history, but they also persuaded Murray of the inherent multiplicity in her identity as a black American.

In Durham, Murray attended segregated schools, with crumbing walls and few books. She avoided streetcars and public institutions, like the movie theatre, so as not to have to submit to Southern apartheid. Growing up hearing about lynchings and other flagrant racial violence, Murray recalled that during her childhood, race was dangerous in more subtle manifestations as well. It was, she wrote later, "the atmosphere one breathed from day to day, the pervasive irritant, the chronic allergy, the vague apprehension which made one uncomfortable and jumpy. We knew the race problem was like a deadly snake coiled and ready to strike, and that one avoided its dangers only by never-ending watchfulness."[3]

In the midst of dangers and indignities of segregation, she grew up in a family committed to education and racial uplift. Murray's grandfather, a Civil War veteran, had been a teacher until he went blind from an injury sustained in the war. Murray inherited her grandfather's commitment to education and took to heart his precept to be trained in more than one trade in order to have skills to fall back on in hard times. Her aunts were both schoolteachers and modeled for Murray a hard-working professionalism that would shape her approach to her several careers. In this household of readers and storytellers,

Murray was often enlisted to read aloud—favorite biblical passages to her grandmother, from the morning paper to her grandfather. Her aunts encouraged her to read novels, history, and poetry and were especially proud when Murray one year won the public library's "first prize among the colored children for having read the most books."[4] Her aunts were leading members of Durham's black Episcopal congregation, in which Murray grew up. Murray's Aunt Sally married an Episcopal priest, which Murray later understood to be the nearest her aunt had been able to come to answer a vocation to the priesthood four decades before the Church would ordain women.

Although Murray's household often struggled to make ends meet, she needed to look no further than her maternal great-uncle for an example of black wealth. Her grandfather's brother was a successful brick-maker who owned an eighteen-room house in a white section of Durham. Also a founder of a local insurance agency, he was among a group of black Durham luminaries who, in the midst of Jim Crow, were carving out a degree of self-determination. In spite of growing up in a loving household and with models of professional and financial success, Murray left the South at her first opportunity. During high school, Murray had visited New York City and marveled at what she saw as an integrated public life. After graduating as the valedictorian of her class, she returned to New York to apply to college. When colleges informed her that her Durham education did not adequately prepare her to enroll in their institutions, she could not afford private tuition, and that she did not meet residency requirements for public education, Murray was not dissuaded. She moved to New York and lived with a cousin until she completed a rigorous additional year of high school to satisfy entrance and residency requirements. In the fall of 1928, Pauli Murray entered Hunter College, New York's vaunted public university for women.

1

The Crusader

The Political Education of a Young Radical (1930s and 1940s)

Pauli Murray was one of hundreds of thousands of African Americans who had left the South in search of economic, social, and political opportunities. In New York City in 1928, Murray found herself at the center of swirling social and political changes that inspired her to engage what she called the ideals of democracy and Christianity. This chapter analyzes Murray's writing and work in the 1930s and 1940s and identifies themes that will animate Murray's democratic thought for the next fifty years, notably identity, history, and democratic eschatology. She wrote publicly about her multiracial identity and privately about her sexual identity. In both cases, she struggled to negotiate the construction of her own experience at the same time that she resisted normative accounts of who she was, either as a multiracial person or as a woman who loved other women sexually. This early self-consciousness about identity will become important to Murray's later claims that a new imagination of identity can inspire greater democratic possibilities for all Americans. Her poetry of the 1940s points to history as a preoccupation in Murray's democratic thought. She demonstrated how our understanding of the American past could be transformed by positing an African slave as the protagonist of historical accounts. Democratic eschatology is a third theme that emerges in Murray's writing of the period, when she repeatedly characterized American democracy in eschatological terms, including contradiction, risk, as partially present, and yet to come.

Harlem provided Murray a diversity of political, social, and theological influences that would resonate for the next fifty years. While a student at the all women's and predominantly white Hunter College, Murray rented a room at the YWCA, a Harlem landmark that served as a community center, boarding house, and hotel. Segregation in public accommodations meant that famous and well-to-do black women, such as Mary Church Terrell, stayed alongside students and working class women.[1] The Y served as an important gathering place for young Harlem women, like Murray and friend Ella Baker. According to Baker's biographer, Barbara Ransby, the Y represented "a new model of black womanhood in this era. Untrammeled by attachments to either birth families or husbands, these women were adventuresome, educated, and ambitious."[2] Having been raised by her two aunts, whom Murray recognized as strong, capable women, she had not immediately realized it was unusual for an institution to be run by and for black women that prioritized all aspects of women's well-being. Years later, she would write, "none of these women would have called themselves feminists in the 1930s, but they were strong, independent personalities who, because of their concerted efforts to rise above limitations of race and sex and to help younger women do the same, shared a sisterhood that foreshadowed the revival of the feminist movement in the 1960s."[3]

Murray also found herself at the crossroads of Harlem's vibrant religious scene. Her room in the fourth floor of the Y overlooked the back windows of the Abyssinian Baptist Church. Murray recalled that she was "in partial attendance" at Abyssinian, because "whenever I was in my room during church services, the choir and the organ so filled the room that I had to stop whatever I was doing to listen." Murray was in fact a member of St. Philip's Episcopal Church, the first major black congregation in Harlem and an important center of social gospel preaching.[4] The Harlem Y was also a center of religious reflection, where Murray became involved in the national YMCA student movement that discussed the compatibility of Christianity and democracy. As a lifelong Episcopalian and niece of a priest, religious reasons and arguments were second-nature to Murray. In this period, Murray would shape her own theological voice—using what she called Christian ideals to diagnose American democratic practices as contradictory and corrupt, and to point a way toward justice.

In the midst of social and religious ferment, however, it was economic realities that circumscribed Murray's daily life. Murray was among the marginal workers who first felt the shock of the Depression. She had been working as a waitress to pay for school and living expenses, but after the stock market crash, tips fell off immediately, and she barely had enough money for weekly rent. By the end of her second year at Hunter, she suffered from malnutrition and dropped out of school in order to look for full-time work. Murray recalled, "with so many thousands of people unemployed in New York City alone, finding a job that would even cover bare living expenses was almost impossible. Downtown along Sixth Avenue, storefront employment offices were besieged by hundreds of men scrambling for a half-dozen jobs posted in hastily scrawled handwriting on a bulletin board out front, only to be erased seconds later." Despairing finding work in the city, Murray decided to head west. Not able to afford train or bus fare, she did what thousands of other poor Americans did to travel cheaply, she hitched freight trains. Riding the rails was a revelatory experience. She recalled, "the national toll caused by unemployment, which I glimpsed in the faces of the hordes of men and boys who haunted freight yards and lived in hobo jungles, and the struggle for survival I had experienced briefly on the road, made my own problems seem comparatively mild."[5] Murray returned to New York City and was committed to finishing school.

She graduated from Hunter in 1933 at "the worst possible time to come out of school and try to begin one's career."[6] Sixteen million people were out of work nationwide, and there were an estimated 10,000 unemployed college graduates in New York City alone. Now Murray was among them. Her ambition had brought her to New York City and motivated her to finish college in the midst of the greatest economic crisis the nation had seen, but Pauli Murray did not have a clear vision of her professional future. Economic realities and segregated workplaces demanded that Murray take whatever opportunities were available. While she did find ful-filling work during this period, notably for Lester Granger at *Opportunity Magazine* of the Urban League, she suffered recurrent bouts of malnutrition and ill health. During healthy periods when she was unemployed, Murray traveled. With compan-ions or alone, Murray took trips around the Northeast and across the country where she saw firsthand the poverty and desperation that gripped the country. But she also reported great generosity that greeted her and her friends as they traveled from town to town, often arriving in a new place with little money and no place to stay. Murray and companions spent nights in county jails and other public accom-modations and were often invited in by townspeople for whom they performed odd jobs. Murray's journals from the period sketched details of her travels.

Repeatedly on these trips, Murray posed as a young man. On one trip, a woman took Murray for a "boy scout" when Murray had offered to carry a pack-age.[7] On another, police at a coffee shop questioned Murray and a friend when they were thought to be two boys using the women's restroom; the incident was later reported in the local paper. Murray's sole-published account of a trans-gender identity came in a 1934 short story about a young boy named Pete, who hitched freight trains across the country in order to return home to take care of his ailing mother. Published in an anthology of Negro writing, "Three Thousand Miles on a Dime in Ten Days" included a photograph of the author that depicted Murray dressed as a boy in britches and newsboy cap with the caption "Pete."[8] Murray's autobiography includes a strikingly similar set of circumstances: After a cross-country trip in 1931, Murray left California to return to the East Coast to take care of her ailing aunt, who was also her adoptive mother. She traveled back across the country by hitching rides on freight trains. She wrote that she felt safer traveling when she passed as a man.[9] Her published account under-theorizes Murray's cross-dressing as solely as issue of safety. It was also a way for Murray to experiment, often playfully, with sexual and gender norms.

Murray dressed in male attire is a recurring motif in an album of photographs from the 1930s and 1940s that Murray titled "The Life and Times of an American Called Pauli Murray." In one set of pictures, Murray and a girlfriend Peggie Holmes pose in various ways that mimic traditional romantic norms. In one photo, Murray was dressed in a sailor's uniform as she cradled a woman in her arms. The photo's caption reads "An armful, Pauli and Peggie."[10] Another collection of photos is a series of portraits, for which Murray dressed up and posed as a number of different characters, including "The Dude," in which she again wore britches and a news cap; "Peter Pan," in which she wore pants and climbed a tree; and "The Crusader," in which she wore a skirt, long trench coat, and held a briefcase. The "Crusader" may have referred to the name of the magazine started by former *Amsterdam News* reporter Cyril Briggs, which advocated an independent and separate existence for black Americans, armed self-defense against lynching, and an immediate end to segregation.[11] The photos depict Murray trying out characters and postures that did not fall within heteronormative sexuality. Of the fantasies of who Murray wanted to become, it would seem that she did her best, ultimately, to become the Crusader, the briefcase-wielding, single person who, perhaps not coincidentally, comes closest to fitting sexual norms. Murray's experimentation will come to a head in the early 1940s when she was hospitalized a number of times for "nervous conditions" that she connected to her sexual interest in women and nonnormative gender presentations.

As Murray searched for categories to describe her sexual identity, she was also writing poems about racial identity. In the early 1930s, Murray socialized with Countée Cullen and Claude McKay and had poems shepherded to publication by Langston Hughes. Murray's poems appeared in the NAACP's (National Association for the Advancement of Colored People) *Crisis*, the Urban League's *Opportunity* and *Common Ground*, but they were not collected into a single volume until 1970. After a portion of Murray's "Dark Testament" was read at a memorial service for Martin Luther King Jr. in Seattle in the days after his assassination, public interest in Murray's poetry grew. The majority of the poems published in the collection *Dark Testament and Other Poems* was written between 1931 and 1945. Murray's poems examine diverse topics and employ various voices. Some are autobiographical, others reflect on the politics of the day; Murray included love poems and blithe critiques about political organizing. In one poem, she called tongues the "taproots of evil" and concluded that if people were mute, "there'd be less need for conferences/caucuses, rallies, meetings, speeches—/ The tongue dragging the body around."[12]

Two of Murray's poems of the 1930s reflect the shifting subjectivity of her racial identity. In "Color Trouble," Murray instructed,

If you dislike me just because
My face has more of sun than yours,
Then, when you see me, turn and run
But do not try to bar the sun.[13]

With a tone of self-conscious playfulness, Murray recognized that the range of color that she can display confuses others, but she refused to "bar the sun" so that she may remain lighter. While the title alluded to a racial problematic, that color means trouble, Murray dismissed the trouble as someone else's.

In "Mulatto's Dilemma," published in *Opportunity*, Murray's tone shifted:

I curse the summer sun
That burned me thus to fateful recognition.

Racial identity is premised on others' "recognition." As in "Color Trouble," in this poem, the sun—that is, the light of day—has the power to reveal who she really is. Murray lamented,

were I but paler by a single tone they would not see me tremble
they stare at me, they note the curl below my hat
They trace the darker line below my chin.

The curl below her hat and the darker line below her chin were two signals of Murray's racial identity. She trembled when people stared to make out whether she fit the racial construct of black or white. The "mulatto's dilemma" was that she fit neither. Murray continued,

If I could lay my quivering brain
Before them, they'd see a brain is but a brain
And know that brown men think and feel, are hurt
And broken even as they.

She wished

Oh for the pride
Of blackness! To stand unmasked before them, Not moved by inquisition.
    Accepted or refused—
Not crucified.[14]

Murray felt misunderstood by a white audience, nor did she identify with blackness. She equated not fitting clearly into the racial construct of black or white with the experience of brutal public execution. For Murray, to be multiracial was to suffer and be rejected. "Mulatto's Dilemma" reproduced, then, the trope of the tragic mulatto or mulatta, the assumption that a multiracial person is confused and rejected by both blacks and whites. This trope has been traced throughout American literature in the works of white- and black-identified authors. Challenging the possibility of a coherent, hegemonic racial identity that is either straightforwardly "black" or "white," the mulatto's "range of color illustrates the instability of racial boundaries."[15] While critical reception of the figure tends to dismiss it as stereotypical, Werner Sollors warns, "by ridiculing the 'conventions' of their representation in literature as 'unrealistic' we may also silently, or not so silently, reinstate the legitimacy of two categories only, black and white."[16] Even as Murray was unable to claim positive aspects of blackness, whiteness, or of an alternative multiracial identity, her poem witnesses that her own experience is not reducible to available categories of whiteness or blackness.

When she was growing up, Murray did not seem to have experienced her multiracial identity as a dilemma. Like Langston Hughes and Zora Neale Hurston, among others, had, Murray chronicled straightforwardly her multiracial ancestry. While she learned as a child that there were two kinds of people, "the race of colored people" and "the white people," she remembered family picnics with relatives of every shade, some blue-eyed with fair skin, some freckled, and yet others with heavy black hair. To a young Murray, family gatherings "looked like a United Nations in miniature."[17] Although she identified a multiplicity of color in her own family, Murray was not always aware of how she could benefit from a white supremacism that rewarded light skin. Murray's friend and fellow activist Maida Springer recalled that when Springer was looking for work in New York City in the late 1920s, she was "too dark to work in a restaurant" chain, in which restaurants were "set up on a plantation theme with light-complexioned waitresses playing the role of house servants." Murray worked in the same chain of restaurants in 1929 and, as Springer's biographer Yevette Richards notes, "Murray did not observe that darker-complexioned blacks were excluded; she only saw that the regular color line was drawn between the higher-paying whites and lower-paying black jobs."[18] Murray was not always self-conscious, then, about own negotiations of intraracial color lines.

In the larger context of her writing over the next fifty years, "A Mulatto's Dilemma," will become the dilemma of racial constructs. Murray will present her racial identity as evidence of the nation's identity, one forged in sexual violence that results in a dangerous but intimate relatedness. Murray's understanding of her multiracial identity will be transformed, therefore, from something that hurts and confuses to something that hearkens democratic possibilities. In these early poems, Murray indicated that neither blackness nor whiteness was available to her as straightforward descriptions of who she really is. Murray did not fully embrace, therefore, available literary and political articulations of blackness by prominent multiracial Harlem intellectuals, among them WEB Du Bois, James Weldon Johnson, Nella Larson, Countée Cullen, and Langton Hughes.[19] Developing a category to describe her identity as an American of multiple ancestries will occupy Murray for the rest of her life.

Even as she successfully published poems in black periodicals, Murray's literary voice did not stand out. She did not make enough money as a writer to support herself and was continually in search of work. In 1936, Murray accepted a position as a labor educator for the Workers Education Project (WEP), associated with the New Deal's Works Project Administration. Murray's supervisor was a young Ella Baker, who would become the great NAACP organizer and a leading force behind the Southern Christian Leadership Council and the Student Nonviolence Coordinating Committee. Murray and Baker remained lifelong friends and each infused their work with lessons from Harlem in the 1930s.

For the WEP, Murray taught night classes in a range of subjects, including remedial English and organizing tactics, to clothing workers, Pullman car porters, domestic workers, transport workers, and the unemployed. According to Murray, teaching for the WEP was "a tremendous intellectual experience for me, because it brought me into contact with young, radical intellectuals of the period, young Communists, young Socialists, young Trotskyites, young Republicans, young Democrats, it was a highly politicized project."[20] Yet economic radicalism, particularly of the Communist Party-USA (CPUSA), was not entirely convincing to Murray. She resisted the CPUSA idea that the so-called Black Belt—a collection of counties that ran through the US South—consisted of a common culture and therefore could declare their independence from the United States and ally themselves with the Soviet Union.[21] Murray decried this position, arguing that African Americans would do better to become fully enfranchised American citizens.

Murray signaled her early commitment to American-centered and anticommunist politics when she joined a Lovestonite grouping 1936. The Lovestonites were followers of Jay Lovestone, the former leader of the CPUSA who had become an avowed anticommunist. Lovestone argued that American communism could take a different shape and course than the universalizing or generic model promoted by the Comintern, because capitalism was more secure in the United States and so more moderate strategies should be undertaken by American socialists than in other parts of the world. Lovestone's forceful dissent from the Comintern led to his removal as the leader of the CPUSA. Subsequently, he became a fervent anticommunist and argued for the unique character of American democracy to bring socialist equality.[22] Murray left the Lovestonites in 1937 because of their support of a communist candidate for president. Murray recalled, "I could not understand the logic of voting for official communists when they disagreed with official communists."[23] Her alliance with Lovestone foreshadowed an aspect of her mature politics: Murray prioritized the American case before a pan-national solidarity.

Her experience at the WEP led Murray to make a decision that would have far-reaching personal and national consequences. In the labor movement, Murray saw connections between economic injustice and race. In organizing with whites, she discovered firsthand that poor whites' experiences of being evicted and struggling to find work resembled blacks' experiences. In order to explore critically American race relations, she pursued graduate education in sociology. In 1938, Murray applied to the University of North Carolina at Chapel Hill (UNC), because it was there that groundbreaking work was being done about theories of race by sociologist Howard Odum. Attending UNC would also mean that she would be close to family. In addition to these motivating factors, her father's memory was likely a consideration in Murray's decision to apply to UNC. Murray had heard stories that her school principal father was an avid reader and that he read sociological tracts of the day which argued that black students would never be equipped to compete with white students. Murray supposed that his great dedication to teaching was a way to "demonstrate . . . the falsity of racial indictment which undermined his influence as a teacher and sought to destroy the ambitions of girls and boys he sought to inspire."[24] Her application was a way to carry forward her father's legacy of challenging institutional limitations levied on black students.

Murray's application was rejected because UNC did not accept African Americans, but the timing of Murray's rejection was important. The same week that Murray received her rejection letter, President Roosevelt visited Chapel Hill to deliver an address on foreign policy in which he argued that America's commitment to liberal and democratic institutions at home was crucial as fascism grew abroad.[25] On December 5, 1938, Roosevelt singled out UNC for being at the vanguard of liberal universities that promote democracy. On the heels of her rejection, this hypocrisy incensed Murray. In a letter, Murray challenged the President, "you called on Americans to support a liberal philosophy based on democracy. What does this mean for Negro Americans? Does it mean that we at last can participate freely, and on the basis of equality, with our fellow citizens in working out the problems of this democracy?"

Murray went on in her letter to connect the failure of democracy in the South with a failure of Christian ideals, she claimed "the un-Christian and un-American conditions in the South make it impossible for me and other young Negroes to live there and continue our faith in the ideals of democracy and Christianity."[26] Murray did not spell out the content of these Christian ideals, but she emphasized contradiction as a guiding principle in democratic understanding. Murray called on Roosevelt to make use of the friction between his vision of the United States as a guiding light for the world and the inhumane conditions in the South. She wanted this contradiction between America's promise and its political realities to prompt FDR to come out on the side of "working out the problems of democracy" at home as well as abroad. According to Murray, democracy was incomplete but demonstrated possibilities for justice in the future.

This letter forecasts guiding themes in Murray's writing about American democracy: Democracy is premised on faith; it is promised in the nation's founding documents but is only partially realized. In Murray's characterization of democracy as partially present and yet to come, we see the earliest formulations of her democratic eschatology. The term eschatology comes from the Greek work for end, *eschaton*, and refers to last things. As a Christian doctrine concerning ultimate or final things, eschatology is variously defined as the conclusion of God's purposes, things yet to be seen, and, simply, things hoped for. Although these end-things will not be realized or seen in this lifetime, eschatology has a practical purpose of instructing Christians about how to pray and work for justice in the here and now. Often, these end-things are described in terms of the coming of the kingdom of God. Eschatology is a category freighted with contradiction between present and future and between experience and hope. The promise of justice is contradicted by experiential realities of suffering and death. Contradiction means that work toward justice always carries risk, risk that the actions chosen will not be effective, risk that the actions will not be appropriate, and even risk that the present situation has been misinterpreted. In her letter to FDR—and in future reflections on American democracy—Murray imagined democracy eschatologically. Murray called for attention to the tension between present realities of injustice and demands for a more fully realized democracy for all Americans. In order to highlight this tension, Murray pointed to the contradiction in policies and practices that treat African Americans as second-class citizens, while they are enlisted to defend democracy. In this writing from the late 1930s is an incipient democratic eschatology that outlined a contrast between what is present and democracy that is to come, used contradiction as a guiding norm to reveal possibilities of justice amid brokenness, and encouraged critical evaluation of democratic efforts.

Just three weeks before Murray's rejection, UNC's president Frank Graham, a noted Southern liberal, had made an argument employing almost precisely Murray's account of democracy and Christianity. On November 20, 1938, Graham delivered the welcoming address at the Southern Conference for Human Welfare, a groundbreaking meeting in Birmingham, Alabama, of southern liberals, socialists, labor leaders and activists. To welcome the diverse group of delegates to the meeting whose mission it was to inaugurate a broad-based social movement to address issues of poverty, violence, and racism in the South, Graham intoned, "in this day when democracy and freedom are in retreat everywhere in the face of totalitarian powers and their regimentation of youth and persecution of minorities, let us raise the flag of freedom and democracy where it counts most." In terms that Murray herself would use only weeks later, Graham asserted, "the black man is the primary test of American democracy and Christianity. The Southern Conference for Human Welfare takes it stand here tonight for the simple thing of human freedom. Repression is the way of frightened power; freedom is the enlightened way. We take our stand for the Sermon on the Mount, the American Bill of Rights and American democracy."[27] It is unclear whether Murray knew of Graham's speech, but accounts of the conference were widely reported in the Southern press. As Murray had, Graham juxtaposed two kinds of ideals. Whereas Murray called on the ideals of democracy and Christianity from a posture of resistance and struggle—resistance to the racist status quo of Jim Crow and a struggle to recognize the worth and dignity of each individual—Graham was not able to take his stand on behalf of Christian and democratic ideals, even in his own institution.[28]

In January 1939, news of Murray's application broke in Chapel Hill and soon became a national story. The black press published letters between Murray and Graham, in which Graham defended the University's decision, citing the provision of the state constitution that required the separation of races in public education. Murray responded, "the Constitution of North Carolina is inconsistent with the Constitution of the United States and should be changed to meet the ideals set forth by the first citizens of our country." A columnist for NAACP's *Crisis* wrote, "when Miss Murray submitted her application to the graduate school she was not merely submitting it to President Graham and a few university officials. In reality she was submitting it to the south, and especially the state of North Carolina."[29]

Murray's application became a public controversy, in part, because of the coincidental timing with the Supreme Court's ruling in *Gaines v. Canada*. In a 6-2 decision, the Supreme Court ruled that the State of Missouri needed to provide Lloyd Gaines, who had been rejected from the University of Missouri Law School on account of race, with law school facilities significantly equal to those available to white students or, if it could not, it needed to admit him to the University of Missouri Law School. The Court found that Gaines' right to a legal education was a personal one, independent of whether other African Americans were seeking the same opportunities. Murray characterized *Gaines* as sending shock waves through the South because it was "the first major breach in the 'separate-but-equal' doctrine in *Plessy*."[30] Perhaps anticipating Gaines, UNC's Dean explained in Murray's rejection letter that he expected the North Carolina state legislature to consider how to make a provision for graduate instruction of African Americans in the state. Murray sent copies of her correspondence to the NAACP where it landed on the desk of Thurgood Marshall, a leading lawyer on the national legal team. Although Murray hoped that her application could be a test of *Gaines*, Marshall did not take the case because he expected that Murray would not meet the residency requirement (while UNC might be obliged to admit a resident of North Carolina, the school might not have the same obligation to someone who had been living in New York).

The irony of Murray's rejection—and of Graham's appeal to a statute that called for the "separation" of the races—was Murray's family's connection to the University. Her great-grandfather had attended UNC; an earlier ancestor had been on the board of trustees. When Murray's great-great aunt died, she left a sizable estate to the University, including a trust fund for scholarships in the family's name. Murray would revisit the irony forty years later when she returned to Chapel Hill to offer her first Eucharist at the church in which her grandmother was baptized into freedom in Christ, but was recorded in church records as a slave.

Murray's application to UNC forged three important legacies in Murray's life. Her letter-writing campaign presented an early example of the rhetorical habit that shaped Murray's future political and religious thought. In letters to FDR and Frank Graham, Murray developed a critical perspective that employed the ideals of democracy and Christianity in order to demonstrate contradictions between democratic promises and realities. Murray's activism would be fueled by the irony she expressed in the wake of her rejection: that the United States was fighting a war against fascism abroad, while fascism in the form of Jim Crow was government policy at home.

Her letter-writing campaign also inaugurated a more than thirty-year friendship with Eleanor Roosevelt that lasted until the First Lady's death in 1962. When Murray wrote to FDR, she sent a copy of the letter to the First Lady, who responded, "I have read the copy of the letter you sent me and I understand perfectly, but great changes come slowly. I think they are coming, however, and sometimes it is better to fight hard with conciliatory methods. The South is changing, but don't push too fast."[31] Throughout their friendship Murray continually challenged Roosevelt on human rights, insisting that black Americans deserve equal rights now, not at some future time. One of Murray's most prized possessions was a photograph of Roosevelt and Murray's two aunts who raised her, who had been invited for a visit to Hyde Park; Murray called the scene a picture of her "three aunts."

Perhaps most important to Murray's political development, her application to UNC was the first of many protests of Jim Crow. Murray pointed to it as the moment when "I finally confronted my fear and took a concrete step for social justice. . . . For me the real victory of that encounter with the Jim Crow system of the South was the liberation of my mind from years of enslavement."[32] Two years later, Murray confronted Jim Crow again, this time by integrating an interstate bus. Against the First Lady's advice, Murray pushed.

In 1940, Murray was living in New York City with Adelene MacBean, a fellow activist who was also likely her romantic partner. On Easter weekend, Murray took MacBean to Durham to introduce her to Murray's family. At a stopover in Petersburg, Virginia, Murray and MacBean found themselves on a half-empty bus. When they moved forward two seats, the bus driver instructed them to move back. MacBean refused, citing a broken seat and uncomfortable riding conditions in the back of the bus. She said that she had paid her ticket in full and that she was not going to sit on a broken seat. In her autobiography, Murray depicted herself as being angry with her friend for causing a scene, yet Murray certainly understood that moving forward on the bus meant challenging law and custom. The bus driver left the bus and returned with two police officers. Murray and MacBean were arrested for disorderly conduct and creating a public disturbance. Murray remembered saying to the driver as she left the bus " 'you haven't learned a thing in two thousand years.' I could not forget that it was Easter Even."

The women had little cash and refused bail. They shared a cell with three other women, in which a "foul-smelling open toilet stood near the door . . . each bed had a grimy straw mattress, one sheet, and a grease-caked blanket... [and] huge water bugs... crawled out of the cracks [in the wall] at night." In spite of these conditions, the women awoke on Easter morning with shared commitment to continue their protest. On paper she had smuggled in with her, Murray wrote a memorandum to the jail's deputy in which she insisted courteously upon humane treatment. In her autobiography, Murray demurred about the calculatedness of her protest, presuming perhaps that it would be untoward for women to seek out opportunities to challenge Jim Crow. Murray would later write to a friend, "we did not plan our arrest intentionally. The situation developed and, having developed, we applied what we knew of *Satyagraha* on the spot."[33] And yet as Murray and MacBean were taken away by police, she slipped a piece of paper into the hand of member of the assembled crowd and asked him to contact the local NAACP office. The case was sent from Virginia to the national office of the NAACP, where a legal team comprised of Marshall, Charles Hamilton Houston, and Spotswood Robinson were looking for a case to challenge segregation laws on interstate travel with a plaintiff who had been accused not simply of disorderly conduct but of refusing to comply with segregation statutes.[34] Murray and MacBean had been charged with disorderly conduct, so the NAACP saw limited possibilities in their case. At trial, Murray and MacBean were convicted. After an appeal was denied, the women refused to pay the ten-dollar fine and returned to jail.

On Easter weekend of 1940, Murray became convinced "that creative non-violent resistance would be a powerful weapon in the struggle for human dignity."[35] Before her trip, Murray had become a student of nonviolence. She had recently joined the pacifist Fellowship of Reconciliation and was among a group of young African American activists, including Bayard Rustin and James Farmer, who studied Gandhi's method and were looking for ways to implement the strategy in the United States. Murray was on the leading edge of the kind of nonviolent activism that would, within ten years, propel the Civil Rights movement.

Murray and MacBean's protest anticipated Irene Morgan's successful challenge of segregation on interstate travel. In 1946, the Supreme Court ruled in *Irene Morgan v. The Commonwealth of Virginia* that states' laws that required segregation in interstate transportation were unconstitutional. Morgan's successful case was the inspiration for the Congress of Racial Equality's (Congress on Racial Equality) 1947 Journey of Reconciliation, in which sixteen activists took trips in the upper South to test enforcement of the Supreme Court's ruling. Founded in 1942, CORE came into being as an interracial group committed to nonviolent direct action. Many of CORE's founding members, including James Farmer and Bayard Rustin, were also members of the Fellowship of Reconciliation. Along with Rustin and Farmer, Murray was part of the planning team for CORE's efforts and wanted to be among the Freedom Riders. CORE decided that women should not be among the Riders, for fear that they would become the targets of violence.[36]

While Murray's application of *Satyagraha* to the American context was prophetic, her experience in the Virginia jail revealed Murray's limitations in theorizing about intraracial dynamics, class, and sexuality. When male prisoners in the adjoining cells called them "New York whores," Murray and MacBean applied the same strategy with fellow inmates as they had with the warden—they insisted courteously on humane treatment. On Murray's account, the two eventually convinced the men of Murray and MacBean's noble cause.[37] Her autobiographical account of her fellow prisoners reads like a primer on Murray's respectability: Taken aback by the sexual banter between what Murray characterized as working-class black men and black women who were prostitutes, Murray and her friend persuaded them of the significance of their own arrest and the ramifications it had for their fellow prisoners' experiences of the Jim Crow legal system.

To refer to Murray's sense of her own "respectability" invokes Evelyn Brooks Higginbotham's study of what she calls the "politics of respectability" among women in the Black Baptist Church during the Progressive Era. Higginbotham explains how "the politics of respectability emphasized reform of individual behavior and attitudes both as a goal in itself and as a strategy for reform of the entire structural system of American race relations."[38] Murray's autobiographical account of her prison stay reflected concerns about sexual decorum, personal behavior, and the importance of propriety. The connections between sexuality and class that Murray did not reflect about in her own writing demonstrate a blind spot in her thinking about the interstructuring of oppression and how her own concerns about respectability may have motivated both her caricature of her cell mates and the under-identification of her traveling partner.

Historian Glenda Gilmore has discovered a fascinating subtext to the Petersburg episode. In May 1940, two months after Murray's arrest, *Opportunity Magazine* published a story about a young black couple who were arrested while integrating an interstate bus. The story drew from an eyewitness' account of a white passenger who was traveling from Washington to Durham in late March 1940 and described the pair as a "light-colored but not very good looking" young woman and a "young man . . . of slight build . . . and sensitive in voice and manner." In all likelihood, the couple was Murray and MacBean. The eyewitness recognized Murray as she had wished to be understood—as a male. The story was written by Harold Garfinkel, then a graduate student in sociology at the UNC. Garfinkel would become the founder of ethnomethodology, a branch of sociology that studies the way people make sense of their social world. Gilmore notes that Garfinkel published work "about shaming rituals and transgendered people. But Garfinkel did not realize that his first published work was about the shaming ritual of a transgendered person." As she had in the decade earlier,

"Murray found in cross-dressing a respite from shouldering the cloak of middle-class female dignity that she had to wear as a black woman activist."[39] The irony, in this case, is that she was at the same time engaged in activism that challenged Jim Crow. Murray's choice to dress as a man for the interstate trip indicates that the bus protest was not planned. As Gilmore points out, Murray would have been aware of the risks of being arrested under the Mann Act if she and MacBean had been caught posing as a straight couple.

Murray did not write publicly about the gendered and sexual dimensions of this (or of many other) incident(s), but in her archives she included journals, letters, and medical records that chart a decade-long struggle to find categories to describe her sexuality and gender identity. These resources shed light on Murray's understanding of herself, offer a fascinating glimpse into transgender and lesbian history, and point to how Murray's experiences of heterosexism influenced her public accounts of her racial and gender identities. Murray's archives include Murray's journals and letters, which discuss love relationships with women, habits of cross-dressing, and Murray's questions to doctors about whether she was, in fact, biologically male. Adelene MacBean, whom Murray discusses in her autobiographical account of her Greyhound arrest, was presumably the "A. MacBean" who wrote a letter to the editor of *Amsterdam News* decrying the alienated experiences of homosexuals as misunderstood minorities of minorities. Murray clipped a copy of the letter and kept it in her files. This and other clippings from Harlem newspapers' reporting about sexuality research demonstrate Murray's abiding interest and engagement with these issues. Aside from a reference to a brief marriage, Murray's autobiography does not discuss sexual relationships.[40]

While her published writings were silent on the subject, Murray wrote openly with family members about her gender identity. Responding to a letter from her brother in which he addressed her by her given name "Anna Pauline," Murray replied "now Brother Love, about this 'Anna Pauline' business, I may be 'Pollyanna' to you, but it is still Pauli to me." Murray signed the letter "Pauli (little-brother-sister-or what have you)."[41] In the early 1930s, Murray renamed herself, replacing her given name "Anna Pauline" with the gender-ambivalent "Pauli."[42] In a letter to her aunt, Murray wrote about the struggle to come to terms with herself,

> this little "boy-girl" personality as you jokingly call it sometimes gets me into trouble...but where you and a few people understand, the world does not accept my pattern of life. And to try to live by society's standards always causes me such inner conflict that at times it's almost unbearable. I don't know whether I'm right or whether society (or some medical authority) is right—I only know how I feel and what makes me happy.[43]

When Murray described herself to her family as a "boy-girl," the terms transgender, transsexual, or intersex were not available to her.

Murray read medical literature in order to make sense of her feelings and attractions. In the 1930s, medical literature offered competing explanatory models for homosexuality, as a physiological or a psychological phenomenon.[44] There was not yet a distinction between biological sex and socially conditioned gender roles. There was, instead, a conflation of the two whereby a person's biological sex determined what is now recognized as a person's gender, demonstrable in social and personality characteristics. Murray supposed, therefore, that her own personality, including a penchant for short hair, wearing pants, forceful speaking, and sexual attraction to women, meant that she was, in fact, a man. Fearful that she inherited her father's mental illness, Murray resisted a psychological explanation, which held that homosexuality was as kind of pathology or psychological deficiency.[45] Murray was sexually and emotionally attracted to women, but she did not consider herself to be a lesbian, rather she understood herself as taking the gendered-male role in relationships as provider. Murray refused a homosexual identity, in part because, according to Doreen Drury, she felt that "her ability to pass was a sign that she transcended the category 'homosexual' and that her inversion, together with the rest of her symptomatology, had to be understood differently."[46] Drawing from medical and popular accounts of sexuality in the 1930s, Murray described herself as a "pseudo-hermaphrodite."

Between 1937 and 1947, Murray was hospitalized three times for what she described as emotional breakdowns. During each hospital stay, Murray wrote letters to her doctors about her symptoms and insisted that they consider hermaphrodism as a possible root of her disturbances.[47] Convinced that she was biologically male as well as female, Murray wanted doctors to perform exploratory abdominal surgery in order to investigate whether or not she had a set of testes. After a surgery that was performed in 1954 revealed that Murray did not possess male reproductive organs, her journals and letters refer less and less to pursuing hormonal treatments. Historian Nancy Ordover reflects, "reading Murray's notes from meetings is excruciating, in part because they demonstrate so clearly how lesbians and gays, including the most well-informed and politically minded, were willing to defer to medical 'expertise.' Ordover characterizes Murray's questioning of medical authority as courageous, yet she concludes that Murray is, nevertheless, an example of how lesbians and gays "have often cooperated in their own pathologization."[48]

Murray's ambivalent publication of her sexual orientation provides a challenge to her biographers. While Murray did not include overt references to her sexuality in her autobiography, she was careful to preserve detailed accounts of her hospital visits and thinking about her own sexuality, as well as photographs and love letters with women. Murray's archival preservation of her struggles with sexuality is particularly important when one considers that she admits to "purging" her professional files from the late 1960s and early 1970s.[49] The preservation of unambiguous references to her sexuality, her love relationships with women, and her desire to seek hormonal treatments serves as a kind of publication—of "making public"—of this aspect of her life. A reader is still faced, however, with the challenge of understanding Murray's reflections and choices in her historical context. A reader must keep in mind the historical development of lesbian and transgender identities, and the individual process we now identify as "coming out."[50] In order to respect Murray's understanding of herself—as she articulated it in letters, journal entries, and photos of the time—contemporary readers should not impose definitions from presently available categories.

At the same time, not identifying Murray as a lesbian or transgendered person could, according to Leila Rupp and Verta Taylor, "contribute to the invisibility of lesbian [and transgender] lives."[51] To meet this challenge, Murray's readers can employ a "deviant historiography," Jennifer Terry's method "for mapping the complex discursive and textual operations at play in the historical emergence of subjects who come to be called lesbians and gay men."[52] Terry is interested in looking at the conditions which enabled or constrained the emergence of sexual identities. To consider Murray's accounts of her sexuality in historical context and with respect to her own definitions of herself can make available, therefore, Murray's thinking about her sexuality as part of a larger consideration of a lifelong investigation of identity.

A careful attention to how Murray described her experiences of multiple identities reveals that Murray articulated her experiences of sexuality in terms that she used to describe her racial identity. In a 1940 note to doctors during one of her hospital stays, Murray characterized herself ruefully as "one of nature's experiments." Almost forty years later, Murray used the metaphor approvingly in the 1978 introduction to *Proud Shoes*, in which she described the process of writing a family memoir as helping her to understand herself as a "New World experiment." In another connection, Murray, also in *Proud Shoes*, described her multiracial identity in terms of being "a minority within a minority." In her autobiography, she used the same phrase to reflect on her experiences as an African American woman.[53] Murray's first connection to the phrase "minority within a minority" seems to be the 1939 letter to the editor of the *New York Amsterdam News* written by "A. MacBean." MacBean wrote to commend the paper for including an article on its front page about a recent experiment with a sex hormone. Referring to people who experience "sex inversion, homosexuality, virility in women, and effeminancy in men," MacBean called them "the minority of minorities, misunderstood by their family and friends, condemned without trial by social custom."[54] Just as her poetry of the period pointed to a racial identity that disrupted binary positions of black and white, Murray's sexual and gender identifications presented a "category crisis," what Marjorie Garber has defined, particularly in reference to cross-dressing, as "an irresolvable conflict or epistemological crux that destabilizes comfortable binarity, and displaces the resulting discomfort into a figure that already inhabits, indeed incarnates, the margin."[55] While Murray did not theorize explicitly about sexuality as an identity category, these connections, according to Patricia Hill Collins, indicate that "her ability to see connections between race, class, and gender also was shaped by her experiences with heterosexism."[56]

By the summer of 1940, Murray had confronted Jim Crow in Chapel Hill and Petersburg, but she was frustrated that her protests did not lead to court action or barriers being broken. And she was again in search of work. In response to her growing reputation as a capable young activist and writer, Murray was offered the position of traveling secretary at the Workers Defense League (WDL) to raise money on behalf of sharecropper Odell Waller, who had been convicted of murdering his white landlord. The case emerged as a national story, as "Odell Waller became a symbol of racial and economic injustice in the United States."[57]

Waller's defense argued that Waller had been denied his Fourteenth Amendment equal protection right to a fair trial, because Pittsylvania County, Virginia, where Waller was convicted, compiled jury lists from voter lists, and people were assessed a tax in order to vote. Waller's defense sought to demonstrate that when one economic class was systematically excluded from jury service, a person's right to equal protection was forfeited. Murray traveled around Virginia and the country alone and with Waller's mother on fundraising tours. Working for the WDL helped to crystallize the direction of Murray's future political and professional commitments. As she traveled the country making the case for equal protection of the laws, Murray felt herself growing into a powerful advocate on behalf of those discriminated against because of race and economic conditions. Impassioned speeches had raised Murray's national profile. At one event, Leon Ransom and William Hastie, leading NAACP attorneys and professors at Howard Law School, were so impressed with Murray's presentation that they invited her to apply to law school. Murray promised herself that she would if she and the WDL failed in their efforts to free Waller. She saw that an individual law that regulated the selection of jury pools in Virginia contributed to a system of apartheid that shaped the character of American democracy. She witnessed firsthand legal luminaries take on entrenched political and economic power and she wanted the tools to do the same.

The WDL positioned its defense of Waller in terms of African American participation in and support for the war. Waller's defense team was "convinced that a strong democracy at home was the first line of defense against the Nazi threat and that through Waller's fight we were challenging the undemocratic poll tax system, which effectively denied millions of poor black and white sharecroppers a voice in their government." Media reports on the case focused on connections between Waller's defense and domestic support for the war. The editor of the

Richmond Times Dispatch wondered whether the "execution of a humble Negro sharecropper" might lessen chances of the Allies to win the war, because it would undermine African Americans' willingness to fight. As she had in her letter to FDR protesting her rejection from UNC, Murray again emphasized the South as "the testing ground of democracy and Christianity."[58] She and others were making connections between the treatment of Jews in Nazi Germany and of African Americans in the American South. She recognized the hypocrisy of the administration, who by this time had entered the war to fight fascism abroad, while "tolerating an incipient fascism within its own borders."[59]

Murray's organizing acumen helped to garner the case its national attention. Murray was faced with a challenge in fundraising because Waller's lead attorney had previous connections with the Communist Party, and as a result local and national organizations were reluctant to be associated with his case. But Murray insisted that a broad-based coalition would be necessary for the Waller campaign to be successful and persuaded others that Waller's case had broad implications for democratic participation. As a result of her efforts, the NAACP and A. Philip Randolph's Brotherhood of Sleeping Car Porters provided legal and financial support. The WDL linked the Waller case with an emerging national campaign to outlaw the poll tax that had growing support on the left. A 1942 WDL flyer included Reinhold Niebuhr, John Dewey, AJ Muste, and Paul Kellogg as signatories who opposed the tax. Murray's work on the Waller case is an early example of the pragmatism and commitment to coalition-building that will characterize her organizing in decades to come.

The WDL and Murray were unable to secure Waller's freedom. He was convicted and sentenced to death by the state of Virginia. After Waller's execution, Randolph, who served on the WDL's board, asked Murray to draft an open letter to the President. Published widely in the African American press and picked up by a national news service, Murray's letter warned, "Negroes are beginning to express a willingness and determination to die right here in America to attain a democracy which they have never had." The letter connected the failures of American democracy with a loss of democratic faith at a critical political moment. The letter suggested that surge in racial violence in response to Waller's execution is "grist for the propaganda mills of the Axis powers, and undoubtedly will be used to destroy the faith of the allied nations in the honesty and integrity of the American democracy, and hasten the deterioration of the morale of the enslaved peoples of the world which hangs precariously on this faith."[60] Murray's final words on the Waller case witnessed a democratic eschatology. Like she had in her letter to FDR about her rejection from UNC, she compared the failure of ideals of democracy and Christianity in the South. In response to Waller's execution, Murray underscored the risks African Americans seemed increasingly willing to take in order to witness the brokenness of Jim Crow justice. These risks would be willingly undertaken because of an abiding democratic faith, even if the faith has yet to be justified for African Americans in the South. Democracy was not yet present, but Murray had faith that, against great odds, it was to come.

Following Waller's execution, Murray kept a promise to herself and entered Howard Law School. At Howard in 1942, Murray was one of only three women in her class and among the next generation of leading civil rights attorneys. While Murray learned legal approaches in the classroom to fight discrimination, she remained committed also to grassroots strategies to confront Jim Crow. In "An Alternative Weapon," which appeared in *South Today*, Murray and fellow FOR member Henry Babcock proposed nonviolence and pacifism as a political strategy for African Americans. Murray and Babcock asserted that the experiences of African Americans, particularly of African American pacifists, have a prophetic role to play for American democracy. Murray and Babcock admitted, "it is a strange thing to believe that out of the Negro's struggle and suffering may come the answer to the very problem which troubles so many Americans today."[61] Murray's connection between African American suffering and pacifism drew from what Anthony Pinn has identified as a theology of redemptive suffering that dominated the African American theological landscape. Redemptive suffering assumes that "God is able to bring about the betterment of African Americans through their suffering."[62]

Pinn has identified two primary explanations for why suffering is considered redemptive. The first deems suffering to be redemptive because it is punitive and the suffering is deserved. The second, and more prevalent approach, is to view suffering as pedagogical; suffering teaches something about the relationship of human beings to each other and about their relationship with God. A pedagogical notion of redemptive suffering became particularly evident in the first few decades of the twentieth century, when "some African-Americans spoke of the personal refinement of African-Americans through suffering endured, as well as the manner in which this suffering sensitized them to the pain of others and put them in a unique position to lead the regeneration of the United States."[63] Murray evinced this second explanation when she insisted that African American suffering can be both revelatory and productive. She and Babcock asserted that African American suffering will reveal "that those people in the United States who support race supremacy belong with Hitler's hordes" and that "victory for democracy must be won at home as surely as it must be won abroad." The suffering of African Americans revealed also that the conflict between democracy and fascism is less a conflict between nations, as it is "more clearly an issue that is internal to every nation."[64] Pacifism provided a method to expose the contradiction between democratic promises and fascist realities in the United States.

Murray and Babcock concluded that "through his suffering, through his bitter conflicts and frustrations of his personal situation, the Negro is led to a thorough-going pacifism at home and abroad which may prove itself the means

of giving the movement in America its greatest impetus." Suffering, then, produces the energy required for nonviolent resistance. They characterized pacifism as "essentially religious . . . in that it operates by and requires faith." Pacifism's
religious character is especially evident in how it seeks conversion to democracy
and freedom, rather than imposing itself violently. But pacifism also holds a
creative tension between the individual and the social, which "is religious
because it demands of the individual an internal discipline and a *controlled* individualism; because pacifism is incurably social it seeks to develop an ever wider
group-conscience."[65] This is exemplary of Murray's emphasis on individualism
in social movements. Even in the context of social movements that made demands
on behalf of a group, Murray insisted on maintaining the integrity of the individual
as a member of this group.

In this article, according to Pinn, Murray "points to the pedagogical benefits
of black suffering, in that it sharpens the African American's ability to analyze
situations and provide creative and healthy alternatives."[66] Murray's characterization of suffering as able to reveal injustice is part of a tradition that extends
from lay public intellectual Maria Stewart and pastor and professor Alexander
Crummell in the nineteenth century to find its most far-reaching expression in
the praxis of Martin Luther King in the twentieth century. For Murray, in the
early 1940s, to endorse unmerited suffering as potentially redemptive was a
means to promote a pacifist political strategy, but it also pointed to her developing notion African American identity. While Murray indicated similarities
between fascism abroad and Jim Crow at home, she nevertheless emphasized
the experiences of African Americans as emerging particularly from the American context.

In the same year that she and Babcock wrote about African American pacifism, Murray experimented with nonviolence in her own activism. With a group
of Howard undergraduates and law students, Murray applied Gandhian nonviolent civil disobedience to protest Jim Crow in Washington, DC. The protest
against Jim Crow began as a response to the conscription of male students who
"unprotected and without any kind of deferment, were being yanked out of their
classes and into a G.I. uniform."[67] Living with the indignities of segregation in
the nation's capital while the government required young black men to make
sacrifices for democracy became too much to bear. After three Howard students
were denied service at a local restaurant, Murray and her classmates mobilized
to form a Civil Rights Committee as part of Howard's NAACP chapter and organized a direct action campaign that used "the stool-sitting technique."[68] James
Farmer had organized a sit-in in a Chicago coffee shop the previous year, and
Murray was eager to apply the technique in the nation's capital.

After a careful study of picketing laws and signing a pledge that they would
conduct themselves with poise and respect, Howard students sat-in and picketed
at two downtown restaurants in April 1943 and April 1944.[69] The direct action

achieved success—in each case, students were eventually served and the Committee reported a majority of supportive opinion from passersby—but Howard administrators demanded that the NAACP chapter suspend the direct action campaign. The university had been threatened with an end to government funding, which comprised 60 percent of its income.[70] Though students initially resisted the administration's call to stop their activities, they eventually relented. Years later, Murray recalled that she and fellow activists "knew the fate of the institution was at stake and we were not willing to take responsibility for that kind of thing."[71] Howard students' use of Gandhian nonviolent techniques was an important example of early efforts by black activists to employ nonviolent direct action and anticipated its effective and widespread use during the height of the Civil Rights movement in the 1950s and 1960s.

An underlying irony of Howard administrators' opposition to the students' protest was the University President Mordechai Johnson's own interest in Gandhi's method. He shared with Howard Thurman, the Dean of Howard's chapel, and Benjamin Mays, Dean of the University's Divinity School until 1940, a commitment to nonviolence and a belief that Gandhi's method could be effectively employed in the American context. In fact, Thurman and Mays had traveled to India to learn more about Gandhi's organizing and how nonviolent strategies could be applied to the American context (Johnson would later also make the trip).[72] Murray's only reference to the coincident connection between the sit-ins and Howard as a center of African American religious thought was a brief mention in her autobiography that in the midst of her despair over whether or not to call off the direct action, she visited Thurman for "spiritual guidance."[73] This reference indicates, however, that Murray knew and engaged with leading black religious thinkers of the 1940s. Her own democratic and theological writing would continue themes integral to Johnson's, Thurman's, and Mays' religious thought, including the interrelatedness of all human rights, the possibility of building the beloved community, and a commitment to nonviolent direct action.[74]

In the aftermath of the sit-ins, Murray found respite at the home of Caroline Ware. A white historian at Howard and American Universities, Ware was instrumental in developing the cultural approach to history that sought to shift historical focus away from the life stories and institutions of elites and toward social realities of a majority of Americans. Ware became a lifelong mentor and friend to Murray. While at Howard, Murray nicknamed Ware "Skipper," because Ware shuttled Murray and others between the District and her farm in nearby rural Virginia so that her guests did not have to use segregated public transportation.

Howard students' actions took place in the midst of growing frustration among African Americans about their role in the war and increased violence against African Americans on the home front. Newly recruited soldiers were trained on segregated army bases, mostly in the South. African American news-papers carried stories of black soldiers being lynched and of gun battles between black and white soldiers. Before 1943, "racial friction, sporadic conflict, and finally outright rioting became commonplace at nearly every army base in the South."[75] Anger over the exclusion of African Americans from defense jobs, about the policy of the Red Cross to segregate blood plasma, and about widespread abuse of black soldiers boiled over in the summer of 1943 and resulted in violence throughout the country.

In 1942, Murray had written that "in common with all Americans, I too want to be a loyal citizen. I want something to believe in, something which challenges my heroism, something I would be willing to die for." As she had in the Waller case, Murray compared fascism abroad to increased racial violence at home. In response to the lynching of a black solider, she wrote, "perhaps we are foolish in not realizing that Hitlerism would destroy us utterly while our fellow citi-zens...would merely burn a few of us each year. But men who confront death and women who see the frustrations of their youth cannot be expected to distinguish between brutalities."[76] She railed against those factions who required that African Americans put aside their demands for equality until after the war was won, "I am also told that in the time of national danger the separate interests of all groups must be submerged in the survival of the whole...does this mean I must accept a synthetic unity, searing the surface of conflicts which are deep and treacherous?"[77] The question would prove moot, for no unity—synthetic or real—would hold. In the summer of 1943, violence shook forty-seven American cities.

By the summer of 1943, Murray was "fed up." She assailed the white press for ignoring the "very existence of the Negro ghetto" and warned that the present "rebellion will stop nowhere short of its goal." She argued that rioting and vio-lence have taken over American cities because the basic needs of African Americans—for equality before the law in housing, employment, education, the right to vote, the most basic democratic rights—continued to be ignored even as black men were called up to fight for democracy abroad. Responding to violence in Detroit, Murray wrote that "I have no easy solution for this deep crisis and I know no one who has...Those of us who will not yield to despair will continue to fight for a solution through long-range and immediate programs of group action. But I think the solution demands a revolution in our individual thinking. It requires a moral ethic which reaffirms a fundamental kinship in all mankind."[78] In the midst of her legal training, Murray recognized the need for legal changes to be paired with a moral ethic premised on a universal anthropology.

In August 1943, violence reached New York City and Murray was there to wit-ness it. In response to a rumor that a white police officer killed an African Ameri-can soldier, Harlem exploded in an "orgy of looting and destruction," leaving five dead and 500 injured. In The Call, a socialist daily paper, Murray reported on the immediate aftermath of the rioting. Street after street was filled with glass as storefront windows had been smashed and all the goods looted. She came upon two Jewish women, who sat stunned and desultory in what remained of their small grocery. Having been in the neighborhood for decades, they asked Murray what the crowds could have against them. Murray wrote, "how could I tell [them] that a mob moves without a head or heart and when the last man down, who had felt the pressure for centuries and can find no scapegoat below himself, revolts, he strikes back blindly and without discrimination."[79]

After Detroit Murray had remained steadfast in her conviction that a moral ethic that prioritized community was part of the solution, but violence in Harlem overwhelmed her. She wrote, "O what to do, what to do in the face of this massed resentment over the centuries? I who believe in a gospel of love, of human kin-ship, of democracy, and of co-operative commonwealth of the dignity of individual personality, of non-violent ways of protesting oppression, what could I offer to stem the flood of hatred against a blank white wall in which there could be no individual exceptions?"[80] In that moment, neither the gospel of love nor appeals to democracy's promises of rights and protections were enough.

In a poem written in the wake of the Harlem violence, Murray recognized that violence would not bring African Americans political or social advancement, but she was at a loss,

> Not by hammering the furious word,
> Nor bread stamped in the streets,
> Nor milk emptied in the gutter,
> Shall we gain the gates of the city.
> But I am a prophet without eyes to see;
> I do not know how we shall gain the gates of the city.[81]

Rioting and looting would not bring the eschatological reward of entrance through the gates of the city, referring to new Jerusalem or the heavenly city of Revelation. Violence would not bring African Americans salvation at some future date, nor would it bring redemption in the here and now of American democ-racy. Despite the hope she had invested in democratic promises, Murray admitted that she was "a prophet without eyes to see." American democracy did not pro-tect black Americans, and she could not offer a viable alternative.

The summer of 1943 was a particularly trying time for Murray. On summer break from law school, she visited a number of doctors in New York and Baltimore to find one who would agree to give her male hormones. Murray read about experimental treatments that might allow her to live as a man, which she hoped would ease her frustration and distress. In a June 1943 letter to her aunt, Murray explained that she was too tired to come home to visit, "yet I do feel the need of getting myself straightened out sort of once and for all." She shared a rumor that had circulated around school that she had been in a relationship with a female undergraduate; Murray was convinced this would be the end of her career before it began. "This conflict rises up to knock me down at every apex I reach in my career," she wrote, "and because the laws of society do not protect me, I'm exposed to any enemy or person who may or may not want to hurt me."[82]

The same summer Murray worked furiously to finish her epic poem, "Dark Testament." In her autobiography, she described finishing the poem in the wake of the Harlem riots,

> for the rest of August I wrote as one possessed, pouring out all my pain and bitterness into "Dark Testament." When the poem was completed, I felt as if a demon had been exorcised and a terrible spell broken. Earlier I had doubts about continuing to study law—it seemed so hopeless— but now a calmer mood prevailed and I was ready to go back and finish my senior year.[83]

The autobiography did not mention questions about sexuality, but the reference to losing hope about studying law likely referred to her concern about circulating rumors. Finishing "Dark Testament" was a cathartic experience for Murray and may have contributed to renewing her faith in American democracy.

"Dark Testament" is twelve–part epic poem that Murray began in the 1930s and was published in *South Today* in 1944.[84] Connecting racial justice in America with God's justice, "Dark Testament" employed a dream motif, declaring that "America was a great and a new world for dreaming," and "America was the dream of freedom." But the dream was turned into a nightmare by the slave trade, the genocide of Native Americans, and the "quest for gold" above all else. "Dark Testament" outlined categories that Murray will develop in her mature theology, including God's preeminent concern for justice and human beings' responsibility to work for justice in the here and now.

The opening stanza introduced the protagonists—an Israelite, an African slave, an immigrant, a Mormon, and a refugee wandering in exile, searching for freedom. Having gestured to diversity among, yet common desires of, human beings, Murray took up the story of the African slave as the central topic of the rest of the poem. Murray pointed out how official government policy and colonial religion diminished an enslaved person's identity, for a white person has "mark[ed] him up in Congress—he's three-fifths human" and "takes a black man's manhood, gives him a white God." Murray connected how the Constitution levied ontological judgments about the worth of Americans of African descent with the forced conversion of enslaved people. Despite the colonial imposition of another's religion, African Americans have recognized who God is,

> A black man down on his knees in the swamp-grass
> Sent his prayer straight to the white God's throne,

Built him a faith, built a bridge to this God
And God have him hope and the power of song.

While whites claimed God for themselves and used religion as a tactic of enslavement, God gave enslaved people "hope and the power of song." Enslaved people
discerned that God was with them and that God is concerned with justice. If
white religion is a perversion of who God really is, then Murray's juxtaposition
of white religion with white justice implied that white justice is not true justice.
Murray's white religion, or white American Christianity, demonstrated how
Christianity promoted and attempted to justify human enslavement. By
connecting racial justice with God's justice, Murray asserted that black Americans
are important to God's plan.

Murray conceded that
ours is no bedtime story children beg to hear
No heroes rode down the night to warn our sleeping villages.
Ours is a tale of blood streaking the Atlantic.[85]

Murray's characterization of slave history as "no bedtime story children beg to
hear" anticipated Toni Morrison's closing of *Beloved* that "it was not a story to
pass on."[86] Murray recognized that painful memories are integral to history, but
there are risks inherent in passing them down. Murray's hope in the power of
song was not utopian, rather it was a gift from God that gave enslaved people
and their descendents the means to struggle for freedom. Murray's hope pre-
saged Cornel West's depictions of hope in spite of a thoroughly racist past. There
is no reason for African Americans to be optimistic about their future in America,
according to West, because American history has repeatedly failed African
Americans. Yet, West promotes a kind of Christian hope that engages "in a form
of struggle in the present moment that keeps the best of the past alive."[87]
Murray's "Dark Testament" is an earlier example of this kind of hope. It confirmed that the struggle for freedom would have to be undertaken in history, for
"not Eden's gate, but freedom lures us down the trail of skulls." According to
Murray, history can teach us important lessons about the meaning of human
being, that the red earth of Virginia is fed "by the white bones of Tom Jefferson/
and the white bones of Nat Turner."[88] The earth knows what white justice
ignores—the ontological equality between human beings.

The connection of God's justice with racial justice in America is a protean
example of how Murray placed religous norms in conversations with democratic
practices. When she insisted that God took a special interest in the forced relocation
and human enslavement of Africans brought to American shores, she emphasized that enslaved Americans were not afforded the rights and protections of
other Americans. Her comparison of God's justice and civil justice was more
than a simple coincidence of two ideals, rather it hinted at a potential relationship

between religious and democratic norms, a give-and-take in which each might be clarified by the other.

In August 1943, after completing "Dark Testament," Murray returned to Howard to finish law school. Even with her prolific writing and organizing activities, Murray graduated at the top of her law school class and was the only woman to graduate. While she had brought to Howard a conviction of the interrelatedness of all human rights, she had been dismayed by her classmates' and professors' exclusion of her and other women from school activities. For example, early in her first year, her complaints that women were not allowed to join the Howard Law Fraternity were met with disinterest. Murray recalled "the discovery that . . . men I deeply admired because of their dedication to civil rights, men who themselves had suffered racial indignities, could countenance exclusion of women from their professional association aroused an incipient feminism in me long before I knew the meaning of the term 'feminism.'"[89]

Murray was similarly disappointed with her colleagues at the conclusion of law school. Traditionally, each year the Howard student with the highest grade point average undertook a year of graduate study at Harvard. Murray, who graduated first in her class, applied but was rejected, because Harvard Law School did not admit women. Some Howard colleagues found her rejection from Harvard comical and teased her about it. Murray was radicalized: "The fact Harvard's rejection was a source of mild amusement rather than outrage to many of my male colleagues who were ardent civil rights advocates made it all the more bitter to swallow. The harsh reality was that I was a minority within a minority, with all the built-in disadvantages that such status entailed."[90] As ever, Murray forged ahead despite setbacks. She matriculated at Berkeley's Boalt Hall instead and feasted on the cosmopolitanism of San Francisco.

Murray had come to Howard in order to gain tools to fight Jim Crow, but she graduated from Howard with a keen awareness of "Jane Crow," a term she used to describe experiences of African American women who are discriminated against because of race *and* sex. Murray distinguished Jane Crow from white women's and black men's concerns, for "within this framework of 'male supremacy' as well as 'white supremacy,' the Negro woman finds herself at the bottom of the economic and social scale."[91] Murray would use this category in her legal and religious writing to explain how African American women experience an interstructuring of oppressions.

Murray's concept of Jane Crow is part of a tradition of African American women theorizing about the intersection of multiple identities. Before Murray, Sojourner Truth, Anna Julia Cooper, and Mary Church Terrell, among others, theorized about the multiple consciousness of African American women. In the late 1940s and early 1950s, a growing chorus of black feminist voices was calling for a recognition of multiple oppressions suffered by black women. A leading Communist, Claudia Jones theorized the triple oppression of black women, by virtue of their race, class, and gender. In a series of articles for *Freedom* magazine, Lorraine Hansberry focused on national and international examples of women's liberation struggles. In the late 1940s and early 1950s—an era that is typically overlooked by periodization of feminist theory—Murray, Jones, and Hansberry theorized about how socially constructed categories intersect to create a system of oppression. A similar theoretical strain would become an important dissenting voice in the 1970s and 1980s to movements in black nationalism and white feminism which tended to overlook the experiences of African American women. For example, in 1970, Frances Beal argued that African American women's status as women *and* as blacks put them in "double jeopardy." Murray was not, therefore, the first or the last person to theorize about what she called "Jane Crow," but she used Jane Crow to make groundbreaking legal and theological arguments. Jane Crow was indicative of how Murray's reflection about her own identity matured into trenchant social critique.

In Murray's writing and work of the 1930s and 1940s, critical attentions to identity, history, and democratic eschatology emerge that will shape her democratic thinking for the next half century. In these decades, Murray also developed a particular political disposition that was at once pragmatic and radical. Murray's insistence on the importance of coalition-building in the Waller case will become the pattern of her legal and organizing activities in the coming decades. Murray will assert that, as an African American woman, her interests are only protected by a broad-based coalition and will continually insist that such coalitions are unique in their ability to defend human rights. At first glance, it may seem misplaced to identify Murray as radical in light of the vigorous economic radicalism of the Communist and socialist parties or of the burgeoning black nationalism articulated by some in Harlem or of a growing commitment to internationalism and Pan-Africanism, all of which shaped these decades. Murray's hope in the possibility of *American* democracy and her commitment to the American framework and tradition may seem conventional, even conservative. Yet radical accurately describes Murray's efforts to reveal what is repressed or obscured by the dominant position. Whether it be poetry that reflected on her multiracial subjectivity, her formulation of Jane Crow, or her experimentation with *Satyagraha*, Murray proposed challenges to moral imagination. Her pragmatism in coalition-building is part of this challenge and indicates her radicality. As someone who lived at the margins of various normative constructions of experience, Murray eschewed any univocal account or strategy. In the 1950s, Murray will continue to reflect on her own and her family's history in order to develop detailed accounts of a new kind of American identity and a new kind of American history. Both will be by enlivened Murray's imagination of American democracy as eschatological—promised, but yet to be fulfilled.

2

Descendents of Hagar (1950s)

After graduating from Boalt Hall in 1945, Murray struggled to find steady work as a lawyer. Her difficulties in finding and keeping work over the next fifteen years demonstrate barriers that prevented African American women from reaching upper levels of the legal profession. In response to these barriers and frustrations, Murray crafted sophisticated arguments about the importance of identity and history for American democratic practices. As chapter 1 demonstrated, the themes of identity and history developed in Murray's writing of the 1930s and early 1940s. It is in the 1950s, however, that Murray moved beyond a description of identity in terms of the multiple axes of her own experience, for example race, sexuality, and gender, and offered a constructive vision of a new kind of American identity that draws strength from multiplicity. While Murray hinted at an interest in history in "Dark Testament" where she presented slavery as principally important to understanding the American past, it is in her family memoir that she developed an argument that a new kind of American history is crucial to democratic futures. This chapter traces Murray's development of identity and history as integral to her democratic vision and points to the continuing development of her democratic eschatology.

From 1945 to 1960 Murray struggled to find work and capitalized on the few opportunities that arose. While she was earning an LLM at Boalt Hall, Murray wrote a thesis on equal opportunity in employment that would garner her first, if fleeting, legal appointment. Published in 1945 in the *California Law Review*, Murray's "Right to Equal Opportunity" argued, "the right to work is an inalienable and natural right."[1] Murray insisted that the right to employment was a logical and necessary extension of the right to life and to the pursuit of happiness, but that the law was doing a fragmentary job of upholding its own antidiscrimination standard. The US government's obligation to prevent discrimination in hiring and promotion should reflect the standards of the recently signed UN charter, which was committed to higher standards of living and full employment. California's Attorney General read the article and offered Murray an interim position as an assistant Attorney General. Her aunt's declining health, and veterans returning home to claim positions conspired to make Murray's tenure in

California short-lived, but the appointment confirmed that Murray was an innovative legal thinker.

After a stop in Durham to tend to her aunt's health, Murray returned to New York to look for work but was frustrated by firms' unwillingness to hire a female attorney or a black attorney. From 1945 to 1949, Murray held a series of clerkships at various law offices but never found a position at which she could practice law under her own license. Two bright spots during these years were her introduction to Dorothy Kenyon and her friendship with Maida Springer. Kenyon was a municipal court judge who interviewed Murray even though Kenyon did not have a position to offer. What Kenyon did offer was advice and encouragement. Kenyon admitted that law practice was difficult for a woman, but that with courage she could survive. Twenty years later, Kenyon and Murray would collaborate on a case that defended a woman's right to serve on juries. In these lean years, Kenyon gave Murray a boost of morale when it was desperately needed and dissuaded Murray from giving up on the law.

During the same years, Murray lived in Brooklyn only a few streets away from Maida Springer, a fellow activist. Springer and Murray met during the Odell Waller case and shared many of the same political commitments, but as importantly Springer provided Murray with a surrogate family and invited her often for home-cooked meals. In 1949, Springer and Murray worked to get Murray elected to Brooklyn City Council. Both had been involved in local Liberal Party politics and when the Party approached Murray to run, it was Springer who convinced her and offered to serve as her campaign manager. Murray later explained, "as a budding feminist I recognized the importance of women actively seeking public office, whatever the immediate outcome, especially Negro women, who were then virtually invisible in politics."[2] Murray had no treasury and no campaign experience, but with contributions from friends like Caroline Ware and Eleanor Roosevelt, she campaigned night after night on street corners until her voice was hoarse. Not expected to win, Murray nevertheless received the endorsement of the New York Post and came in a respectable second place (beating out major party candidates). While the grueling campaign was enough to convince Murray that she did not again want to run for public office, it was an important distraction in an otherwise difficult time of not finding meaningful work.

A breakthrough came for Murray in 1949 when she was approached by the Women's Division of the Christian Service Board of Missions of the Methodist Church to develop a pamphlet on states' laws dealing with racial segregation. Thelma Stevens, a white woman from Mississippi, sought out Murray; their working relationship exemplified Murray's multiracial professional collaborations (especially with white women) and multiracial friendships. Historian Susan Hartmann suggests that white women's support of Murray's work also "showed the unequal power configuration of their relationships, a bias that reflected racial discrimination."[3] Despite multiplying professional qualifications in the coming decades, Murray, as a single woman and as an African American woman, would struggle throughout her professional career to support herself.

What was intended as a preliminary study developed into a more than 700-page accounting of each state's statutes relating to racial segregation. Murray's compendium was an exhaustively damning rebuke of the thoroughgoing infrastructure of segregation. Published in 1951, *States' Laws on Race and Color* had what Murray described as a "short but strategic career."[4] The American Civil Liberties Union distributed 1,000 copies to its staff attorneys and allied groups who were litigating against segregation. Thurgood Marshall deemed it "the bible" of segregation laws and described it as instrumental in the NAACP's preparation for the case that would become *Brown v. Board of Education*.[5] It was the *Brown* ruling that quickly made the book obsolete.

States' Laws showed the strength of Murray's research skills. She combed through statutes from every state in order to catalog any law, ordinance, or regulation that made reference to race or color. She began the project with the intention of documenting laws that addressed people of African descent, but she discovered that many states also had restrictive legislation against Native Americans, and Americans of Chinese and Japanese ancestry. Murray's compilation included "segregation and anti-miscegenation statutes, laws relating to public accommodations and which are popularly called 'civil rights' laws, fair educations practice acts, fair employment practice acts, statutes directed against lynching and the activities of the Ku Klux Klan, alien land laws, and miscellaneous anti-discrimination measures."[6] The result was a phenomenological triumph, a digest of laws from every corner of the country that witnessed both the legal enforcement of white supremacy and fledgling efforts to oppose discrimination. The State Department recognized Murray's expertise and invited her to apply for a position as a research assistant for a Cornell University School of Industrial and Labor Relations project to codify the laws of Liberia. The project was part of President Truman's Point Four program, an initiative designed to provide technical assistance to developing nations. An important aim of the program was to win support of nonaligned nations.

During the job application process, Cornell grew concerned about what it termed Murray's "activist" background and that none of her recommenders—among them Thurgood Marshall and Eleanor Roosevelt—had stated explicitly that Murray was *not* a communist. Murray filed her application in 1952 at the height of the second Red Scare, when activists, intellectuals, and artists who were thought to have ties with the Communist Party were under suspicion. In a discourse where homosexuality and black activism were coded as communist, Murray was vulnerable to suspicion on two fronts.

Murray had worked or volunteered for a number of the organizations singled out by the House Un-American Activities Committee (HUAC). This, she claimed, compelled her to submit a six-page memorandum detailing "pertinent data on my background and organizational affiliations which may be useful to you in the event that the State Department requires a loyalty investigation of all prospective personnel."[7] Murray explained in each case how her contributions were not communist and how, more often than not, she took an anticommunist position in internal organizational struggles. Murray asked recommenders to send follow-up letters that confirmed her loyalty to the United States. Regardless of her exhaustive explanations and eminent recommendations, Cornell passed over Murray's application because of concerns about so-called "past associations."[8] In the wake of her unsuccessful appeal, Murray reflected that she did not know the reason for her rejection. In a letter to Caroline Ware, Murray lamented that "the issues are so intertwined—race, sex, liberal academic tradition—each of us must hold his ground wherever he is."[9] As she had five years earlier in her articulation of "Jane Crow," Murray again pointed to an interstructuring of oppressions, which prevented her from pointing to a discrete reason for the dismissal of her application.

Cornell's rejection spurred Murray to reconsider her past. She recalled:

> In one of those inexplicable flashes of insight, the phrase that had tormented me suddenly took on a new meaning. The Fitzgeralds, my mother's family, with whom I had grown up, were actually my earliest and most enduring "past associations." They had instilled in me a pride in my American heritage and a rebellion against injustice . . . the example they set had fueled my own political activism. My best answer to Cornell in defense of "past associations" was to turn the phrase on its head and present the doughty Fitzgeralds as my first exhibit.[10]

Murray crafted her answer into a family memoir, which retrieved her "past associations" as archetypically American and patriotic, and she presented them as evidence of her loyalty to the United States.

Proud Shoes: The Story of an American Family was written in the midst of and was influenced by the political climate of anticommunism in 1950s' America. As growing anticommunism increasingly "turned left or progressive dissent into an act of disloyalty, even treason," Murray asserted her and her family's commitment to a specifically American democratic faith.[11] The tone of *Proud Shoes* is defiant of the insinuation that Murray had communist connections or that she was disloyal to the American government and to the ideals of American democracy. Yet, Murray's project can also be read as deeply apologetic: Murray was testifying to her commitment to American democracy, contextualizing it within her family's history of public service.

Instead of calling into question the state's use of suspicion to discredit people involved in freedom struggles (or with marginalized sexualities or gender identities), Murray went to great lengths to show that she did not deserve suspicion. Penny von Eschen has documented a shift in the meaning of anticommunism among

African American leaders after the Truman Doctrine. When Truman proclaimed the United States as leader of the free world, he paired the moral authority and obligation of such leadership with an ardent anticommunism. The Truman Doctrine paired anticommunism, therefore, with a defense of American institutions as the only viable alternative to Soviet expansion. Domestic civil rights efforts, which had during the war been largely understood as part of a worldwide effort for colonial and oppressed people to achieve self-determination, began to emphasize the need for civil rights legislation in order for the United States to serve as an example to the international community. In the early 1950s, therefore, anticommunism took on a new meaning that included an implicit endorsement of American exceptionalism. This new ideological outlook employed "anti-Communism to justify the fight against domestic discrimination and for civil rights," argues Von Eschen, and thus "conceded the high ground to anti-Communism."[12] While Murray had described herself as anticommunist before World War II even as she had situated the black freedom struggle in the United States as part of the worldwide struggle against colonialism, her anticommunism took on a different meaning in the Cold War when she implicitly credited the government's suspicions of communist activists in her assertion that she was not a communist.

Murray's memoir failed to interrogate the ideological equation the government drew between communism and disloyalty, but it did provide innovative accounts of American identity and introduced what she called a "new conception of history."[13] *Proud Shoes* may be read as an example of what Gary Gerstle has identified as an emerging articulation of civic nationalism in the 1950s. Gerstle argues that until the Cold War, American citizenship had largely been defined by racial nationalism, an assumption defended by the Constitution and Supreme Court precedent that only certain kinds of Americans were equipped for self-government. Fervent anticommunism in the early Cold War, however, provided the context for the development of a civic nationalism, in which democratically excluded groups asserted their Americanness by loyalty to the United States.[14] Murray's memoir models both of Gerstle's categories. Throughout *Proud Shoes*, Murray argued that her family was archetypically American and was devoted to American ideals of freedom and civic participation. Murray's family memoir can be seen as an effort to underscore her patriotism and loyalty. In the process of telling her family's story, Murray attempted to recast the very object of patriotism. Using her own multiracial family as an example, she demonstrated how a new understanding of relatedness could contribute to an enlarged civic nationalism. She mined her family's story for a new conception of American history.

Themes that suffuse Murray's other writings are evident here, including a self-conscious regard for identity categories, a tradition of storytelling, and an emphasis on the role of education in racial uplift. As she researched her family's history, the conviction grew in Murray "that one of the best ways to incorporate social and political history into one's own experience is to embark on a search into one's family's history."[15] Murray was two generations removed from slavery, but *Proud Shoes* shares literary features with slave narratives. Slave narratives, which Toni Morrison has identified as the print origins of black literature, presented a personal story that was to represent the race and were written, in part, to persuade white readers that enslaved and formerly enslaved people were "human beings, worthy of God's grace."[16] In *Proud Shoes*, Murray developed these literary features to make a case about democratic possibilities. She wrote to persuade readers that her multiracial family is paradigmatic of the American family. *Her* family's story, replete with violence, contradictions and, yes, hope, could serve as a model for understanding the *American* story. Writing *Proud Shoes* was transformative for Murray. By reflecting critically on the histories of her multiracial family, she developed a new understanding of herself and what it means to be American. As a forceful response to Cornell's rejection, Murray's memoir embraced an often overlooked tradition of black activism and promoted relatedness as the American existential condition.

Proud Shoes charted how Murray's grandmother's and grandfather's different accounts of American history competed for prominence in the household. After her mother's death and her father was committed to an asylum, three-year-old Murray was sent to live with her mother's sisters and parents in Durham, North Carolina. Murray's grandfather was born a freeperson in Delaware, of African, French, and Irish descent. For Murray, Robert Fitzgerald represented a proud tradition of free people of African descent and formerly enslaved people who demonstrated democratic faith through contributions to American civic life. Murray was less certain about the legacies of her grandmother's family. Cornelia Fitzgerald was born enslaved in North Carolina, the daughter of an enslaved woman of African and Native American descent and a white, slave-owning lawyer. Throughout the memoir, Murray struggled with the complicated inheritance of enslavement and family ties.

The principal character of the memoir is Murray's grandfather, who serves as an exemplar of patriotism. Murray framed her grandfather's life in terms of the legal debate about citizenship. The Dred Scott decision of 1857 was handed down when he was a teenager and threatened his status as a free person. In the Scott case, the Supreme Court ruled that descendents of African slaves, whether born to free or enslaved parents, were not to be considered among the citizens to whom the Constitution referred, nor were they intended to be included among the people whom the Declaration of Independence claimed were born equal. According to Murray, this decision "stripped every vestige of citizenship from free persons of color and left them indistinguishable from slaves."[17] The case had a great impact on her grandfather, reported Murray, for after the decision he made it his life's work to prove himself a worthy citizen and thereby expand the notion of citizenship to include African Americans. Throughout the memoir, Murray identified closely with her grandfather's efforts and imagined her own commitment to civil rights as a way to carry forth his legacy.

She appealed to her family's memories of her grandfather's civil war service as a way to both dispute and transform a normative version of Civil War history, which held that whites bestowed freedom on blacks. Murray was most proud of her grandfather's civil war service and teaching career. Initially, Robert Fitzgerald joined the Quartermasters Department as a civilian. Later in the war, when the Union conscripted black soldiers, he became a uniformed soldier and was part of the Union assault on Petersburg, Virginia, in 1864. The assault on Petersburg, among many other contributions of black troops to the Union cause, "would be an armor of pride for their descendents, for there were those in later years who would have these descendents believe that freedom was a gift bestowed upon them by a magnanimous North to whom they owed an eternal debt of gratitude."[18] The memory of her grandfather's and other blacks' service was an important witness that African Americans were instrumental in securing their own freedom. After her arrest in Petersburg in 1940 for integrating an interstate bus, Murray reflected in her journal about the connection between her own efforts and her grandfather's service. Murray wrote that while her grandfather "was fighting to free his colored brothers. His grandchild has been arrested and imprisoned in the same town nearly 80 years later for standing up for Negro rights."[19]

Her grandfather's service was critical to her family's understanding of itself as American, as each a citizen in her own right, and so transformed for Murray what it is to be American. "Because of him," Murray reflected, "we felt that we belonged, that we had a stake in our country's future, and we clung to that no matter how often it was snatched away from us."[20] As she addressed a sense of belonging, Murray gestured toward a tension between assimilation and transforming what is the subject of belonging. In *Proud Shoes*, Murray did not endorse a simple assimilationism in which African Americans should be included within a dominant white culture. Instead, she argued that to recognize Americans of African descent as necessarily belonging to the American nation transforms the meaning of the nation.

Murray framed her grandfather's efforts after the war as a commitment to American democracy. Having trained as a teacher at the Ashmun Institute (what would later become Lincoln University), Robert Fitzgerald decided to travel south to teach in a school for emancipated people in North Carolina. While many of his classmates prepared to serve as missionaries in newly appointed schools in Liberia, Robert decided that his own country deserved missionary attention. In a series of rhetorical questions, Murray characterized her grandfather's choice to stay in the United States in terms of a commitment to the promise of American democracy, despite its shortcomings: "Was it not the *promise* of America rather than its *fulfillment* which had lured the men and women of so many nations to her shores?...Should he leave his native land because the promise had not yet been fulfilled in this case?"[21] Murray used an eschatological register to describe her grandfather's commitment to American democracy. The dialectic of promise and fulfillment carries significant theological weight. The pair refers to a theme of redemption that runs through Jewish and Christian Scriptures that God gives promises at one stage and brings them to fulfillment at subsequent stages. By distinguishing democratic promise from its fulfillment, Murray characterized her grandfather's imagination of democracy as similar to her own—American democracy was partially revealed but yet to come and demanded people's participation in order to make it more fully present.

Murray depicted her grandfather as dissenting from the group of Americans of African descent who wanted to return to Africa in order to construct a nation of freepersons.[22] Robert chose not to participate in the nation-building project in West Africa and insisted instead on the need to strengthen American institutions so that freedom may be nourished in the United States. Portraying her grandfather's choice to stay in the United States as a heroic commitment to racial uplift may have been a way for Murray to assuage her disappointment. She had wanted to leave for Liberia in order to serve as a kind of legal missionary but had been denied the opportunity. This passage of *Proud Shoes* foreshadowed Murray's decision to return to the United States from teaching in Ghana six years hence. Murray will insist that her energies should be spent on making American democracy more fully present, rather than committing herself to African efforts.

Her grandfather's service was central to Murray's "new kind of history," because "if Grandfather has not volunteered for the Union in 1863 and come south three years later as a missionary among black freedmen, our family might not have walked in such proud shoes and felt so assured of its place in history." Though mainstream history did not record Robert Fitzgerald's accomplishments, Murray and her family considered her grandfather "our own personal statistic, our invisible footnote which we added mentally to textbooks where references to the Negro was at best bleak or disparaging."[23] In so doing, Murray and her family began to sketch a new kind of American history, transformed by family memories that include African Americans as subjects of American history. As Murray wrote in the early 1950s, black activism was branded as disloyal, but in her grandfather's service Murray offered a paradigm of black activism that had worked to keep the Union intact. African Americans were patriots and should share in the credit not only for securing freedom but also for securing the integrity of the Union itself.

In contrast to the august portrait of her grandfather, Murray presented her grandmother's story as enmeshed with violence and disputation. Murray's discussion of her grandfather repeatedly invoked civic values and democratic ideals, but it may be in her grappling with her grandmother's story that Murray articulated most robustly a new conception of American history. Murray concluded that the Smith family drama represented the American family writ large. Murray's grandmother was the daughter of an enslaved woman, Harriet, and a white, slave-owner, Sidney Smith. The Smiths were a prominent family in Chapel Hill—Sidney was a lawyer, his brother Francis a doctor, and their sister Mary oversaw the household. Past generations of Smiths included a US Senator, state legislators, and trustees of the University of North Carolina. In what Murray characterized as a struggle between the brothers for control of Harriet, Sidney and Francis repeatedly and alternatively raped Harriet and eventually Francis, the older brother, won out. But Harriet had become pregnant and gave birth to Sidney's daughter. Murray related that Mary despaired over local gossip about the brothers' fight over Harriet, and, in order to spare the family more attention, Mary Ruffin Smith "grudgingly...brought the baby into the house and kept a private nurse for her until she was six years old." Murray's grandmother had complicated relationships with her mother and the woman she called "Miss Mary," her aunt who became her pseudo-adoptive mother. Miss Mary looked after her in the house apart from her mother, and she treated Murray's grandmother as a servant, "if of a special class."[24] Murray's grandmother's special status was recorded in the local church's baptism registry, in which she is counted as among "five servant children of Mary Ruffin Smith."[25] Murray recalls that her grandmother would insist that she and her sisters "were free. We were just born in slavery, that's all."[26]

When Murray was growing up, her grandmother's insistence on identifying proudly with her white father and adoptive mother was a source of confusion and disgrace for Murray. Murray remembered her grandmother telling her, "hold you head high and don't take a back seat to nobody. You got good blood in you—folks that counted for something—doctors, lawyers, judges, and legislators. Aristocrats, that's what they were, going back seven generations in this state."[27] Murray emphasized the existential quandary of many African Americans, who are descended from enslaved people and the people who enslaved them. Contemporary legal scholar Patricia Williams recalls a similar comment when Williams left for law school; her mother told Williams that the Millers, her white ancestors, "'were lawyers so you have it in your blood.'"[28] Williams explains that her mother "wanted me to reclaim that part of my heritage from which I had been disinherited, and she wanted me to use it as a source of strength and self-confidence. At the same time, she was asking me to claim a part of myself that was the dispossessor of another part of myself."[29] Murray presented her grandparents' stories in much the same way—her grandfather was a source of pride while her grandmother's reverence for the white side of the family was an embarrassment. Near the beginning of the memoir, Murray had asserted, "grandmother's uncritical love for her father was intensified by her urgent need for acceptance and for an identity of which she was not ashamed. Her father and his people represented everything desirable in life—power, wealth, privilege, and respectability. All her life she would strive to identify herself with the best of her father's world and reject all associations which linked her to slavery."[30]

Yet the memoir implicitly attributed to Cornelia an ethic of liberation and resistance. As a girl, Murray spent hours reading to her grandmother from the family bible, which had been given to Cornelia by her white aunt. According to Murray, Cornelia's favorite passages were Daniel in the lion's den and Ezekiel's account of the dry bones. Each passage exemplifies a tradition of African American biblical interpretation that compares the experiences of exile with the struggle to survive in the midst of slavery. When Daniel is thrown into a den of lions, God delivered him as a reward for his faithfulness. In Ezekiel's vision of the valley of dry bones, the prophet responds to the destruction of Jerusalem from exile in Babylon. Struggling to find a language to describe the Israelites' experiences, Ezekiel makes a case for the abiding presence of God among the exiles. The bones represent the Israelite exiles, who have seemingly no hope of resuscitating the kingdom of Israel.

Murray did not describe the texts, nor offer an interpretation. It could be that Murray felt the texts were well known enough not to merit it or that a particular tradition of interpretation was so familiar to her that she chose not explain the importance of Daniel and Ezekiel for enslaved and free Americans of African descent. By specifying these texts as her grandmother's favorites, Murray situated Cornelia in the midst of a tradition of biblical interpretation that portrays a God who liberates. James Cone has argued that African Americans retell the story of Daniel because "blacks reason that if God could lock the lion's jaw for Daniel...then God could certainly deliver black people from slavery."[31] According to Allen Callahan, the power of the Ezekiel passage in African Americans' imagination stems from "the exiled Africans and their descendants...yearn[ing] for a collective resurrection that included the resuscitation of their brutalized bodies. They neither looked back to Jerusalem nor looked forward to heaven; their text of choice was an oracle spoken in the midst of a community of exiles."[32] While Murray did not discuss the significance of her grandmother's favorite biblical passages, her recollection that Cornelia had Murray read these biblical passages demonstrates that Cornelia introduced young Pauli to a hermeneutic of hope that God is on the side of the oppressed and those living in exile. This is a hermeneutic that Murray will revisit in her sermons, when she will specifically acknowledge her grandmother's reading of Ezekiel.[33]

Murray credited her grandmother as the family memory keeper and historian, for "out of her own vivid memories and the tales she heard from her mother and the older Smith slaves, she literally breathed their history." The history that she breathed, however, at times exceeded the limits of the telling. When Cornelia's daughters and husband angrily demanded that she not pollute Pauli's mind with stories of the white slave holders, she responded that "the truth's the light and the truth never hurt nobody. I'm proud of my kinfolks. Besides, I'm telling this child pure history." Cornelia told Murray about Smith family's accomplishments in medicine, law, and politics; of particular family pride was the Smith family's involvement in the endowment of the University of North Carolina. Murray's grandmother could trace the family's history back to home counties of English settlers. Murray noted that "years later when I looked up the records I found Grandmother's family history to be remarkably accurate."[34] When Murray compared her grandmother's accounts of Smith family's history with archival records and found that they agreed, Murray considered her grandmother's memories as a primary historical source. Family memories were integral to Murray's new kind of American history, because the kind of memories to which Murray appealed had been ignored by official historical records and thus were not part of normative history. The historiographical authority she granted her grandmother made available family stories that were not part of official history.

There was "one haunting story" Murray's grandmother told about "the Smiths and Great-grandmother Harriet which did not appear in the records." Cornelia described that when Sidney Smith repeatedly raped Harriet "ear-splitting shrieks tore the night . . . night after night he would force open her cabin door and nail it up again on the inside so that she could not get out. Then he would beat her into submission. She would cry out sharply, moan like a wounded animal and beg for mercy." Cornelia Fitzgerald told the story of her mother's rapes with "such passionate single-mindedness it was like the recounting of a long-buried wrong which had refused to die and which she expected me to right somehow."[35] Historian Catherine Clinton notes, "unlike most autobiographies and testimonies which tend not to give full accounts of forced sex, Murray's work reveals that [Cornelia] was born after her mother suffered a series of violent rapes. Murray's level of detail is rare."[36] For Murray, rape was the family's crucible experience and was fundamental to the larger American story, in which violence is a primary way whites relate to blacks.

Murray's use of her grandmother's memories anticipated postcolonial feminist theorist Trinh T. Min-ha's discussion of the fluid boundaries of storytelling and history-telling in postcolonial women's storytelling. Trinh argues that in postcolonial situations, when a woman tells a story, it is considered "just a story," whereas when a man tells a story, it is considered "history."[37] History sets itself apart from storytelling, according to Trinh, by "consigning story to the realm of tale, legend, myth, fiction, literature." History moves to make itself out as fact, mutually exclusive from the story as fiction—where fact comes to mean "truth" and fiction becomes shorthand for "lies."[38] History and storytelling become distinguished by their form, which in turn determines their content. Trinh resists the identification of storytelling with fiction and lies. She argues that the form and activity of storytelling are as important as the content and that both exceed measure. The content necessarily exceeds meaning and measure because every word involves past, present, and future. The form exceeds measure because "what is transmitted from generation to generation is not only the stories, but the very power of transmission."[39] In *Proud Shoes*, Murray demonstrated how her grandmother's storytelling is history-telling. Murray grants her grandmother's authority as an historian by avowing the accuracy of her genealogical accounts. In so doing, Murray affirms as history the family stories about the sexual violence done to her great-grandmother.

Murray complicated the accounts of her great-grandmother's repeated rapes with her portrayal of her grandmother Cornelia's loving relationship with her father. In Murray's account, Sidney was the family troublemaker and was eager to disrupt social custom. Even though Francis forbade his brother from being with Harriet, Sidney delighted in his daughter Cornelia and was proud of her keen intelligence. When no one else was allowed in his study, Sidney would invite her in and taught Cornelia to read. Murray explained, "although a slaveowner himself after his father died . . . he instilled in her that she was inferior to nobody. He gave her pride in her Smith-Jones ancestry."[40] Murray's depiction of her grandmother in the memoir is shot through with contradiction. While Murray faulted her grandmother for extolling the white side of her family, Murray also noted Cornelia's testimony of the violence done to her mother and to her favoring biblical passages that promise delivery from bondage, which implicitly pointed to her grandmother's critique of white violence that shaped her family and her own faith that God would deliver enslaved people from bondage.

In the original text of the family memoir, Murray did not address the conflict between the brutality of her great-grandmother's rapes and her grandmother's love for her great-grandfather, who had raped her birth mother. In the introduction to the reissue of the memoir written in 1978, Murray reflected that although she had resented her grandmother's reverence for the slave-owning side of her family, she credited her grandmother's "view of her own life as a symbol of the possibility of the reconciliation between the races and classes, however fragmentary the symbol may have been." Reconciliation does not mean forgiveness or glossing over historical relationships, rather it points to a future possibility that stemmed, at least in part, from recognizing family history. Murray realized that "in the telling of my grandmother's story I had to embrace *all* the tangled roots from which I had sprung, and to accept without evasion my own slave heritage, with all its ambivalences and paradoxes."[41]

Throughout *Proud Shoes*, Murray wavered between a proud association with her grandfather's legacy and a complicated, at times resentful, relationship with her grandmother's family history. But through the process of writing the family memoir, Murray discovered that while she had always attributed her commitment to democracy and human rights to her grandfather's legacy, it was perhaps from her grandmother that she inherited a conviction in reconciliation between the races. Murray's grandmother had indeed prophesied what would become a cornerstone of Murray's accounts of identity and history—the need to come to terms with one's entire past.

One's entire past, for Murray, included her family's ambivalent encounters with racial categories. Murray reported that her great-grandparents' generation, who came of age a generation before the Civil War, "traveled back and forth through this corridor of mixed bloods as they chose, depending on their appearance and the strength of their ties." Murray explained, "since racial identification was ultimately a matter of appearance...the census enumerators had a hard time of it because in many cases they had to take a person's word as to which race he belonged to." Murray admired her grandfather's family for choosing to anchor themselves in the "Negro race," for "such anchorage was not an automatic process for them; in fact, considering the later history of their close relatives, it was a deliberate choice. Anyone who has been part of a family of mixed bloods in the United States or West Indies has lived intimately with the unremitting search for whiteness."[42]

This "search for whiteness" was, according to Murray, "first a search for safety and then a quest for acceptance." Yet as long the American legal system organized itself around race, Murray saw how the quest for an illusory racial purity supplanted justice: "I daresay that if the country had been settled by black men who enslaved white men, we might have witnessed a relentless search for blackness instead of the other way around." Murray emphasized that the central achievement of her memoir was the lesson that "multi-racial origins of both blacks and whites are realities." In fact, a new kind of American history that accepted this "relatedness," Murray hoped, "might ease the transition to a more humane society."[43] Relatedness provided Murray with a new way to think about racial identities on a national scale. While her poetry of the 1930s described her own racial identity in terms of "trouble" and "dilemma," the family memoir foresaw her family's multiracial identities as indicative of the American story. Murray's "relatedness" was not a call to transcendence; rather it challenged the ontological logic of racial categories. When Murray described her family's experiences of traveling back and forth between or even among racial categories, she intimated how racial identities are, in some sense, performed. Such performances come with real existential risks, of being caught on what is determined to be the inappropriate side of line drawn according to apartheid logic. Murray also noted that these performances took place on the stage of white culture, which determined the strictures and punishments for a person who is caught "passing" for someone she was "not." To understand American history rightly, Murray made that case that the "entanglement of the races" must be at the center of historical work. Murray appealed to a biblical story to describe this entanglement.

The memoir characterized Cornelia's story as "a human story as old as the biblical narrative of Abraham and his bondswoman Hagar, and their son Ishmael."[44] As told in Genesis, Hagar was a woman enslaved by Abraham and Sarah. When Sarah was not able to conceive a child, she handed over Hagar to Abraham so that he might have an heir. Hagar gave birth to a son, Ishmael. But soon Sarah too conceived and gave birth to Isaac. Concerned about her son's inheritance, Sarah told Abraham to banish Hagar and Ishmael. Abraham sent Hagar and their son out into the desert with nothing more than a flask of water. Murray's consideration of Hagar as representative of African American women's experiences of slavery is part of a rhetorical tradition that compares the experiences of enslaved Americans of African descent with the biblical archetypes of Hagar and Ishmael.[45] In her influential account of the meaning of the family drama to the American story, womanist theologian Delores Williams considers Hagar's wilderness experience as a way for African American women to understand their experiences of "standing utterly alone, in the midst of serious trouble, with only God's support to rely on."[46] Murray had retrieved Hagar's story similarly in her family memoir, thus implicating Americans, black and white, in Hagar's story.

In *Proud Shoes* Murray's primary concern is not theological—to offer an account of God and of God's relationship to human beings—but Murray nevertheless critically engaged with a biblical story to develop a broad moral vision of American democracy. By describing the national character as Ishmaelite, Murray underscored that white violence and legislated inhumanity were part of the nation's founding and continued to sabotage democratic possibilities. Murray insisted that to recognize the American story as Ishmaelite—that is, to embrace a new kind of American history—can transform how contemporary Americans understand themselves as related through histories of violence, coercion, resistance, and even hope. In this way, every American is implicated in the family drama. For Americans to pursue democratic ideals such as equal protection and human rights, Murray argued, they need to face the legacies of enslavement. When we understand ourselves rightly, affirmed Murray, reconciliation becomes a possibility for the descendents of Hagar.

The question remains, however, if Murray's new kind of American history has the capacity to enact the kind of reconciliation she imagined? Ashraf Rushdy doubts that it does. In response to Murray's Ishmaelite account, he argues, "if purity is always tentative, based on partial memories, false constructions, and incomplete narratives, the discovery and acceptance of impurity does not produce certainty, liberate memory, and give a sense of fullness to family narratives. Rather, the recognition of impurity produces a difficult and wearying set of contradictions."[47] Murray would likely agree with Rushdy, perhaps to his surprise. While he seems to read Murray's faith in relatedness as optimism, Murray's own text dwells in the difficult and wearying set of contradictions that impurity begets. The result of Murray's insistence on the Ishmaelite character of the United States was not a naïve optimism that wanted to recast America as one big (happy) family. Murray's argument that the American character is Ishmaelite is not a simple rejection of racialist assumptions about who were full citizens, rather it dispels the assumptions that some Americans can, in fact, be meaningfully excluded from participating democratically by the constructs of race.

Years later, Murray would insist that acceptance of her historical roots "is a reminder to white Americans that we are in fact related and cannot be excluded from the family table."[48] Murray's use of memory and her development of a new American history are efforts in aid of remembering but are never finally complete. Murray believed that democratic faith can go hand in hand with the critical memory of a macabre and tragic African American past—and present. Although Rushdy implies that Murray's aspirations for relatedness were naïve and have, in the intervening years since the publication of her family memoir, been disproved, this chapter argues that Murray understood the great challenges that needed to be overcome in order for relatedness to be possible. Indeed, Murray admitted that her aspirations for relatedness were often in the face of all historical evidence to the contrary.

With her new kind of American history, Murray does not simply advance another version of history as the normative account, rather Murray makes the case that the reason to pay attention to history is much more complicated than any simple use of it. Murray argues that history will always exceed the telling; this means that the particular narrative that we have chosen as normative at any particular moment has important democratic implications. In Murray's family memoir, she offered what Emilie Townes has called countermemory. According to Townes, "countermemory begins with the particular to move into the universal and it looks to the past for microhistories to force a reconsideration of flawed (incomplete or vastly circumscribed) histories."[49] The development of countermemory has potentially important democratic effects, for, as Townes asserts, it "can open up subversive spaces within dominant discourses that expand our sense of who we are and, possibly, create a more whole and just society in defiance of structural evil."[50] As the story of an American family, Proud Shoes offered an alternative account of American history distinguished by entanglement of the races and so too of relatedness in order to expand our sense of who we are. Murray's family story as microhistory reveals further how typical historical accounts ignore—or at the very least tragically underestimate—the wagers of white violence.

Proud Shoes was well reviewed but did not have a wide readership in 1956. After its publication, Murray was recruited by Lloyd Garrison, great-grandson of the famous abolitionist, to join the prestigious New York Law Firm of Paul, Weiss, Rifkind, Wharton, and Garrison. Garrison was attuned to the political climate for African American intellectuals; he had served as Langston Hughes' attorney when the poet was called to testify before the HUAC. As the only female and only black attorney at the firm, Murray was lonely and sensed that some coworkers and many clients were not comfortable with a black woman attorney.

As ever, Murray was involved with a network of fellow activists and immersed herself in political activities. She remained close friends with Maida Springer and lived near her in Brooklyn. Springer was a leading figure in the Pan-African labor movement and often hosted visiting labor and nationalist leaders at her apartment. In 1956, for example, Springer enlisted Murray to pick up Tom Mboya from the airport. Mboya was a nationalist leader who would later become Kenya's minister of labor. Murray characterized conversations with visitors like Mboya and Julius Nyerere, who would become the Prime Minster of Tanzania, as "challenging."[51] In the late 1950s, Murray was thoroughly engaged in Pan-African conversations, even if she did not identify herself as a Pan-Africanist. She had her doubts about American blacks' increasing focus on democratic movements in Africa. These hopes and energies, Murray concluded, should be invested in making American democracy more fully present.

Yet Murray recognized, and defended, the importance of a committed internationalism. In the spring of 1959, she represented Robert F. Williams, an NAACP chapter president from Monroe, North Carolina, who connected the experiences of Southern blacks with subjugated people worldwide. Murray served as counsel for Williams when the national NAACP tried to remove him from his position as president of the Monroe Branch. Roy Wilkins, then executive secretary of the NAACP, called for Williams' ouster when Williams was quoted in the national press that it was time "to meet violence with violence" and that "we must be willing to kill if necessary."[52] Williams made these comments in the wake of local courts dismissing two cases brought by black women who had been assaulted by white men: one woman had been working as a hotel maid when she was thrown down a flight of stairs by a white man staying at the hotel; another woman, though visibly pregnant, had been raped by her husband's employer.

The Monroe dismissals came the day after the body of Mack Parker had been found. In February, Parker had been arrested under suspicion of kidnapping and raping a pregnant white woman in Poplarville, Mississippi. In April, two days before he was to stand trial, Parker was taken from the jail by a group of white men, beaten and shot. Ten days later—and the day before the Monroe dismissals—Parker's body was discovered bound in chains, floating on the river. The lynching was reported in newspapers nationwide. Timothy Tyson argues that in the wake of Mack Parker's lynching and the white racism of Monroe Courts, Robert Williams reflected the mood of much of black America that spring, which had lost faith in the possibility of justice from white courts and turned to armed self-defense.[53] In defending Williams before the NAACP national board, Murray did not endorse violence, but she recognized Williams' call for self-defense in the context of violence routinely being done to African Americans. Murray insisted, "I would recommend the NAACP not condone violence. I think that the statement Robert Williams made on May 5 was made in anger and there was provocation—the same day that Mack Parker's body was found...the same day the

President of the United States of America said he would not call for stronger civil rights legislation. Violence was the order of the day."[54]

The lynching of Mack Parker had a profound effect on Murray. In a poem about Parker's murder, Murray used the Evening Prayer from the *Book of Common Prayer* to frame experiences of fear and dread of white violence. Murray wrote "Lighten our darkness, we beseech thee, O Lord; Teach us no longer to dread hounds yelping in the distance, the footfall at the door, the rifle butt on the window pane." She concluded, "Give us courage to stand firm against our tormentors without rancor—Teach us that most difficult of tasks—to pray for them, to follow, not burn, thy cross!"[55] According to Elaine Caldbeck, Murray wrote "of a faith of prayerful resistance instead of revenge, a theology of naming and rejecting evil and calling the self to rise above the actions of those who hate. This is not an easy, assimilative theology, but a trumpet decrying a twisted, cross-burning Christian culture."[56] Like her earlier "Dark Testament," Murray's poem in response to Poplarville (the Mississippi town in which Parker had been lynched) called on God to show special concern for those who face white violence. Though Murray counseled standing firm against tormenters, in the wake of Poplarville Murray decided to leave the United States. In a 1980 interview, Murray explained that "each of us reaches a point where we can't take it anymore. I reached it with Poplarville. My depression was so deep I had to get away."[57]

The opportunity to quit the United States came in the fall of 1959, when Maida Springer, upon returning from a conference in Accra, Ghana, forwarded Murray a job announcement to teach at the newly formed Ghana Law School. Springer, who was by then the representative to Africa for the AFL-CIO Department of International Affairs, wrote letters on Murray's behalf to Kwame Nkrumrah, Ghana's president, and Ako Adjei, Ghana's ambassador to the UN. Springer characterized Murray as a lawyer with superior qualifications, "dedicated, has a sense of history, the love of teaching, and the ability to challenge searching young minds."[58] In spite of her hesitations about Pan-Africanism, Murray accepted the challenge of teaching constitutional law in the newly independent nation.

In the 1950s Ghana was a primary object of African American and international Pan-African democratic imagination. The first African nation to achieve independence, Ghana was led by Kwame Nkrumrah, a charismatic leader and committed Pan-Africanist who was well known throughout Europe and the United States. During the Middle Passage, Ghana was a central locus of the slave trade, its coast dotted with so-called castles that served as docks for moving untold numbers of human beings into ships' holds for the torturous trans-Atlantic journey. That African independence was born in Ghana had special resonance for African Americans; Ghanaian independence meant freedom and self-determination for those who traced their ancestors to the same kin as did many Americans of African descent. Murray's arrival in 1960 preceded the arrivals of fellow intellectuals WEB and Shirley Du Bois, Maya Angelou, and Julian Mayfield.

In Accra, Murray taught classes about Ghana's new constitution and offered comparative lessons about the American constitution. She believed that her role was not simply to be a law professor, but to mentor students how the constitution revealed newly available freedoms and democratic possibilities. Murray was the first to teach the Ghanaian constitution (arriving as she did the year after it was ratified) and collaborated with a South African scholar on the first textbook about the new constitution.[59] Reviews of the textbook by African scholars criticized Murray and her coauthor's wont to argue that the Ghanaian constitution was based largely on the American model.[60] Reviewers contended that the Ghanaian constitution was better understood in the model of British and French jurisprudence. These critiques pointed to Murray's insistence on privileging American constitutional tradition, an insistence that would levy an emotional and political price. In her autobiography and in her journals of the period, Murray reported that Ghanaian students doubted her claims about the possibilities of constitutional law to affect justice because of the international headlines about racial brutality in the United States. Murray had left the United States out of frustration with the failure of the legal system to provide justice for African Americans, but once she arrived in Ghana, she found herself in the unlikely position of extolling the virtues of the American Constitution, particularly its Bill of Rights.

Murray's commitment to American constitutional principles was not limited to the classroom. From Murray's perspective, Nkrumah's government was becoming increasingly dictatorial. It was an open secret that Murray was helping jailed opposition politicians JB Danquah and Joseph Appiah, both of whom were being held under the Preventative Detention Act.[61] The Act allowed detention for up to five years without trial for "political" offenses. Appiah and Danquah were members of the National Liberation Movement, a party that supported Ghanaian independence but was seen as more socially and economically conservative than Nkrumrah's Convention Peoples' Party. Danquah was considered the elder statesman of Ghana's independence movement while Appiah was a member of Parliament who had argued against the Preventative Detention Act when it came up for debate because he foresaw that those who voted for it might someday be imprisoned under its auspices. In the process of mounting a defense of those who had been imprisoned under the Act, Danquah himself was detained. Before his imprisonment, Danquah had approached Murray for help to build an argument that would appeal to the right of the writ of habeas corpus, or relief from unlawful detention.

Murray was aghast at what she interpreted as the young nation's curb on basic elements of the rule of law. Murray felt targeted because her "approach to constitutional law represented a threat to authoritarian rule."[62] She sensed she was being watched and was warned by Ghanaian professors that she should return to the United States, lest she be imprisoned as many of Nkrumah's opponents had been. Naturally, Murray was frightened by this possibility, but she was frustrated also that the postcolonial government that had given so much hope to African Americans was, from Murray's perspective, disintegrating into corruption and violence. According to Murray, Ghana had taught her the bitter lesson that black politicians had the same capacity for treachery as whites.

While in Africa, Murray rejected Pan-Africanism as a constructive political identification and focused instead on American resources to define and address the situation of black Americans. Murray had hoped to experience a homecoming, but her time in Ghana convinced her instead that "my peculiar racial history has made me irrevocably an American, a product of the New World."[63] In an unpublished essay "A Question of Identity," Murray concluded that, for better and for worse, the United States was her home.[64] In this essay, she developed a positive account of African American identity as archetypically American. The diverse hues of Americans of African descent did not fit neatly with African racial categories: a black American is not simply a transplanted African, according to Murray, who employed the generic masculine to make her argument, rather "multiracial in his biological origins, he is microcosm for the American people as a whole, the physical embodiment of their political and cultural unity coupled with infinite variety."[65] Murray recognized, however, that "the dilemma of multiple origins" presents a Catch-22. If a black American emphasized them, he is accused of "miscegenation." If he appeals to his multiple origins to "point up the hypocrisy of his oppressors" then it might appear that he is "ashamed of his race." Murray wrote that the black American has long been aware of multiple origins,

> but he has not yet learned to accept them as a matter of course or to interpret them to his fellow Americans. He has too often asserted, "I am American, too," instead of "I am American, period." The "too" reveals an unsureness of his position, an implied acceptance of the notion of something added rather than something integral to the whole.[66]

This is an important development in Murray's theorizing about racial identity. Whereas her poetry from the 1930s demonstrated confusion and dismay about racial identity categories in which she does not neatly fit, in Ghana she developed an account of a new kind of identity, which drew strength from its inherent multiplicity and was quintessentially American.[67] Paired with her reflections about relatedness in her family memoir, Murray's essay in which she understood African Americans being integral to the American whole foreshadowed theological language she would use in her sermons to advocate for reconciliation. As Murray developed a new sense of American identity while she was in Ghana, she resisted a growing movement among African Americans to identify closely with African politics and cultures. She claimed that she understood why African Americans looked elsewhere for affirmation about who they are, yet she worried that a too close identification with Africa effaced African Americans' multiple origins and evaded the kind of democratic work that needed to happen in the United States. Murray's readers should be circumspect about her portrayal of alienation between black Americans and Africans, which resembled myths from the Old South that blacks, even if enslaved, preferred life in America over returning to Africa. Such arguments sought to undermine the potential for Pan-African identity or for the black freedom struggle in the United States to position itself as a part of a worldwide struggle of oppressed people to achieve self-determination.[68] In 1960 from Ghana, Murray argued that American identity, if a new kind, should be prioritized above a Pan-African or internationalist identity.

Murray was not alone in feeling alienated from African roots. In *Black Power*, Richard Wright recounted his travels through what was then known as the Gold Coast.[69] Wright was a leading figure in Pan-African efforts in Paris and was profoundly influenced by ongoing discussions with CLR James and George Padmore, who had recommended that Wright visit the Gold Coast. Wright departed for Ghana in 1953 in order to see firsthand Nkrumah's independence movement. Wright's travels sharpened his critique of colonialism as a system of exploitation of human and natural resources, but *Black Power* revealed also his ambivalent and often negative impressions of village life. Wright did not seem to be able to make sense of particular kinds of ritual expressions and found them unremittingly foreign. Wright's account of the Gold Coast was stunted by experiences of culture shock and feelings of alienation.[70]

Like Wright, Murray expressed surprise that Ghana did not feel more like home to her. The contradictions Murray saw between the newly independent government and the Preventative Detention Act sparked in Murray a similar outrage as when she called FDR to explicate the contradiction between the ideals and realities of American democracy. Murray chose to side with the ideal of the rule of law and habeas corpus instead of Nkrumah's government. While many other African American activists and intellectuals made use of their position in Ghana to call for political change in the United States while they remained mum about the political climate in Ghana, Murray worked behind the scenes with the Ghanaian opposition to fight what she saw as government's abuse of power.[71]

Kevin Gaines points out, however, that an important difference between Wright and Murray is her defense of American values and institutions in response to her misgivings about Ghanaian politics. Gaines argues that Murray's difficulties in Ghana stemmed from her faith in American constitutionalism and color-blind principles, which "placed her at odds with the Ghanaian government and its left-wing expatriate sympathizers of all backgrounds."[72] This faith also precluded her, according to Gaines, from embracing African identity as central to African American cultural and political projects. Murray's portrayal of African American identity as peculiarly American was shortsighted for two reasons, insists Gaines. Murray's exclusive connection of Negro identity with American identity "denied the validity of transnational solidarities," while at the same time it promoted a "dominant color-blind American individualism that mirrored the ideology promoted overseas by US officialdom."[73] Gaines is right to point out how Murray's defense of American constitutionalism put her at odds with her students and fellow African American intellectuals, but Gaines overlooks Murray's exploration of black identity. Murray did not discount the importance of recognizing racial identity to describe a particular community's experiences and to demonstrate how the American justice system falls short of satisfying these ideals. Gaines misrepresents Murray as advocating race blindness, because he conflates her suspicions about African Americans identifying closely with Africa with a refusal of any racial identification. Following the argument in *Proud Shoes* that her own multiracial family is exemplary of the American family, in Ghana Murray posited an African American identity with multiple origins. Gaines undertheorizes why Murray hesitated to embrace a black nationalism as constituent of Pan-Africanism. While Murray did indeed want black Americans to understand themselves as Americans, not Africans, this was not in response to a color-blind ideal, rather it was partly in response to her dismay in what she saw as increasing corruption in the Nkrumah government and partly in response to what she was convinced was a uniquely American black identity.

Murray saw firsthand Africans struggling with new democratic governments and issues of self-rule, and she concluded that these were African problems needing African answers. While she recognized that Countée Cullen's question "What is Africa to me?" will always be important to Americans of African descent, Murray insisted that this question is only intelligible in the context of American history. Black Americans had just recently been able to make out "the broad outlines of the promised land," the promise of equality and liberty in the context of American democracy.[74] The possibility of reaching the promised land, according to Murray, depended on black Americans developing American answers to American problems. As she had in *Proud Shoes*, Murray described American democracy in an eschatological rubric of promise. The United States, not Africa, insisted Murray, would have to be the location where liberation from oppression would occur.

Murray's long-time friend Maida Springer was not surprised by Murray's short tenure in Accra. Years later, Springer would characterize Murray as "301 percent American. We always had a difference of opinion [...] Pauli was a sharp critic of all of the undemocratic practices in the United States and all of the injustices that black people were victims of. My passionate feeling about Africa she certainly did not share. She was too coolheaded and intellectually searching and was unwilling to make any compromises for undemocratic practices in

Africa."[75] It is not clear, however, how and why Murray overcame the sense of frustration and depression that had, in part, motivated her to leave the United States. In the wake of Poplarville, Murray left the United States because the rule of law and constitutional protections were not preventing black people from being lynched and were not bringing their murderers to justice. While she did indeed counsel for hope for justice in the future, she did not seem ready to embrace America as a promised land.

Personal reasons likely contributed to Murray's return to the United States. Loneliness and self-doubt plagued her while she was in Ghana; her journals from the period are full of accounts of homesickness and feeling "terribly cut off from my world, my roots."[76] She attributed her loneliness to being single: "There are usually couples and they share one another's hardships. I have no one with whom to share and it makes it all the more difficult."[77] Murray had left her romantic partner, Renee Barlow, in New York City. Barlow and Murray had met in 1956 when Murray was hired by Paul & Weiss and Barlow was the firm's personnel manager. Their romance blossomed when they discovered that they were both Episcopalians and began attending church together. Although Murray's careers would take her to Ghana, New Haven, and Boston, Murray and Barlow remained close until Barlow's death in 1973.

Murray remained in Ghana for only a year and a half. When a former colleague from her New York firm and a law professor at Yale visited Murray, he invited her to Yale Law School to pursue graduate work. He assured her that with a Doctor of Laws she could teach law in the United States. Murray hoped that he was right and in 1960 she left Accra for New Haven. Murray's short time in Ghana seemed to have convinced her that, for better and for worse, the United States was her home. Over the course of the decade, Murray had developed constructive accounts of American history and American identity. In each case, Murray posited a democratic eschatology in which promises of liberty and freedom could be fulfilled for all Americans. In *Proud Shoes*, her democratic vision prioritized relatedness and the possibility of reconciliation. From Ghana and in spite of growing enthusiasm about independence and democratic movements in Africa, Murray insisted that black Americans should renew their efforts to make American democracy more fully present. But Murray's analysis was limited by her failure to address the looming Cold War. In the period when civil rights activists like Paul Robeson and Claudia Jones were being jailed under the Smith Act, Murray continued to insist American democracy was partially present and yet to come.

In the 1960s, Murray achieved perhaps her greatest professional accomplishments: she played an instrumental role in broadening American legal theory and was among the pioneers of a feminist court strategy to expand civil rights for all American women. In her JSD (doctorate of laws) dissertation, she traced the historical roots of African American identity and further explored how democracy can recognize difference. In spite of these successes, she will turn away from the law, partly in reaction to her failure to communicate effectively with a younger generation of students who embraced Black Power. The next chapter charts Murray's landmark legal contributions and increasing attentions to what she called "moral and spiritual problems."

3

Jane Crow (1960s)

During the 1960s, Murray made significant contributions to American jurisprudence and the women's movement, earned a doctorate of law (JSD) from Yale Law School, and, as a professor, struggled to reach a younger generation of activists as the Black Campus Movement made nationwide gains. In Murray's legal briefs, dissertation, and journal entries, readers discern familiar themes of identity, history, and democratic eschatology. Carrying forward her emphasis on identity as a primary category of democratic experience, she argued that equal protection is a democratic ideal that must be responsive to actual identities instead of promoting equality in spite of differences. Expanding the historical work of her family memoir, Murray's JSD dissertation undertook an historical investigation of identity as a way to address contemporary democratic debates. Standing at the intersection of two of the century's great social movements, Murray called for faith in American democracy that was to come.

Immediately upon her return to the United States Murray enrolled at Yale Law School to pursue a JSD. At the same time, Murray immersed herself in a new civil rights cause. In 1961, she was invited to serve on a subcommittee of Kennedy's President's Commission on the Status of Women (PCSW), chaired by her friend Eleanor Roosevelt. Even with her heavy workload at Yale, Murray jumped at the chance to devote her talents to a new horizon of human rights, and she was moved by the opportunity to work on behalf of the former First Lady. Since their first exchange in the 1930s, Roosevelt and Murray had sustained a steady correspondence, punctuated by Murray's visits to Roosevelt's apartment in New York City and home in Hyde Park. Murray's influential work for the PCSW would be completed in December 1962, one month after Roosevelt's death.

Murray's contributions to the PCSW influenced feminist legal strategy and exemplified Murray's continued application of Jane Crow. Synthetic discrimination on the basis of race *and* sex needed to be addressed in order to protect the rights of African American women. The PCSW was convened to explore legal issues related to women and to make proposals about employment policy, education, and property rights. Until the 1960s, employment legislation concerning women was generally protective legislation, which was understood to protect women from injury and exploitation. An unintended consequence of protective legislation, however, was that depending on the particular job a woman might be seen to require so many accommodations that it would be cheaper and easier to hire a man. The legislation that many first wave feminists had hoped would protect women *in* their jobs, second wave feminists increasingly saw as protecting women *from* higher paying jobs. Debate about whether or not to endorse the Equal Rights Amendment (ERA), first proposed in 1923, had gone on for decades among women's organizations and took center stage in the PCSW's discussions. Supporters of the ERA promoted it as a way to invalidate protective legislation all at once. Opposition to the ERA ranged from a concern that the Amendment would ignore women's special role as mothers to little hope that the ERA would be ratified in the number of states required.[1] A central focus of the PCSW, then, was to find an alternative to protective legislation, but one that would not necessarily promote the ERA.[2] Murray would theorize this alternative.

Murray had been assigned to the Committee on Civil and Political Rights, which was charged with dealing with this most contentious issue of the PCSW—whether to support the ERA. Murray did not oppose the ERA on the merits, but she felt that it would likely prove to be politically inexpedient. Many feminists recognized the shortcomings of protective legislation but nevertheless felt that women's special role as mothers deserved protections. While she did not endorse any legal position that viewed women simply as people who functioned maternally, Murray acknowledged that some women at some times did, of course, and that any legal strategy that sought to address women's status would need to be sophisticated enough to address women as workers *and* mothers (Murray noted repeatedly that for African American women, working outside the home was much more often the norm than for white women).

In search of an avenue of compromise, Murray looked to the Fourteenth Amendment's Equal Protection Clause for redress of sex discrimination. Different from other categories that were considered under equal protection, including race, religion, and national origin, "sex" had been considered a reasonable basis for legislative classification, referring to a less stringent standard of review that meant that laws could discriminate on the basis of sex when a set of facts was seen to justify the discrimination. In the case of "sex," courts defended a biologically inspired paternalism that sought to protect women in order to safeguard mothers and families. Murray argued that this was retrograde, however, since the Universal Declaration of Human Rights included a sex provision among its fundamental freedoms. In order to pursue women's rights under equal protection, Murray needed to demonstrate that there was not necessarily reasonable basis for a classification according to sex. She insisted that the problems of women are not as unique as the courts had assumed. The Supreme Court had made the mistake, Murray argued, of conflating a person's biological sex with her social role.[3] Of course not only were all women not mothers, Murray recognized, but often women who were mothers undertook different functions as well.

In order to formulate a principle of equal protection under the laws that would include "sex," the courts needed to take into "account both the special needs of women and their individuality."[4] In a memo to the PCSW, Murray argued for courts to recognize that women can seek the freedom of choice "to develop their maternal and familial functions primarily, or to develop all other individual capacities as fully as the male, or to develop different capacities at different stages of life, or combinations of these choices."[5] Murray agreed with courts' rationale that society has a legitimate interest to protect women's maternal and familial functions. A recognition of women's roles as functionally chosen, rather than ontologically prescribed, would also recognize women who worked in the home, because it would consider women's work as mothers and wives as functions performed rather than as endemic to their persons. Murray's appeal to the Fourteenth Amendment mediated between factions: Murray's solution recognized that it was imperative to protect the functions that some women performed through giving birth, raising children, and working in the home while allowing that not all women performed these roles. Murray's legal perspective understood each person's identity as always already existing at a number of intersections. In this case, she asserted that an individual woman ought not to be reduced to any particular social role she happens to perform.

In her PCSW memo, Murray advocated for women a court strategy that had recently succeeded in addressing race-based claims in *Brown v. Board of Education*. As an alternative to the ERA, Murray argued that women should go through the courts. Marguerite Rawalt, a leading PCSW member and ERA supporter, was doubtful that the courts, staffed as they were by an overwhelmingly (white) male judiciary who had been ruling against women's claims for centuries, would recognize women's rights. But Murray persisted that the courts provided the most immediate way to chip away at discrimination against women. And unlike legal approaches that emphasized formal equality or gender neutrality—the idea that "men and women are similarly situated and, therefore, should have the same rights and opportunities"—Murray believed that a court strategy would be flexible enough to recognize that not all laws that specified differential treatment were necessarily discriminatory (a position that the ERA could not accommodate).[6] Murray specified that women may be subject to differential treatment as a class if and only if the law is designed to protect maternal and family functions and is limited to a class of women who provide these functions; is a valid health regulation that takes into account special health needs that advanced scientific discoveries see women as having; and that differential treatment should not imply inferiority of women or single out women as a class. Any law that applied differential treatment to women, but did not meet these standards, would be based on an arbitrary and unreasonable standard within the meaning of the Fourteenth Amendment.[7] Completed in 1962, Murray's memo not only found a solution to a long-standing disagreement in the women's movement, but it also challenged the premise that "sex" was a reasonable basis for legislative classification. Murray's careful distinction between social roles and biological sex would serve as a critical distinction in legal battles for women's rights in the decades to come.

In the PCSW memo, Murray included an ancillary argument about the intersection of race and sex discrimination, what Murray had called Jane Crow in light of her experiences as a student at Howard Law School. While the Fourteenth Amendment's Equal Protection Clause had been successfully deployed in Brown and served as a cornerstone of civil rights legislation, Murray concluded that, because of the interstructuring of racism and sexism as Jane Crow in black women's lives, African American women would be fully protected by equal protection until "sex" was added to equal protection standards. In so doing, Murray confirmed that the "women" addressed by the President's Commission included necessarily African American women, other women of color, and poor women.

In the 1960s, Murray found herself at the intersection of two burgeoning movements. In the midst of Murray's efforts to change the American legal landscape, she used Jane Crow to confront male leaders of the Civil Rights movement, whom she felt did not recognize women's contributions. Murray's most pointed critique came in the run-up to the 1963 March on Washington when she addressed an open letter to A. Philip Randolph, a chief organizer of the March.

Murray protested that not only were women not scheduled to speak at the March, but Randolph accepted an invitation to speak at the men's only National Press Club on the eve of the March. In an open letter to Randolph, Murray challenged,

> I have been increasingly perturbed over the blatant disparity between the major role which Negro women have played and are playing at the crucial grass-roots levels of our struggle and the minor role of leadership to which they have been assigned.... The time has come to say to you quite candidly, Mr. Randolph, that "tokenism" is as offensive when applied to women as when applied to Negroes.[8]

But the March was also a hopeful time for Murray. She later described it as "the nearest thing I've seen the nearest thing I've seen to judgment day. You know our romantic notions about judgment day? Well, these were great throngs, you know, it was like the great gettin' up morning."[9] By referring to a familiar hymn which describes the coming judgment day, Murray appealed to an eschatological vision of American democracy. Murray considered the massive peaceful protest of hundreds of thousands of Americans to demand fair employment as a sign of coming redemption. American democracy must repent and live up to its Constitutional guarantees of justice. When she described the crowd as the "great throngs," she called on biblical scenes when multitudes would assemble to greet Jesus and hear his teaching, *and* she reflected on these many Americans exercising their right of peaceful assembly in order to call for a law prohibiting discrimination in public and private hiring, a major public works program to provide jobs, school desegregation, an end to police brutality, among other demands. The throngs have gathered to testify to the possibilities of American democracy and the distance the nation must yet travel.

Murray's decision to call Randolph, the elder statesman of Civil Rights, to account caused a rift in Murray's lifelong friendship with Maida Springer. Murray and Springer had met in New York City in the 1930s and both had been schooled in the radical politics of the city's labor organizing, central to which was Randolph's March on Washington Movement. Murray had been staying in Springer's Washington apartment in the lead up to the March and voiced her frustration about Randolph's leadership. Murray was organizing a picket should Randolph go forward with the speech. Springer's refusal to participate inaugurated "one of several long periods of noncommunication that arose in the course of their friendship because of strong disagreements."[10] After the March, Murray continued to call for recognition of women's leadership. In November 1963, the National Council of Negro Women met to discuss what should happen next. Murray delivered a speech entitled "The Negro Woman in the Quest for Equality." According to Dorothy Height, Murray's speech "captured the feeling of black women about their exclusion from direct participation in the March on Washington, as well as their feelings about their treatment in the overall movement."[11]

Murray's choice of an open letter to Randolph was indicative of her habit of making sense of the world through writing and of her distance from the grassroots of the growing movement. While Murray had been on the vanguard of black activists in the 1930s and 1940s, who organized sit-ins and integrated interstate buses, Murray's work in the intervening decades had moved away from the street and lunch counters and toward her desk and typewriter. This transition was not a foregone result of middle age. Ella Baker, Murray's friend and former colleague at the Worker's Education Project, had become the NAACP's most accomplished organizer and was a leading staffer of the Southern Christian Leadership Conference and the Student Nonviolent Coordinating Committee. Springer remained a Pan-African labor organizer in a class by herself. Bayard Rustin, whom Murray knew from her FOR and CORE days, was a chief advisor to King about how to apply nonviolent techniques to the Civil Rights movement. While Murray supported the movement's strategies, she had left her organizing days behind her. In the mid-1950s, the demand for civil rights had shifted from desks and dossiers (what James Cone has characterized as "the slow legal work of an elite group of officials and lawyers") to a grassroots movement in Montgomery.[12] During this transformative period, Murray was hard at work on her family memoir and was struggling to make a living as an attorney. In the early 1960s, she developed a transformative legal strategy. While thousands marched through the South, Murray typed. Murray was not quietist or disengaged, but her contributions were now largely intellectual and theoretical. Murray fits the description of the vocation of public intellectual that Cornel West has used to describe Du Bois' "Victorian social criticism":

> Intellectual and political leadership is neither elitist nor populist; rather it is democratic, in that each of us stands in public space, without humiliation, to put forward our best visions and views for the sake of the public interest.[13]

Representative of Murray's best visions and views was the crucial role she played in lobbying to retain an amendment to the Civil Rights Act of 1964 that would witness the interrelation of civil rights and women's rights. Evidently to undercut the seriousness of the bill, Representative Howard Smith of Virginia had added "sex" to the existing equal protection provisions of "race, color, religion, or national origin" outlined in Title VII of the Act, which prohibits discrimination in employment.[14] After the bill passed the House, it was expected that "sex" would be removed from the bill. But Marguerite Rawalt saw Smith's gambit as an opportunity to forward women's legal standing. She asked Murray to write a second memo, this one in response to legislative developments surrounding the sex amendment.[15] Murray's "Memorandum in Support of Retaining the Amendment to HR 7152 to Prohibit Discrimination in Employment Because of Sex" argued that race and sex discrimination should not be separated, for they were "only different phases of the fundamental and indivisible issue of human rights."[16] Opponents of the amendment of "sex" believed that it would distract from the bill's primary purpose—to end discrimination against blacks—but Murray sought to demonstrate a natural affinity between the status of (white) women and of (male) blacks. Murray cited evidence from contemporary social scientists about similarities between sex and race discrimination. She emphasized that while courts had worked to remedy race discrimination, they were almost completely oblivious to sex discrimination. To convince lawmakers about the importance of the amendment, Murray laid out a number of parallels between race discrimination (which Senators were ready to legislate against) and sex discrimination (which was largely overlooked). The memo was sent to a select group of Senators, Attorney General Kennedy, and Lady Bird Johnson, whom Rawalt knew personally.[17]

Murray wrote the sex amendment memo to persuade Senators to support the amendment, but she also implicitly addressed leaders of the Civil Rights movement who were mostly men and leaders of the emerging feminist movement who were mostly white. Murray argued that similarities between race and sex discrimination were "not accidental, but originated in the paternalistic order of society." Rather than simply parallel, race and sex discrimination were connected in that they served a similar end—to bolster "the paternalistic order." Wanting to assuage the concerns of some white women who grumbled that African Americans' rights were being prioritized over their own, Murray universalized civil rights and characterized white women as "natural allies of disadvantaged minorities." The interrelation of all human rights underlay Murray's argument for the inclusion of "sex." "The employment rights of all must be protected or the rights of none will be secure," she insisted.[18]

Just as the victory in *Brown* had depended on attorneys educating the court about the psychological damage caused by segregation, Murray undertook a campaign to educate her white female and black male readers about the multiple axes of oppression that black women experienced. After developing a comparison between historical discrimination against African Americans and against women, Murray invoked the experiences of African American women to demonstrate overlapping and interconnected forms of inequality. Murray argued that "these two types of discrimination are so closely intertwined and so similar that Negro women are uniquely qualified to affirm their interrelatedness." As Murray had argued in the late 1940s with her category of Jane Crow, she testified again that black women rarely knew the source of the discrimination they suffer. Murray cited demographic reports that evidenced the synthetic forms of inequality that a black woman endured, for she had less education, earned less, was in the labor market longer, and bore a heavier economic burden of heading a family. Murray concluded that "in a more sharply defined struggle than is apparent in any other social group in the United States, she is literally engaged in a battle for sheer survival."[19] Embedded in a memorandum to support the inclusion of "sex" among equal opportunity provisions, Murray cautioned leaders of the Civil Rights and women's movements against making a false choice between rights for African Americans and rights for women, which would ignore the experiences of those at the intersection of race and sex.[20]

With white feminist legal scholar Mary Eastwood, Murray published her argument about legal remedies for Jane Crow. Eastwood, a lawyer at the Department of Justice, had served as the Secretary of the PCSW's Committee on Civil and Political Rights. Their article was among the first published considerations of African American women's legal status and is an important precursor to critical race feminism, a theoretical movement that emerged in the late 1980s that addresses the legal rights of women of color. Murray and Eastwood argued, echoing Murray's memo, that the addition of sex to Title VII was crucial because "it is exceedingly difficult to determine whether a Negro woman is being discriminated against because of race or sex."[21]

Murray again appealed to affinities between the Civil Rights and women's movements at a 1965 conference sponsored by the National Council of Women, when she argued that it may become necessary for women to march "to assure equal job opportunities for all."[22] Although the Equal Employment Opportunity Commission (EEOC) has been created to enforce employment antidiscrimination laws under the standards set in Title VII, the EEOC had been reluctant to take sex discrimination cases. In response to the EEOC's seeming indifference to sex discrimination, Murray advocated that feminists take to the streets to articulate their demands for equal protection under the laws. Drawing on a tradition of civil rights protest about employment opportunity, Murray called for a feminist version of the March on Washington. Betty Friedan did not attend the conference but read about Murray's comments in the following day's New York Times. Friedan was intrigued by Murray's comparison of civil rights to feminism and the potential for feminist activism that the comparison implied.[23] Nine months later, Friedan, Murray, and thirteen others who had gathered at a women's conference decided that the time was right for a national civil rights organization for women and established the National Organization for Women (NOW).

Although a founder of NOW, Murray soon became disheartened by what she saw as the organization's almost exclusive focus on white women and by its strategic decision to focus on the passage of the ERA as its primary objective. Since the 1920s, support for the ERA has been centered in the National Women's Party (NWP), a largely white, middle- and upper-class women's group that had a contentious history with civil rights. As recently as the previous year, the NWP had ostensibly sided with Murray in support for the addition of "sex" to Title VII, but for much different reasons. The NWP supported the addition in order to ensure that white, Christian women would receive the same legal protections as African Americans. Murray was concerned that by focusing on the ERA, NOW would alienate potential coalition partners in civil rights and labor. As Serena Mayeri argues, "while Murray did not oppose the ERA per se, she felt that concentrating on the amendment in light of other groups' misgivings compromised the multiplicity of her own identity and her aspirations for the feminist movement."[24]

In light of her experiences at Howard, Murray was not naïve about the potential for members of a marginalized group to have their own analysis be limited by critical short-sightedness. When Murray felt her own and the contributions of other older women and African American women being passed over by the growing movement, she felt the familiar pangs of alienation and of not being recognized, as activists overlooked the importance of critical evaluation of multiple axes of oppression. In an unsent letter to a friend, Murray revealed that she had begun to "reassess my entire relationship to the women's movement and to ponder how I can remain effective without exposing myself to humiliation—for it is humiliating to be deliberately excluded from participation in an area to which one has devoted many years of one's life." She perceived that NOW and the larger women's movement were

> beginning to display the same characteristics as other "minority groups;" they have so long been left out of important decision making processes that any small recognition causes a scramble for mere crumbs and bones. In some ways this can be likened to the situation among Negroes in the 1940s when a Congressional politico said to me: "Why are you Negroes like crabs in a barrel? When one of you climbs up to the top, the rest reach up and pull him down again?"[25]

Murray broke her ties with the national organization just a few years later because she felt that it represented primarily the interests of white, middle-class women and that NOW reflected the general pattern of segregation that characterized feminist groups. Susan Hartmann concludes that Murray's alienation from NOW "was all the more striking in light of Murray's abundant contributions to the resurgence of feminism."[26]

Despite these frustrations with the women's movement, Murray had made her mark. The race–sex analogy that Murray employed in her argument in support of the amendment to Title VII would, according to Mayeri, "profoundly shape women's rights advocacy under the Fourteenth Amendment and through civil rights legislation well into the 1970s and beyond."[27] Almost immediately, the analogy was put into practice in an argument supporting women's right to serve on a jury. In 1965, Murray joined the Board of Directors of the American Civil Liberties Union (ACLU) and dedicated her energies to the Board's Equality Committee. The ACLU would provide Murray's court strategy with institutional support. While her PCSW memo had argued for women to model equal protection claims on the success of *Brown*, her court strategy depended on potential cases being "deliberated, selected, and litigated by some group or coalition."[28] While Murray and others had hoped NOW would serve this purpose, it was in fact the ACLU that would take up Murray's strategy with great energy.

In 1966, Murray and fellow Committee member and leading legal scholar Dorothy Kenyon cowrote the ACLU brief that framed women's rights to serve on juries according to the standards of protection detailed in the Fourteenth Amendment. They argued that the recognition of "sex" among equal protection standards accorded women the right to participate in the most basic of democratic activities.[29] Murray and Kenyon's argument was successful, and the ruling proved to be a precedent-setting decision that "sex" was included in equal protection standards. To the ACLU's chagrin, however, the decision was not appealed, thus thwarting the possibility that Murray and Kenyon's argument would be considered by the Supreme Court.

Murray's contributions to ACLU's efforts coincided with the hire of a young attorney, Ruth Bader Ginsburg, to head the ACLU's newly formed Women's Rights Project, which "quickly dominated the field, entering far more cases than any of the women's rights organization." Between 1968 and 1980, the ACLU participated in two-thirds of sex discrimination cases decided by the Supreme Court.[30] Ginsburg was so impressed with Murray and Kenyon's work that years later Ginsburg attached their names as coauthors to a brief Ginsburg wrote on behalf of the appellant in *Reed v. Reed*, a case in which the US Supreme court "would rule for the first time that discrimination on the basis of sex is an unconstitutional denial of equal protection of the laws."[31]

In the 1960s, Murray made groundbreaking contributions to feminist legal theory, including outlining a court strategy for women that followed the success-ful approach the NAACP had pioneered in the previous decade. In her arguments for the inclusion of "sex" to Title VII, Murray anticipated ongoing efforts in con-temporary critical race theory to have the law be responsive to the synthetic nature of identity. Discrimination that occurs at the intersection of race and sex (as well as class, on the basis of sexuality, etc) has received its most influential treatment by Kimberlé Crenshaw, a legal theorist who has developed the category of intersectionality to describe the experiences of African American women (in particular, but the term can describe others' experiences as well) whose "intersec-tional experience is greater than the sum of racism and sexism."[32] Crenshaw follows Murray in asserting that an African American woman may experience sex discrimination or race discrimination, and that often there is no clear source of harm. To presume one clear source of harm, or what legal theorists refer to as a single-axis framework in antidiscrimination law, typically results in privileging whiteness in sex claims and privileging maleness in race claims. Murray antici-pated Crenshaw's critiques of a single-axis antidiscrimination approach and imagined, it would seem, that black women would be able to cite "sex" in Title VII in order to make a claim from the intersection of race and sex.

But African American women who have appealed to Title VII for redress of race discrimination and sex discrimination in employment have been ruled against for their failure to make claims about a discrete kind of discrimination. The language of the Title employs "or" as the conjunction between the kinds of discrimination that are outlawed.[33] The courts have interpreted "or" to mean that a plaintiff may only appeal for redress for one kind of discrimination. Emble-matic of the courts' inability to conceive the intersectional nature of identity is the ruling in *DeGraffenreid v. General Motors* (1977). To the claim of five African American women that they were adversely affected because of their race *and* sex by a "last hired-first fired" policy, the court ruled,

> the plaintiffs are clearly entitled to a remedy if they have been discrim-inated against. However, they should not be allowed to combine statutory

remedies to create a new "super-remedy" which would give them relief beyond what the drafters of the relevant statutes intended. Thus, this lawsuit must be examined to see if it states a cause of action for race discrimination, sex discrimination, or alternatively either, but not a combination of both.[34]

In her arguments in support of the addition of sex, Murray had indeed hoped that Title VII would be able to respond to the synthetic nature of identity, for example to her own experiences of Jane Crow. But courts have not interpreted the statute in this way and "have been reluctant to allow plaintiffs to aggregate evidence of discrimination when it encompasses more than one legally-protected category."[35] To make way for intersectional claims that employ Title VII, Bradley Allen Areheart advocates that the statute be amended to include "or any combination thereof" to follow the list of categories according to which discrimination is prohibited.[36] Crenshaw and Areheart push for interpretations of Title VII that Murray intended, for Title VII to protect against the kind of interstructured discrimination African American women experienced.

During her years on the PCSW and at the forefront of the second wave of feminism, Murray was also working toward a doctorate of laws at Yale. During the course of her studies from 1961 to 1965, Murray turned her academic attention to a genealogy of African American identity and investigated the process through which legal subjects have been formed. Like and her contributions to the PCSW and on behalf of Title VII, Murray's dissertation challenged presumptions about who is the subject of the law. American liberalism presumes a universal subject, stripped of any particular racial, gender, or class, among other identities. But feminist legal scholars have argued that this universal subject or individual is more often than not characterized by whiteness and maleness.[37] Legal scholar Tracy Higgins advocates that feminist approaches to constitutional remedies take into account developments in feminist theory that recognize ongoing social construction of self in order to challenge traditional approaches that privilege an implicitly white, male subject. Murray's work provides a model of this. Murray's theoretical appeal to the "individual" is always already in reference to an individual who is implicated in particular historical and material conditions. Murray wanted to unsettle the very notion of "American" that implicitly presumes that whiteness and maleness characterize the subject of the law. Murray affirms that an American citizen is an identity formed in a web of relationships shaped by histories and traditions of race, sex, class, and so on. When Murray is committed to the potential for legal remedies of sex discrimination, she did not do so by advocating neutrality or formal equality, rather she recognized historical differences between men's and women's roles that have resulted in women doing the work of raising children and maintaining a home.

Murray noted it had always been the norm for African American women to work inside and outside the home. Before second wave attention to the "second shift," Murray recognized that women as subjects of the law should not be presumed to be just like men but instead should be recognized as people who tend to perform work that is unrecognized and unremunerated. She premised her legal theory on historical realities of women's, particularly African American women's, experiences even as she appealed to liberal standards of equal protection. In a similar way, her dissertation sought to understand the subject of American jurisprudence in light of white racism and African American identity.

While still convinced that social protest and legal changes were important to ameliorating the position of African Americans in the United States, Murray was also looking for more radical explanatory approaches to American race relations. As she had in *Proud Shoes* and in theorizing African American identity while in Ghana, Murray was focused on what she understood to be the unique situation of Americans of African descent. In order to effectively address contemporary realities of segregation and violence, Murray insisted that an historical investigation of African American identity was necessary. Although the dissertation was never published, it demonstrated important developments in Murray's attentions to identity and history. While *Proud Shoes* had focused on her family's history as emblematic of the Ishmaelite identity of American democracy, the JSD dissertation engaged on a broader scale of questions about the identities and histories of Americans of African descent.

"Roots of the Racial Crisis: Prologue to Policy" was a multidisciplinary exploration of the history of race relations in the United States.[38] Spanning twenty chapters and more than 1,200 pages with notes and appendices, Murray's law school dissertation employed history, psychology, and emerging behavioral sciences to describe the situation of Americans of African descent. Written in the midst of the civil rights legislation of 1964–65, the dissertation argued that the "Negro problem" cannot be solved with legislation and court decisions, no matter how radical. The roots of American racism, argued Murray, are "social pathologies which are the outgrowth of centuries of racial injustice." The primary pathology of white racism is a foundational self-contradiction in American philosophy. The contradiction is between the claim that each person is born free and endowed with certain inalienable rights and the legal definition of African American enslaved women and men as less than human.[39] America was "endowed at birth with the genius of the egalitarian ethos of the Declaration of Independence," which declared the universal worth of the individual and an inalienable claim of every person to human dignity. Murray reminded her readers, "the Declaration, however, was not more than an *assertion* of these democratic claims, a *promise*, not a realization." "All too often" she continued, "Americans have overstated the nature of their society by speaking and acting as if democracy in the United States were a reality instead of a *process of becoming*."[40] This foundational self-contradiction defers American democracy to a future date. Once again, Murray insisted that democracy is best understood in terms of a promise that has yet to be fulfilled. This democratic eschatology means that American democracy has been promised but not yet fully realized. How could one nation's history contain so much revolutionary promise and inhumanity and violence at the same time? Murray set out to find out.

Race-based slavery was a "congenital defect" argued Murray, "and the ideology which supported it, compromised the vision of individual worth at the moment of its conception; it stimulated growth of racism, created a divided people, generated a bitter civil war, corroded other human values, and poisoned the institutions of the United States with its baleful influence." The assignment of individuals to racial categories—even though it was an arrant betrayal of Enlightenment commitments to the individual—created the habit of division that would later divide American regions, institutions, and even families. Murray recognized that given this American habit of dividing people into opposing groups, it is difficult not to slip into the error of generalization. Indeed, the "very language of the racial struggle—'the white man,' 'the black man'—reflects the pathology which gives it birth, the deadly generalizations of color which levels individual variations."[41] Recognizing risks in speaking in broad identity categories, Murray nevertheless employed the comprehensive category of "Negro." Her use of "Negro" was qualified, however, and recognized it as a provisional and imprecise category.

Analyses of two of Murray's chapters indicate the sweep of her argument, the kind of evidence she employed, and the broad conclusions she drew. In a chapter on "The Effects of Slavery Upon the Personality of the Negro," Murray investigated the development of family life and black communities after Reconstruction. In an effort to explain why emancipation in itself was not a sufficient condition to resolve the "cultural disruption" of centuries of racial slavery, Murray turned to Erik Erikson's child development studies that argued for the crucial role which family life and early experiences play in intellectual and personality development. Murray noted that it is dangerous to generalize about the effects of slavery on family life, because of variables such as individual personality, regional variations, and differences between rural and urban slavery, yet she did generalize. The thrust of her argument was to upend the historiographical trend of blaming African Americans for the failure of Reconstruction, but in order to do this she depended on far-reaching generalizations about black families and communities. For example, Murray used Erikson's studies to draw blanket conclusions about African American families during slavery. In reference to Erikson's finding that a child who grows up with no clear parental attachments enacts similar relationships for future generations, Murray concluded that "these conceptions of the role which family life and early experiences play in intellectual and personality development and the further recognition that parents tend to raise their children as they were raised throw immense light upon the effects of aggravated family disorganization of Negroes during slavery."[42] Murray could have looked to her own family's history (and to her own life), as of course she had done in great detail just ten years earlier, to see that black families, slave and free, certainly experienced cultural disruption, but also they nurtured loving relationships against all odds.

In a chapter on "The Reality of African Heritage," Murray appealed to Stanley Elkins' *Slavery: A Problem in American Institutional and Intellectual Life* (1959), which considered slaves to be casualties of a closed and repressive system similar to Nazi concentration camps. Elkins' concluded that slavery infantilized slaves, producing adults who were like children. Many historians responded critically to Elkins' assertions, pointing out the irony that he neglected to consider enslaved persons' own points of view as he presented a psychological explanation.[43] Murray noted the "critical reaction" to Elkins' work, but she insisted that his psychological explanation could help her to understand the effects of slavery. Murray cited Elkins, but also referred to slave sources that were available to her, slave narratives and histories, as well as the standard-bearers of African American history, including John Hope Franklin, Du Bois, Carter G. Woodson, William Leo Hansberry and African sources, such as KA Busia and JB Danquah.[44]

At moments, Murray's dissertation seems to share logic and categories with a "legacy of slavery" argument, which held that African Americans emerged from slavery without a culture. Attempting to provide an explanation of black inequality, the "legacy of slavery" argument attributed the lack of middle-class values among African Americans to profound cultural disruption. While "cultural disruption" may be an apt, if underwhelming, turn of phrase to describe the trauma of linguistic, epistemological, historical among other elements of deracination that accompanied the Middle Passage and continued to be a central feature of enslavement, cultural disruption more often functioned as a kind of code to communicate that black communities did not meet the social standards established by whites. A prime example of social science research that employed this argument was the 1965 Moynihan report, which argued that blacks can only end the cycle of cultural disruption with help from whites.[45] Murray shared metaphors like "roots" and "pathology" with the report, which, some have argued, sought to sanction a "legacy of slavery" argument as the official policy of the federal government.[46] Though she characterized the pathology as profoundly American, rooted in white racism, her argument might have been more compelling had she not employed freighted categories.

Integral to Murray's argument was her avowal of her highly personal involvement in her dissertation topic. As an African American only two generations removed from slavery and with established credentials in the Black Freedom movement, Murray characterized her epistemological position as that of an "involved observer," and qualified that her analysis was affected by her "identification with the rising expectations of the Negro minority with whom

I share both impatience with dilatory tactics and the desire for radical approaches to problems of racial inequality." These commitments precluded the
kind of scholarly detachment—a presumption that an academic observer can
and should be personally and politically distanced from her object of inquiry—
still considered *de rigueur* in the American academy in the early 1960s. Murray
argued that scholarly detachment was not only impossible but was not salu-
tary in this case:

> It is a delusion that any American, white or black, can write with
> complete objectivity about the racial issue in the United States, more-
> over it seems unlikely that any American who does not feel deeply
> involved in the outcome of a domestic conflict which continually dis-
> turbs the social equilibrium and at times approaches guerilla warfare
> would have anything worthwhile to say about it. Disengagement is not
> a sure path to truth.[47]

Murray rejected scholarship that ignores each American's entanglement in
race relations.

The primary purpose of her dissertation was "an effort at self-enlightenment,
an attempt to achieve intellectual integration of an intensely felt life experience.
A conscious process of individual integration may well be necessary to the achievement of genuine racial integration in the United States."[48] Here, Murray considered herself a datum of her research, a party to the pathology that has divided
the United States against itself. Murray turned to history in order to integrate
and heal this self-contradiction, a term Murray used to describe America but
could well describe herself, as an African American who was firmly committed to
an American constitutionalism that had historically not recognized her rights or
citizenship.

Murray's self-conscious articulation of her epistemological perspective anticipated standpoint theory, which investigates relationships between power and
production of knowledge and how they are co-constituted. Developed in the late
1980s in opposition to positivist epistemology that asserts a single, authorita-
tive description of reality, standpoint theory identifies how entanglements of
class, gender, race, and imperialism, among others, produce interstructured oppressions from which emerges different descriptions of reality. Standpoint epistemology argues that different social positions provide different opportunities
and limitations for interpreting how social order works.[49] Twenty years earlier,
Murray had asserted that every American is necessarily ensnared by the contradiction between American founding documents' promise and the violence and
oppression that white racism provokes. She rejected a positivist or "objective"
account of race relations and instead underscored her standpoint as a locus of
scholarship.

Murray's dissertation also pointed toward an emerging historiographical debate. It came on the cusp on what has been described as a fourth generation of African American history,[50] a generation for whom Civil Rights and the growing Black Power movement forced a reassessment of black experiences in America. Following Du Bois' *Black Reconstruction* that demonstrated how American history had been abused to oppress black people, a new generation of scholars set up to "penetrate the interior lives of slaves and to outline a distinct Afro-American culture."[51] The significant historiographical move in African American history in the 1960s was to consider "various types of black cultural expression—including folklore, spirituals, language, and religion—that sheltered and nurtured African-Americans throughout their nightmarish ordeal of slavery."[52] Historians understood African American history not only within the context of American history but also in an international context of African history, the African diaspora, and postcolonial independence movements. Murray wrote her dissertation in the early 1960s, but she came of age in the 1930s and 1940s and shared the disposition of the previous generation of scholars "that lived the optimism generated by early victories against segregation and the despair of realizing the limitations of courtroom victories."[53] Yet she also foresaw black feminist and white feminist analyses that each scholar's experiences shape her epistemological standpoint.

If Murray had been prescient about standpoint epistemology, she did not fully appreciate the burgeoning energy of Black Power. Murray presented her dissertation as an effort to discern various historical, economic, and psychological roots of African American experiences in the United States as specifically American experiences. In so doing, she undertheorized connections between African American identities and diasporic identities. Murray worried that a close identification with Africa misunderstood that black experiences were uniquely American. To understand what she calls the "Negro problem," she looked primarily to American history and institutions.

In the dissertation's conclusion, Murray presented integration as a rallying cry. She believed that integration, on a personal level and on a national scale, demanded that Americans face realistically the whole history of American racism. Allowing that what she called an "overly heavy" sense of history can leave people unprepared to face radical social changes, Murray nevertheless maintained that historical perspective can be transformative of American race relations. She pointed to the "many Negroes involved in the civil rights movement [who] have, for the first time, caught that sense of mission and destiny said to be part of the American democratic faith and have felt themselves to be a conscious element in the great sweep of American history."[54]

Murray believed that a robust accounting of African American identity is possible only if African American memories and a new kind of American history are recognized by both African Americans and white Americans. This connection between identity and memory was, for Murray, the precursor to integration, which she described as "the development of internal cohesion, a core of integrity, which gives one stamina and the self-acceptance to review one's past and correct past errors as well as to confront and solve difficult problems of the immediate present. This would seem to be true of nations as well as individuals."[55] This shows how Murray's project was intensely personal. In her poetry, Murray had written about her identity in terms of "trouble" or "dilemma," and in *Proud Shoes*, she described herself as a "nobody, without identity." In the dissertation, Murray turned to the possibility of integration as an answer to her questions about identity and history.

Murray considered the contemporary "Negro revolt" as potentially the kind of democratic crossroads that Emancipation had promised to be. Murray wondered whether a majority of Americans were now "prepared to live together *as one people* on the basis of liberty *and* equality as they were not prepared to do in 1865." Murray thought the answer was yes, but that the success of any policy initiatives, no matter how imaginative or comprehensive, depended on a new sense of a connection between identity and history that would offer a more accurate picture of American history. Yet Murray was also forthright about the anger that fueled the "Negro revolt." She characterized "the present hostility" as coming from "younger Negro intellectuals who are taking a long look at the contradictions in American values and saying to themselves, 'Do we want to integrate in a burning house?'" In an effort to respond to Baldwin's demand, civil rights organizations, religious groups, and African American intellectuals called for a "payment with interest for a long-standing moral and material debt." The leaders of the "Negro revolt," according to Murray, argued that American history is synonymous with "lawlessness and violence, extermination of weaker peoples, and the ruthless exploitation of the powerless, which has paralleled its quest for the enduring values of human dignity."[56]

African Americans' tragic experiences of the American contradiction, according to Murray, gave them special authority with which to call on the conscience of a nation and articulate, despite their anger and suffering, a new kind of democratic faith. Murray admitted that "this newly-conceived missionary role is an ironic twist of history, of course, but it is an important therapeutic phase of the reconciliation of Negro Americans with their national heritage in their painful movement from alienation to full cultural assimilation." Although Murray recognized "the Negro revolt," a reference to urban violence and increasing unrest within civil rights organizations about the efficacy of nonviolence, Murray was not prepared to accept a change in movement tactics. Even in the face of violence and exploitation, Murray counseled nonviolence and faith. The black revival of democratic faith would help "to fill a vacuum caused by an increasing secularization of American society." She characterized the civil rights movement as a religious movement when she described how "it has forced many white Americans to re-examine their own moral and ethical values" and that many white Americans who had involved themselves in the movement had "experienced something akin to religious conversion."[57] Murray's JSD dissertation adopted a theological tone when her new kind of American history would be premised on an American democratic faith, motivated by a sense of mission and populated with prophetic voices. In the dissertation's introduction, Murray described American democracy as involved in "*a process of becoming*," a promise but not yet a reality. Her conclusion recognized the prophetic call of the Civil Rights movement to nurture a democratic faith that is premised on a profound hope for what is yet to be seen but will be revealed.

For her readers, Murray's dissertation serves as a companion piece to her family memoir from the previous decade. Both outlined a particular American identity rooted in the historical experiences of the people of the United States, free and enslaved, and were interested to refocus historical study on the experiences of black Americans. The sweeping generalizations of the dissertation failed to address the tragic particularities of American history. Nor did they answer implicit questions about *why* African Americans should have faith in American democracy. Continued state-sanctioned violence against blacks in the South and persistent segregation indicated that the faith Murray's dissertation counseled was naïve and perhaps even self-destructive. Even as it addressed white racism, the dissertation focused on the "Negro problem" and so did not accomplish the new kind of American history that *Proud Shoes* promoted. As an historical project, *Proud Shoes* was, in many ways, more effective and perhaps more true. It had demonstrated that interpreting American history through the rubric of relatedness would encourage all Americans to understand themselves differently. The professed aspiration of the dissertation was to develop an historical account of race relations, but the result took on, at times, the tone of an *apologia* of American democracy. The strength of the dissertation was Murray's repeated insistence that critical investigations into identity and history are at the heart of the American democratic project.

Murray was not alone in connecting identity and history to democratic ambitions, of course. Two of Murray's contemporaries, Ralph Ellison (born 1913) and James Baldwin (born 1924), also presented the search for identity and the possibility of a new kind of American history as principal democratic concerns. Investigating Baldwin's and Ellison's attentions to identity and history sheds light on Murray's critical work. Murray's, Ellison's, and Baldwin's paths crossed in personal and circumstantial ways. Baldwin and Murray spent a summer together with other writers, artists, and musicians at the McDowell Artists Colony in New Hampshire in 1954, when Murray was hard at work on *Proud Shoes*.[58] Nowhere in her autobiography or in her archived correspondence did Murray mention a personal acquaintance with Ellison, but both came of age politically in 1930s' New York City. Ellison's formative political experiences as "part of a generation of working class intellectuals" were evident in his stories collected in *Flying Home*. Just as Murray made connections between experiences of whites and blacks in the working class, Ellison wrote about "the shared humanity across racial lines [and of a] shared economic plight that encourages the connection."[59]

Murray, Ellison, and Baldwin were eyewitnesses to the 1943 Harlem riots. Murray and Ellison wrote accounts for local newspapers while Baldwin recalled that the riots erupted on the same day as the funeral of his father, a preacher. In "Notes of a Native Son," Baldwin wrote, "I had declined to believe in that apocalypse which had been central to my father's vision; very well, life seemed to be saying, here is something that will certainly pass for the apocalypse until the real thing comes along." In the same essay, Baldwin identifies the burden of white racism that he would spend the rest of his life writing against, "I had discovered the weight of white people in the world. I saw that this has been for my ancestors and now would be for me an awful thing to live with and that the bitterness which helped kill my father would also kill me."[60]

Five years after the Harlem riots, Baldwin left the United States for Paris. Even in Paris, Baldwin faced nagging questions about black identity. About a group of African American students studying in Paris on the GI Bill who meet African students also studying in France, Baldwin wrote, "they have each other, the Negro and the African, over a gulf of three hundred years—an alienation too vast to be conquered in an evening's goodwill, too heavy and too double-edged ever to be trapped in speech. This alienation causes the Negro to recognize that he is a hybrid. Not a physical hybrid merely: in every aspect of his living he betrays the memory of the auction block." Like Murray's experiences in Ghana had, Baldwin's encounters with African writers in Paris convinced him that Americans of African descent are tragically, but nevertheless indelibly, American. Baldwin connected this revelation about African American identity to the articulation of a new kind of American history, "it is difficult to make clear that he is not seeking to forfeit his birthright as a black man, but that, on the contrary, it is precisely this birthright which he is struggling to recognize and make articulate. Perhaps it now occurs to him that in this need to establish himself in relation to his past that he is most American."[61]

But Baldwin characterized this need to establish oneself in relationship to the past in terms of panic and nightmare. In "Many Thousands Gone," originally published in 1951, Baldwin traced a labyrinth of connections between American identity, "Negro identity," and American history. Throughout the essay, Baldwin negotiated between subject positions, at times to imply that his use of "we" included all Americans, at other times to imply that "we" was a separate group from black Americans.[62] At the beginning of the essay, Baldwin couched the ramifications of black identity in psychological terms: "Our estrangement from him is the depth of our estrangement from ourselves. We cannot ask: what do we *really* feel about him—such a question merely opens the gates on chaos. What we really feel about him is involved with all that we feel about everything, about everyone, about ourselves." Here, Baldwin juxtaposed "the Negro" with the rest of "America," and emphasized "our" estrangement from "him." Yet, in the following paragraph, Baldwin elided "the Negro" with "Americans" when he wrote, "the story of the Negro in America is the story of America—or, more precisely, it is the story of Americans. It is not a pretty story: the story of a people is never very pretty." Here, the antecedent to "people" seems to be "Americans," but to consider African Americans as Americans, and to have such a consideration inform our sense of history, inspires panic. Baldwin concluded that Americans understand black Americans—here the subject position has split once more—in social, not human or moral, terms such that "if he [the Negro] breaks our sociological and sentimental image of him we are panic-stricken and we feel ourselves betrayed."[63]

In a 1962 essay, "As Much Truth As One Can Bear," Baldwin revisited panic, this time connecting it to history, "our impulse to look back on what we now imagine to have been a happier time. It is an adulation which has panic at the root." The panic is in response to the past that will reveal a truth with which we are not equipped to grapple. Baldwin continued, "and that panic then . . . comes out of the fact that we are now confronting the awful questions of whether or not all our dreams have failed. How have we managed to become what we have, in fact, become? And if we are, as indeed, we seem to be, so empty and so desperate, what are we to do about it? How shall we put ourselves in touch with reality?"[64] While Murray had faith that facing history will enact a reconciliatory process, Baldwin wondered at our capacity to make sense of history in any meaningful way. In "Stranger in a Village," Baldwin confirmed that Joyce "is right about history being a nightmare—but it may be a nightmare from which no one *can* awaken. People are trapped in history and history is trapped in them."[65]

Ellison wrote similarly of the difficulty for Americans to reconcile their history. In a 1964 essay, "Blues People," Ellison reckoned that "perhaps more than any other people, Americans have been locked in a deadly struggle with time, with history. We've fled the past and trained ourselves to suppress, if not forget troublesome details of our national memory, and a great part of our optimism, like our progress has been bought at the cost of ignoring the processes through which we've arrived at any given moment in our national experience."[66] Murray discussed her own experiences of writing *Proud Shoes* as coming to terms with "suppressed memories." And throughout her discussion of the development of American identity in her JSD dissertation, Murray employed similar psychological analogies, diagnosing American racism as a pathology.

In her dissertation, Murray argued that this pathology prevents Americans from realizing their democratic ideals, for white racism has engendered a deformity in the body politic. Yet Murray remained committed to these ideals, even in the face of centuries of failure to realize them. Ellison shared this sense of hope.

In "The Little Man at Chehaw Station," Ellison referred to the Declaration of Independence, the Constitution, and the Bill of Rights as the sources of democratic ideals, though he affirmed that "we stand, as we say, in the name of these sacred principles that we ceaselessly contend, affirming our ideals even as we do with violence."[67] Like Murray's, Ellison's faith in American ideals was premised on his belief in both the possibility of wholeness and, at the same time, the ongoing process of defining what it means to be American.

For Ellison, the process by which Americans search for an identity was dynamic and democratic. In a 1976 essay on the "Perspective of Literature," Ellison wrote, "the struggle between Americans as to what the American is to be is part of that democratic process through which the nation works to achieve itself."[68] In her 1978 introduction to *Proud Shoes*, Murray would also write about the search for an American identity in terms of a "slowly evolving *process* of biological and cultural integration, a *process* containing the character of many cultures and many peoples."[69] The result of this process, according to Murray's family memoir, was a kind of wholeness in which the integrity of differences is maintained. Ellison articulated a similar ethic of wholeness. Arguing against what he called recent attempts to reduce American cultural diversity to "an easily recognizable unity," Ellison proffered a vision of a "complex and pluralistic wholeness," which he calls "our 'Americanness.'"[70]

Like Baldwin and Murray, Ellison described African American identity as a special kind of American identity, for "though as passionate believers in democracy Negroes identify themselves with the broader American ideals, their sense of reality springs, in part, from an American experience which most whites not only have not had, but one with which they are reluctant to identify themselves even when presented in forms of the imagination."[71] This attention to the important character of African American identity in making sense of democratic ideals was central to Ellison's and Murray's democratic faith.

Similarities between Murray's and Ellison's espousal of democratic faith might prompt Houston Baker to discount Murray's account of history for not being sufficiently critical. A leading American literary critic, Baker has excoriated black intellectuals and politicians for downplaying dire material conditions of many African Americans in post-civil rights America.[72] In *Critical Memory*, Baker offers Ralph Ellison as an exemplar of a black intellectual who refuses to wrestle with the historical exigencies of black experience. To do so, Baker necessitates critical memory, which "not only hurts and outrages but also produces critiques, strategic collaboration, intervention, and public-sphere institutions" that can support and help the black community flourish.[73] But Baker warns that the potential of black critical memory is often blunted by black Americans' desire to be like and to be liked by white Americans. Baker employs "like" in two ways, as a preposition and a verb, to describe relationships between white and black Americans. If black Americans apply their efforts in the prepositional way, that is, to be "like" white Americans, then they might have the experience of the verb, to be "liked" by white Americans.

Making a connection between critical memory and likability, Baker insists that

> critical memory—that and almost that alone—has always conditioned black Americans' likability and danger quotients in the mental life of white America. Now, this realization carries its own melancholy weight. For in sometimes sad, complicitous, self-destructive ways, we have assumed that if blacks simply step back and erase our memory we will be allowed to remain healthily on American soil—and even be liked.[74]

According to Baker, Ralph Ellison is an African American intellectual who wanted to be like white Americans in order to be liked by white Americans, and who, thus, cannot contribute to African American critical memory. Baker takes particular aim at what he characterizes as Ellison's naïve democratic faith. Baker presents an early scene in Ellison's *Invisible Man* as exemplary of such faith: After the protagonist is being beaten, he stands "bloody and unbowed in his American faith." Baker argues that Ellison's democratic faith was misplaced and strangely anachronistic, since Ellison's reading "misses, of course, all the nascent energy of Civil Rights and Black Power." Baker criticizes Ellison for choosing to "recline in butter-soft seats at exclusive Manhattan clubs" instead of taking an active part in the black freedom struggle. Baker finally dismisses Ellison's democratic hope as "pure poppycock."[75]

Baker does not address Murray's work, but Baker's frustrations with Ellison's democratic faith raise questions about whether Murray's democratic faith can contribute to critical memory. Baker's evaluation of Ellison provides Murray's readers a critical lens to apply to Murray's theorizing about history and democratic faith. On Baker's reading, Ellison shied away from speaking truthfully about a history that is "embarrassing, macabre, and always bizarre with respect to race." Ellison's and Murray's writings repeatedly express a faith that American democratic principles can both protect and give meaning to lives of black Americans. Baker argues that Ellison fails to contribute to African American critical memory because, by implication, Ellison's democratic faith is a strategy to be like white Americans, so that he might be liked by white Americans. Baker calls for African American intellectuals to undertake the work of critical memory in order to "lead the American majority to understand the real war against decency that has been waged against it, in the name of race, during the past forty years.... The difference critical memory can make depends in large measure on the honesty of black intellectuals who are not seeking to be liked."[76] If, on Baker's account, Ellison failed because he was seeking to be liked, we might look to Murray's honesty as a measure of how critical were her contributions to African American memory.

While Murray was "liked" by many whites, that is, she nurtured close friend-ships and collaborative professional relationships with influential white women, including Eleanor Roosevelt, Caroline Ware, Lillian Smith, and Ruth Bader Ginsburg, among others, she never reclined in the butter-soft seats of Manhattan clubs. In fact, alienation and loneliness typified Murray's experiences and her critical reception. Whether in light of her fellow activists' rejections of her rad-ical demands that racism and sexism be considered in equal measure, or her lifelong struggle to find and keep meaningful work, Murray's democratic faith in the face of ongoing rejection would seem to be faith in spite of being liked. But perhaps more the point, Murray did articulate an American history that is, as Baker requires, "embarrassing, macabre, and always bizarre with respect to race." Her family memoir refused to erase memory, as Baker worries shying away from critical memory entails. Instead *Proud Shoes* shared a complicated inheritance of sexual violence and the unremitting search for whiteness. Her dissertation insisted that the fundamental deformity in the American body politic is a result of white racism. Baker's criticism of Ellison points, however, to critical questions about Murray's reaction to the nascent energy of Black Power.

A debate during a 1967 ACLU equality committee meeting was representative of how Murray's commitment to women's rights put her at odds with a younger generation of black activists and intellectuals, but it also demonstrated Murray's reluctance to credit the democratic potential of Black Power. Murray and Floyd McKissick, then President of the Congress of Racial Equality (CORE), were ACLU equality committee members, who debated its future priorities. Murray wanted the committee to place women's rights among the top items on the agenda, but McKissick disagreed. The committee's secretary recorded McKissick as saying that "at the moment CORE is emphasizing black male power, and tomorrow will concentrate on the equality of women. He will defend the ACLU position, but at the same time must maintain his organization's position. He further noted that the black woman in America has traditionally been the spearhead of the movement while the black male leadership has slept."[77] Meeting minutes do not include Murray's response to McKissick's prioritization, but in a journal entry from the following year, Murray wrestled with a response to McKissick. In a draft of what she planned to be a book length polemic "from the viewpoint of a long personal experience that racial equality and sex equality are part of the principle that human rights are indivisible" entitled "Black Power for Whom?" Murray wrote,

> Until my black brothers and white brothers recognize white racism and
> male supremacy as equally immoral and unjust and just as dangerous to
> the future healthy development of the United States, we are not likely
> to make any permanent progress toward racial equality.[78]

Murray was frustrated by what she perceived as an emphasis on male domination in the Black Power movement, which therefore could not recognize the
interrelatedness of all human rights.

Murray and McKissick shared political commitments before their disagreement in the 1967 meeting. A native North Carolinian, McKissick was among the
first group of freedom riders in CORE's 1947 campaign, for which Murray served
on the organizing committee and in which she had wanted to participate first
hand. Following Murray's unsuccessful bid to integrate the University of North
Carolina in 1938, McKissick had been among the first African American students
admitted to UNC's the law school in 1951. McKissick had been a youth organizer
for CORE and later, as an attorney, was arrested for participating in sit-ins in
North Carolina. Although they shared a pedigree, by the late 1960s McKissick and
Murray disagreed about the strategic direction of the Black Freedom movement.
When McKissick took over the leadership of CORE in 1965, he shifted the organization's priorities from nonviolent direct action and integration with whites to
Black Power, including programs to build black people's political and economic
power. CORE's shift was representative of similar moves in organizations like
SNCC, which moved away from an exclusive commitment to nonviolence in order
to explore expressions of black nationalism and possibilities for self-defense. The
growing influence of other groups that emphasized Black Power politics, including
the national ACT and Detroit-based Revolutionary Action Movement, signaled a
shift in the Black Freedom movement when a younger generation of activists
chose a new direction against the wishes of some of Murray's generation.[79]

While Murray disagreed with the direction of CORE, it was what Murray took
to be a personal slight that occasioned reflection on how McKissick's and her
own politics had diverged. It had been ten years or more since they had last seen
each other. When Murray and McKissick met in the elevator on the way to the
meeting, McKissick turned to a CORE staffer who accompanied him and, by way
of introduction, said "this chick really has something on the ball." At this, Murray
was livid. She recalled,

> this incident triggered a chain reaction in me. Why should I be upset by
> a colloquialism? Certainly McKissick meant no offense. . . . Was I so
> "brain-washed" with "white middle class values" that I wanted to disso-
> ciated myself from expressions popular in the black ghetto? Turning
> the question around, I wondered if McKissick and I had been fighting
> all these years for the same things? True, as a woman who had sought
> the quieter more scholastic paths of the struggle I had been more
> protected from the fury of the battle.[80]

Allowing their different locations of struggle, Murray asked but did not answer
a provocative question about her ability to appreciate McKissick's political

program. About their encounter, she concluded, if "I stress human rights rather than Negro rights, it is because I have a double minority status and that achievements of Negro rights would leave me only partially protected. Nor do I believe that one set of rights must take priority over the other, but all must be achieved simultaneously or none will be permanently secured."[81] As she had since her years at Howard Law School in the 1940s, Murray refused to choose between civil rights and feminism. Instead, according to Susan Hartmann, she "reinterpreted civil rights, insisting that women's rights were critical for black women's civil rights to be realized."[82] Murray's rejection of Black Power was not, therefore, a result of a kind of naïve democratic faith. Instead, Murray rejected McKissick's position because she concluded it was a false choice between the advancement of rights for African Americans and rights for women. Once again, Murray's commitment to Jane Crow shaped her strategic perspective and, in the spirit of Baker's critical memory, provided her a constructive way to wrestle with realities of black experiences, which included white racism and male domination.

The following year, in her own classroom, Murray confronted her frustrations with the changing course of black activism. In the summer of 1968, Murray received an offer from Brandeis University to teach in the American Studies Program and to help to develop a Black Studies curriculum. Murray was hired in the wake of King's assassination when Brandeis and other universities were looking to increase the number of black faculty and develop programs to address growing interest in black history and diasporic identity. Murray looked forward to developing a curriculum that considered black experiences as an integral part of American civilization and emphasized the impact of African and European heritages on New World identities. Murray saw Black Studies as "a part in the effort of reintegrating our national heritage, of making whole the American psyche, of bringing into the intellectual current of our past significant tributaries of 'Black Experience' [and as] a creative mission of high order, one that in its potential for reconciliation had religious as well as social and political implications." She would soon discover, however, that her students did not share her vision of black identity. On her first day of teaching at Brandeis, she was challenged by an African American man who dismissed her use of "Negro" as outdated and insisted instead that she use the term "black." Murray strongly objected to the "*exclusive* use of 'black' as an official designation." The content of what Murray called Negro experiences should not be reduced to a shade of color. She was concerned that "making 'black' do double duty to describe (the color) and to name (the race) gave the term a confused meaning."[83] That day Murray was able to gain control of her classroom, but she remained at odds with growing black nationalism on campus and struggled to connect with the younger generation.

Murray had arrived at Brandeis with "the vision of carrying forward Dr. Martin Luther King's dream of the 'beloved community,'" but almost immediately she felt it "receded like a mirage."[84] In January 1969, a group of students took over a university building and presented the administration with nonnegotiable demands, including an African Studies Department, an Afro-American center designed by black students, and ten fully funded scholarships for black students.[85] Murray experienced the takeover deeply personally because her office, which housed all her papers and files, was in the chemistry building, which students had occupied and threatened to blow up. Brandeis students' actions were part of a larger Black Campus Movement that undertook similar protests across the country and resulted in over 300 departments, centers, and institutes in Black Studies. Ibram Rogers estimates that "the Black Campus Movement probably had more of an effect on its segment of society than any other sector of the Black Power Movement."[86]

Yet in the moment, Murray was frustrated by the students' tactics. In her journal, she wrote:

> Why can't I be proud of these kids for what they have done? Because I think they have used the lowest, crudest form of protest and they are getting away with it and this will lead them to believe that that this is the only was to win victories. Is it? This is the great question in my mind. Whatever the outcome, force, the threat of destructive force will have produced it. And can force of that nature produce anything but a pyrrhic victory?[87]

Among the first African American activists to experiment with *Satyagraha* and nonviolent direct action in the early 1940s, Murray could not countenance what she interpreted to be antagonistic and coercive tactics by young people in the late 1960s. She also questioned the politics that underlay students' demands. Murray had misgivings about what she interpreted as students' dependence on a monolithic black identity. She saw the separation that some black students demanded as artificial at best and destructive at worst. To assign classroom space and living arrangements based on existentially improbable classifications seemed to Murray not only false but also reminiscent of the kind of nostalgia for origins that fueled Jim Crow. She admitted also that "my barely disguised hostility toward the Black Revolution was in reality my feminist resentment of the crude sexism I perceived in many of the male leaders of the movement."[88] Murray was demoralized by her failure to reach young men and women with whom she expected to share political goals. She grieved at what she took to be "a complete reversal of goals that had fired my own student activism."[89]

Murray did not want to concede connections between her own activism and Brandeis students' demands. Brandeis students' political program emerged out of a Black Freedom movement characterized by internationalism, Pan-Africanism, and calls for black self-determination. Historian Peniel Joseph is among a group of historians who are outlining a Black Power historiography that refuses to reduce Black Power to the "'evil twin' that wrecked civil rights."[90] Instead, Black Power historiography traces the broad movement's roots to antebellum black conventions, Garveyism of the 1920s, and calls for self-defense in the South in the 1950s. It reveals how, for example, Brandeis students inherited arguments Murray and her colleagues have been making in the 1940s, which compared the struggle for rights for African Americans in the United States with struggles of oppressed people around the world.[91] The students emphasized an identification with Africa partly in response to this earlier internationalism and especially from African American interest in African freedom movements in the late 1950s and early 1960s. Murray herself had left the United States for Ghana in hopes of discovering a sense of home. While Murray struggled to identify closely with Ghanaian politics and culture, she revered others who had, including her dear friend Maida Springer, who devoted her professional life to Pan-African labor organizing.

Student demands did not arise out of thin air, rather they emerged out of a diverse collection of speeches, writings, and radio broadcasts by Malcolm X, Stokely Carmichael, Huey Newton, and Robert F. Williams, among others, who promoted political and economic programs to target white supremacy and give black people platforms to address community issues, such as access to health care, education, and employment, and to respond to police brutality. The details of Murray's democratic vision differed from these spokespeople for Black Power, but Murray had literally defended Robert F. Williams when he was ousted from his position as Monroe, NAACP chapter president. In 1959, Murray recognized reasons why Williams had called for armed self-defense. While Murray disagreed with Williams, she saw fit to defend his leadership of the local black community and credited, therefore, that he represented its interests.

Murray criticized Black Power's seeming male supremacy, but so did many other black women including Frances Beal and the Third World's Women Alliance who "crafted a multipositioned political space through which they fashioned feminist politics that also theorized and enacted central ideological commitments of the Black Power Movement as part of their feminist politics."[92] Murray's feminist criticism pointed to a key to her democratic vision—a synthetic understanding of social movements as co-implicated in their demands for human rights. Given Murray's prophetic ability to see connections between movements, it is surprising that she was not better able to perceive legacies of her own politics in her students' demands. Murray's misgivings about Black Power politics will continue in her sermons of the coming decade. In spite of early trials at Brandeis, Murray remained at the university until 1973 and reached the rank of full professor.

Murray's Brandeis years have been characterized as a kind of "dark night of the soul" that helped her to discern a call to ordination.[93] In an oral history interview that was conducted in the months before Murray was ordained, she described her vocation a "much more closely related to my feeling of standing in the tradition of Martin Luther King, Jr. and my strong conviction that basically, all these problems of human rights in which I had been involved for most of my adult life, race, sex, all the problems of human rights, that basically these were moral and spiritual problems." She felt called toward the ministry because "the particular profession to which I had devoted the larger section of my life, law, was—that we had reached a point where law could not give us the answers."[94]

A lifelong Episcopalian, Murray had begun to experience grave doubts about the Church in the late 1960s. She recalled one Sunday in 1966 leaving in the middle of the service, because she could no longer countenance that girls were not allowed to serve even as acolytes. Although she stopped regularly attending church, Murray became involved in the growing movement in support of women's ordination. In 1969, a staffer for the Executive Council of the Episcopal Church described Murray as "on fire about participation of women in the church."[95]

Murray entered New York City's General Theological Seminary in 1973, four years before the Episcopal Church would officially ordain women. Was this a political as well as a spiritual calling? One of Murray's colleagues at seminary accused her of as much, suggesting that she take her political campaigning elsewhere.[96] Murray answered the charge: "I did not decide to come into the priesthood to advance the cause of women.... I came because I had no other alternative. I fought Death, God and my own articulated plans—but the *Call* would give me no peace until I made the decision. My interest in the cause of women in incidental but important because I cannot fulfill my own Call unless all women can fulfill theirs."[97]

Murray turned to the church as a way to answer the moral and spiritual questions to which she had devoted her professional life, but her ordination also had a strong personal component. In 1973, Murray's companion, Renee Barlow, died after a year-long struggle with cancer. With no priest available as Barlow lay dying, Murray "stood by her bed reading the Twenty-third Psalm."[98] After she had organized the funeral, picking hymns and arranging the order of service, Murray realized that she had taken a priestly role, even if unofficially. Providing for Barlow in her hour of greatest need played an important part in leading Murray to the priesthood. In the months after Barlow's death, Murray characterized their relationship in language of the marriage rite: "God brought us together to comfort and help one another when each needed it most. And we both grew and matured (I hope in grace) in the warmth of that friendship...I had the consolation that I had done my best, that I had not let her down, in sickness or in health."[99] Murray described the first time she assisted in a church service—with Renee's cross around her neck—as "a natural progression from R's illness and death and my reaction to it, as if one of the meaningful ways to express what she meant to me was to move in this direction and try to express more fully the joys of Christian sisterhood/brotherhood." Murray concluded, "R—by her life, her love, her example and her death— pointed me toward this road."[100]

In the next decade and a half, Murray was among the first women to be ordained in the Episcopal Church. The next chapter outlines Murray's developing theological and homiletic voice, with which she uses religious categories to critique American democracy *and* uses democratic norms to challenge the church to live up to its endemic egalitarianism.

4

Murray Among the Theologians
(1970s and 1980s)

While still a professor at Brandeis, Murray had become involved in the grass-roots movement for women's ordination in the Episcopal Church. In response to the church's 1969 annual fund-raising campaign, Murray wrote that the bishop's call for women to support the church financially amounted to "taxation without representation."[1] With a rallying cry for American independence, Murray underscored that women in the Episcopal Church were unfairly excluded from leadership in their own churches. Murray's somewhat tongue-in-cheek protest to the Bishop had serious theological implications and exemplified a habit whereby Murray used a democratic ideal, in this case of fair representation, to challenge a church hierarchy that did not reflect Jesus' egalitarian teachings. By appealing to another set of egalitarian ideals, Murray reminded the church of its endemic history of women's leadership in the earliest communities. Murray's case for women's participation at all levels of the church's hierarchy was supported by Christian ideals and history, but she employed democratic ideals and history to infuse fresh logic into staid debates. At 62 years of age Murray was preparing to undertake yet another career change. She entered seminary in the hopes of becoming an Episcopal priest.

Challenges that Murray had faced as a lawyer, activist, and academic followed her to seminary. She experienced once more the loneliness and self-doubt that she attributed to being a minority within a minority. As a student and later from the pulpit, she pressed for incipient (male) black and (white) feminist liberation theologies to recognize each other as allies. As she had been doing for thirty years, she appealed to the concrete historical experiences of African American women as a way for liberatory movements to enact their rhetorical promise. Murray retained her abiding attentions to identity and history as she developed a theological account of identity that pronounced differences as integral to God's creative work and featured historical examples of African American women's participation in freedom movements as harbingers of the coming kingdom. Murray had been using theological language and metaphors throughout her life, notably her appeal to the paradigm of promise and fulfillment in order to describe American democracy. While her earlier writing more often used theological categories to challenge American democratic principles and institutions, her sermons invoked democratic ideals to remind the church of its endemic egalitarianism. Murray's sermons demonstrated, therefore, a collaborative relationship between democratic and theological norms and provides contemporary readers with a model for a relationship between religion and public life.

This chapter traces the development of Murrray's theological voice through her seminary training and years as a priest in the 1970s and 1980s. Murray began at New York's General Theological Seminary (GTS) in 1973, in the midst of a church-wide debate about whether women should be ordained. In 1970, the question of women's ordination was brought before the General Convention, the governing body of the Episcopal Church, where it was narrowly voted down. After the question was voted down again at the next triennial Convention, a group of those in favor of women's ordination chose a different tact. In the wake of the second no vote, community organizer and deacon Suzanne Hiatt realized, "my vocation was not to continue to ask for permission to be a priest, but to *be* a priest."[2] In the July of 1974 on the feast day of the Saints Mary and Martha of Bethany, Hiatt and ten other women were irregularly ordained by three bishops (two retired, one who had resigned his post). The irregular ordinations, meaning without permission of the Convention, sent shock waves through the church's hierarchy, but only two years later the General Convention allowed women to be regularly ordained when it affirmed that the canons for admissions of candidates to the orders of deacons, priests, or bishops "shall be equally applicable to men and women."[3] Regular ordinations of women as Episcopal priests began with the New Year in 1977.

But in 1973, when Murray entered GTS, she was unsure whether women would be ordained in the coming years. Despite uncertainty, Murray immersed herself in course work and became well-versed in the emerging theological projects of Black theology and feminist theology. Murray had spent the previous decade trying to persuade leaders of the women's and Civil Rights movements of the interrelation of their claims for rights, liberty, and full personhood. As a seminary student, Murray continued her quest to demonstrate the movements were co-implicated, this time in a theological key.

Just as she had encountered Black Power in her teaching at Brandeis, she continued to be challenged by the movement as a seminary student. The development of Black theology out of Civil Rights and Black Power indicated for Murray "the difficult theological questions being asked in the racial ghettoes were quite different from those being raised in white middle-class suburbia. Blacks were seeking...a meaningful theology of hope in the *here* and *now* in the midst of racial oppression."[4] Murray's engagement with Black theology focused on close readings of its two leading spokespersons, James Cone and Deotis Roberts, and was limited to their texts of the 1960s and 1970s. I offer a brief overview of Cone's and Robert's works from the period before I engage Murray's response.

Now widely recognized as the father of Black theology, James Cone wrote the signal texts of the theological movement in the late 1960s and early 1970s. Published in 1968, *Black Theology and Black Power* sought to demonstrate that "Christianity is not alien to Black Power, it is Black Power." Writing in the wake of King's assassination and a resurgent interest among young intellectuals and activists in the possibilities of black nationalism and Black Power, Cone rejected integration as a primary goal for black people in a white racist society. Instead, Cone called on blacks to reclaim and reimagine black identity from the "distorted self-image" that white society projects to an understanding of blackness as "a special creation of God himself."[5]

The Christian Gospel speaks directly to blacks' experience of oppression in the United States, argued Cone, for the Gospel is a message about the ghetto, it "proclaims that God is with us now, actively fighting the forces which would make man captive." Black theology thus demonstrates what the Gospel means for blacks in the United States and, at the same time, determines white denominational churches to be unchristian in their willingness to tolerate and perpetuate a racism that is anathema to the Gospel message. Cone pushed back against many blacks' commitments to civil rights, pointing to the impossibility of reconciliation on white racist terms and the necessary failure of any movement that has as its primary goal appealing to white consciences and merely "asking for black Americans to be included in the total structure of the white American way." Cone took the side of self-described revolutionaries who prioritize liberation for the black community and the ability of blacks to define themselves on their own terms. Cone recognized God's reconciling work in Jesus Christ but argued that for any reconciliation between blacks and whites to be possible, that whites need to be able to meet blacks in the fullness of blacks' humanity "and be prepared to address black men as *black* men and not as some grease-painted form of white humanity."[6]

In *A Black Theology of Liberation*, published in 1970, Cone continued to develop the central tasks of Black theology—to analyze the black community's condition in light of God's revelation in Jesus Christ and to apply the freeing power of the Gospel to black people. This volume advanced a systematics, presenting doctrines of God, human being, Christ, and eschatology from a black theological perspective. Cone identified the norm for his systematics (or any other) that "if theology is to be relevant to the human condition which created it, it must relate itself to the questions which arise out of the community responsible for its reason for being." Blackness was Cone's primary description of the human condition out of which Black theology emerges. As a physiological trait, blackness refers to black-skinned people in the United States who have been subjected to white brutality; as an ontological symbol, blackness refers to "all people who participate in the liberation of man from oppression."[7] According to Cone, blackness as an ontological symbol points to the universal note in Black theology and shaped Cone's doctrines of God, human being, and Christ.

Cone identified a God who acts in history in order to liberate the oppressed. From this understanding of God, argued Cone, necessarily emerges an identification of God with blackness, for "the blackness of God means that God has made the oppressed his own condition." As God who became incarnate in order to bind the wounds of the afflicted and liberate those who were in prison, Jesus is similarly associated with blackness. According to Cone, to understand the historical Jesus as an oppressed Jew tells us who Christ is today. If Jesus associated himself with those who are the most rejected and marginalized, then in the American context Christ takes on blackness. Cone explained, "in a society that defines blackness as evil and whiteness as good, the theological significance of Jesus is found in the possibility of human liberation through blackness. Jesus is the Black Christ!"[8]

At the same time that Cone was storming the theological ramparts, Deotis Roberts was making his case for a Black theology premised on liberation *and* reconciliation, as the title of his major work attests. Merely 11 years Cone's senior, Roberts, positioned himself as a member of an older generation, on the border between revolutionaries and what he characterized as "the old-fashioned civil rights integrationist." In *Liberation and Reconciliation: A Black Theology*, Roberts engaged with Cone repeatedly, criticizing Cone's work as not clearly situated in the discipline of theology. In 1971, Roberts wrote "James Cone is on the fence between the Christian faith and the religion of Black Power. It will be necessary for Cone to decide presently where he will take his firm stand." Having identified his own concerns as primarily theological, Roberts sought to dispel what he saw as bluster behind a black nationalism that is "a fantasy more akin to rhetoric than to reality."[9] In response to Cone's minimization of reconciliation, Roberts defended reconciliation as a primary theological concern and postrevolutionary political goal.

Roberts elaborated a Black theology that self-consciously recognized an abundance of raw materials and sources from the black community, including spirituals, folklore, sociology, and black religious heritage. Yet Roberts was, at the same time, seemingly more circumspect than Cone about descriptions of the black community and the meaning of blackness. Whereas Cone repeatedly equated whiteness with sin, Roberts indicated that "from the position of theological ethics, the 'black nation,' should it exist, would be not only sinned against, but also a sinning community."[10] When Roberts emphasized reconciliation, therefore, it was not simply blacks' reconciliation with whites but also blacks' reconciliation with God and within the black community.

Roberts shared with Cone, however, a theological commitment to Christ's blackness. Comparing Black theology to emerging theological projects in the

Third World, Roberts affirmed the need for black Americans to make Jesus meaningful in their own context. In place of the Christ of the slave master, "the visualization of Christ as black may enable the black person to have a real encounter with self and God through Christ." The Black Christ may enable black Americans to discover "his or her own dignity and pride in a self-awareness that is rooted in black consciousness." In his appeal to black consciousness, Roberts demonstrated another affinity with Cone's work. While Roberts was cautious about an ideal of the black nation (as demonstrated in a chapter title, "The Search for Black Peoplehood"), at times he referred to Black Power and black consciousness without ambivalence, for example, when he affirmed that "revelation to blacks is a revelation of Black Power, which includes black awareness, black pride, black self-respect, and a desire to determine one's own destiny."[11]

Whereas Roberts criticized Cone's early work because it eschewed reconciliation as a goal, other criticisms of Cone emerged about the sources Cone used to develop his black theological paradigm. While talking about the importance of blackness as the subject and object of Black theology, Cone nevertheless depended on white sources for the heart of his argument. Whether Sartre, Camus, Tillich, or Barth, white (and male) voices predominate Cone's early texts. (Cone addressed this criticism directly in his third book *God of the Oppressed*, published in 1975, which opened with Cone tracing his own religious experience to the AME church of Bearden, Arkansas. In this and later works, Cone outlined and drew from black religious experiences in order to further his own theological project.)

Another criticism addressed Cone's application of particularity. In the theological anthropology forwarded in *A Black Theology of Liberation*, Cone was careful to recognize that claims about a so-called universal humanity tend to obscure experiences of oppression. Cone pointed out that God did not become incarnate as a universal human being but as an oppressed Jew and that particularity tells us something important about who Christ is for us today. And yet throughout his text, Cone employed the generic masculine uncritically, referring exclusively to "men" even as he argued for the importance of particularity to address experiences of oppressed people. While generic masculine was certainly the norm in academic and theological writing in the late 1960s and early 1970s, Cone's rhetorical choice is striking when read alongside Roberts' use of "people," "human beings," and occasionally "his or her." While Roberts does not plumb the importance of inclusive language, his use of it serves to highlight a limitation of Cone's early work (which Cone himself recognizes in later editions of both texts).

In seminary papers about Cone's and Roberts' work, Murray argued that Roberts presented a more constructive theological paradigm. Murray rejected outright Cone's exclusive theological attention to black experience. When Cone argued that reconciliation could not be based on white racist terms, Murray, like

Roberts had, inferred that Cone was not at all concerned with reconciliation. She characterized Cone as "so obsessed with the liberation struggle itself—and its exclusiveness—that it is difficult not to characterize his language as 'racial exclusiveness' bordering upon arrogance."[12] In her autobiography and in these seminary papers, Murray indicated that her disapproval of Black Power and its influence on Black theology came from her frustration with its misogynist tendencies.[13] But it was also more than this. Murray was alienated by Black theology's emphasis on blackness, in Cone's work in particular. When Cone explained the need for a specifically "*Black theology*, a theology whose sole purpose is to apply the freeing power of the Gospel to black people under white oppression," Murray read a false polarity between black and white, neither of which was an adequate category to describe complex experiences implicated in class, gender, and other power relations.[14] Murray did not address the distinction Cone made between ontological and physiological blackness, a distinction that may have diffused some of Murray's concern. In *A Black Theology of Liberation*, Cone affirmed that blackness was not simply a physiological trait that describes black-skinned people, but it is also (and perhaps more importantly) an ontological symbol that can describe oppressed people engaged in liberation struggles. Cone's appeal to blackness describes, then, not simply men who are black-skinned, but all those who work to liberate themselves and others from oppression. In his later work, Cone has made concerted attempts to articulate more clearly his commitment to fight all sorts of oppression. Murray did not live to read Cone's assertion that "we must fight sexism, classism, and heterosexism as fiercely as we fight racism. To embrace blackness is to embrace humanity in all of its manifestations."[15]

Frustrated by what she read as Cone's exclusive concern for black men, Murray overlooked critical and specifically American sensibilities she shared with Cone. Cone's claim that "I am critical of white America, because this is *my* country; and what is mine must not be spared my emotional and intellectual scrutiny," echoed Murray's claim in her family memoir that democratic criticism was her birthright.[16] Yet Murray's steadfast commitment to nonviolence and belief in the possibility of reconciliation (and even integration) kept her from embracing Cone's project. Cone did not advocate violence, but he recognized that the violence whites continuously inflicted on African Africans limited black strategies and meant that nonviolence might be self-destructive. The crux of Murray's resistance to Black theology was likely her resistance to Black Power. While she recognized that the novelty of Black theology meant that its inconsistencies had yet to be teased out, Murray nevertheless criticized Cone for a "desparate [*sic*] effort" to respond to a secular movement, Black Power, which Murray argued "in its most militantly radical stages threatened to discredit both the Black Christian Church and the legacy of Dr. Martin Luther King Jr."[17] This was perhaps the most stinging indictment Murray could level against Cone's theology—its departure from King's ethic of reconciliation and nonviolence.

Murray believed that Deotis Roberts' project was more viable than Cone's because of a correspondence between Roberts' theological program and King's ethic. Murray had followed King's activism from a distance and saw in it commitments that she shared and had acted upon. Murray celebrated King's application of Gandhian principles and she agreed with his emphasis on the transformative power of nonviolence. Even after King's assassination, Murray remained committed to King's theological account of a beloved community. She saw in King's work a realization she had come to herself, namely that though legal changes were absolutely necessary, there is yet another horizon of human relationship.

In her autobiography and sermons, Murray did not address the questions that King voiced later in his life about whether integration was possible. While Murray often quoted from King's *Chaos and Community* in sermons and speeches, she did not mention King's discussion in this book about Black Power and his recognition of its value for black Americans, even if he did not feel that he could embrace it fully himself. In a coincidence she reports in her autobiography, she recalled that she was reading the final chapters of the autobiography of Malcolm X the moment she received word of King's death. Whether this was a subtextual connection about King's recognition that separation may have to precede integration is unclear, but publicly Murray espoused King's nonviolence and commitment to a beloved community. While Roberts had put aside King's goal of integration for the time being, he held out hope that black and white relations could be interracial, which for Roberts meant that blacks and whites have the ability to treat each other as equals. According to Murray, Roberts' focus on interracial relations showed a "profound appreciation for Dr. Martin Luther King's ethical stance" even if he did not adopt it wholeheartedly.[18] Roberts balanced reconciliation with liberation, noting that reconciliation between races cannot come at the cost of black liberation.

Just as Murray was critical of Cone's appeal to blackness, so was she of Roberts' employment of the Black Messiah, which Roberts had insisted was a powerful symbol in order for Christ to be meaningful to black people. Roberts' development of a black Christology resembled Murray's own efforts to forward a doctrine of God in her 1943 poem "Dark Testament," in which she distinguished between "white God" and God who gave people "hope and the power of song." Almost thirty years later, Roberts was imagining a Christ who might give African American people hope. But from Roberts' Black Messiah, Murray inferred "a preoccupation with black liberation which tends to narrow his focus and suggests an insensitivity to the oppression of women, who, after all constitute one half of the black community." Murray was concerned that Roberts' Black Messiah engaged only with one kind of oppression. She wondered, "Is Dr. Roberts prepared to suggest that a 'female' image of Christ, or a 'female Christ' would be valid as a symbol for women fighting to affirm their personhood? And if a woman is also black, what images or symbols of Christ would have meaning for her?"[19]

Murray went on to suggest that Black theology would benefit immeasurably from a dialogue with feminist theology. She predicted that "a dialogue between the two would serve as a continual reminder of our common humanity and solidarity in the 'groaning toward freedom.'" A conversation would encourage in white women "the growing awareness of their own oppression and the analogies between racism and sexism can enable white women in the United States to gain a deeper insight into the depths of racial oppression and help them to become instruments of conversion and evangelism in white America." As she had a decade earlier in lobbying for African American women's legal rights, Murray saw strategic opportunities in allying with white women. Murray concluded forcefully that "until Dr. Roberts and other black theologians have demonstrated in their writings an effort to overcome a male-oriented bias, it will be difficult for thoughtful black women, who are crucial to the reception of their message, to take Black theology seriously."[20]

In her seminary thesis, Murray carved out a theological space for African American women. As she had in appeals to male leaders of the Civil Rights movement and white leaders of the women's movement, Murray argued that Black (male) theology and (white) feminist theology are natural allies. She pointed out that until each project realized the strengths of the other, the theological significance of African American women's experiences would go untheorized. Murray argued that Black theology and feminist theology were limited by monolithic analyses that name one kind of exploitation as the ultimate evil. The emerging American theologies shared with other liberation theologies a common theme of specifying the "relation between Christian theology and social action," and Murray was interested in the possibility of Black theology and feminist theology informing each other in order to be more effective "forces for liberation within the context of the Christian message."[21] While Murray recognized the strength of liberation theology as a strategic and contextual methodology, her 1976 seminary thesis argued that single-axis analysis of identity prevented black and feminist theologians from articulating a universal message of salvation and liberation.[22]

Feminist theology's analysis of sexism as the ultimate evil precluded white feminist theologians from recognizing the interstructuring of sexism with other kinds of oppression. Led by Mary Daly, Rosemary Ruether, and Letty Russell, the first generation of white feminist theologians was interested in, to paraphrase Daly, moving "beyond God the Father" in order to put women's experiences at the center of theological reflection, making women the subjects and authors of theology. But Murray warned that if feminist theology failed to account for the intersection of sexism and racism, for example, it could cater only to middle- and upper-class white women at the expense of poor women and women of color. Similarly, Black theology's particularized analysis of race limited its potential to proclaim the good news of universal liberation. Murray criticized Black theology, specifically Cone, for revealing "little understanding of the problems of Black women as women and [for] almost totally ignor[ing] feminist theology." She worried about the "dearth of Black women theologians" and announced that "interlocking factors of racism and sexism within black experience awaits analysis." According to Murray, the "greatest danger to the effectiveness of specific theologies is a tendency to compete with one other in definition of particular form of oppression as the 'source of all evil' and thus losing sight of the goal of universal liberation and salvation."[23]

Published in 1978 in *Anglican Theological Review*, Murray's MDiv thesis anticipated black feminist theology and womanist theology, theologies that consider tradition, scripture, and human being in light of black women's experiences and in order to promote in black women's and black men's liberation. Drawing from Alice Walker's 1983 definition of womanism, black women theologians and ethicists who identify as womanists underscore a multiplicity of experiences and colors contained in blackness and emphasize black women's moral agency as a guide to resist dominating structures of oppression.[24] From the groundbreaking early works of Katie Cannon, Jacquelyn Grant, and Delores Williams, among others, womanist theologians and ethicists employ African American women's experiences as their point of departure and African American women as the community to which their scholarship is primarily accountable. According to Stephanie Mitchem, womanist scholars consider the "operations of the ordinary theologies of black women's daily lives as rich sources of theological constructions, emphasizing the importance of spiritual and communal life."[25]

Joanne Terrell has cited Jacquelyn Grant's unpublished 1985 essay on "Becoming Subjects in the Christological Debate" as "the first proto-womanist essay employing a critique of black and feminist theologies' assumptions and methodologies."[26] Murray's 1978 comparative account of black and feminist theologies deserves to be part of the discussion of proto-womanism, because she was among the first to recognize publicly the shortcomings of existing liberation projects. In fact, in *White Women's Christ, Black Women's Jesus*, Grant herself cites Murray's article as an early source, which "lays the groundwork for the development of a Black woman's perspective in theology."[27] In a similar way, Anthony Pinn has characterized Murray's seminary thesis as providing "the early ideological and technical framework for womanist thought."[28] Yet to identify Murray as a proto-womanist risks obscuring her identification as a black feminist.

Sociologist Patricia Hill Collins and Christian ethicist Traci West each identifies as black feminist and draws distinctions between black feminism and womanism. Hill Collins seems somewhat reluctant to draw such a distinction in the first place, for she worries that preoccupation with naming neglects social issues that affect the black community. However, she allows that it may be beneficial to attend to how a distinction is drawn if it "forces a rethinking of long-standing notions of racial solidarity that have been so central to Black women's community

work."[29] Hill Collins values how womanism fosters stronger relationships between black women and black men and commends its theological articulations
that reject all forms of oppression and are committed to social justice. But Hill
Collins wants womanists to be more attentive to the difference between "identifying the liberatory *potential* within Black women's communities that emerges
from concrete, historical experiences" and a claim that these same "communities
have already *arrived* at this ideal, 'womanist' end point." While she recognizes
that racial segregation in the United States has tended to make feminism shorthand for white feminism, Hill Collins insists that *black* feminism does important
work both to disrupt the racism inherent in the assumption that feminism is a
white concern and to disrupt "the false universalism of this term" for white and
black American women. By identifying as a black feminist, Hill Collins demonstrates her commitment to a global feminist movement that advocates for wom-
en's economic and political rights and charges her with understanding how issues
affecting black women in the United States are part of a worldwide struggle for
women's emancipation. Hill Collins, echoing her Brandeis professor Pauli Murray,
concludes that the strength of black feminism is its capacity to "come to terms
with a White feminist agenda incapable of seeing its own racism, as well as a
Black nationalist one resistant to grappling with its own sexism."[30]

Like Hill Collins, Traci West resists the assumption that feminism necessarily
indicates whiteness, because this "problematically eras[es] the contributions of
generations of black feminist foremothers." While West celebrates womanists'
articulation of black women's subjectivities, she worries about "the dangers of
parochialism that might be inherent in this project."[31] West cautions womanists
against capitulating to taxonomies of race and racism by adhering to a critical
project that is exclusively accountable to a particular racial group. In identifying
as a black feminist, West sees the most strategic potential to privilege black
women's wholeness while also providing opportunities to ally with others' liberation movements. Murray anticipated Hill Collins' and West's concerns about
narrow delineations of identity that prevented people from forming coalitions.
We should heed Hill Collins' suspicion that the debate about whether black
women should identify as womanists or black feminists is largely academic and
draws attention away from critical engagement with social issues. Yet Murray's
work demonstrates why a self-conscious articulation of identity has democratic
ramifications. Murray insists that reflection on identity becomes crucial in the
kind of moral imagination that coalition building requires and that is demanded
by human rights campaigns. Murray's MDiv thesis witnessed a black feminist
theological standpoint that worked to disrupt racism and sexism in emerging
theological projects.

Murray was ordained in Washington's National Cathedral on January 8, 1977.
Among a group of three men and two other women, Murray was the last to be

ordained that day. She was told that when she received the laying on of hands "the sun burst through the clouds and sent rainbow-colored shafts of light down through the stained glass windows."[32] The *Washington Post* reported that almost 1,500 gathered to witness the ordinations and "as the new priests themselves pronounced the traditional exchange of the 'peace of the Lord,' the scene before the altar erupted into happy chaos. The nearly 50 priests of the diocese who had joined in the consecration surged forward to embrace the new priests, each other, and members of the congregation who rushed up to join in the joyous occasion."[33]

Even after ordination, Murray continued to be assailed by others' accusations that she was not fit to be a priest. The Coalition for Apostolic Ministry (CAM), a group organized to fight women's ordination, wrote to the standing committee of Murray's diocese that it objected to her ordination.[34] Murray welcomed CAM's letter for giving her "an opportunity to respond in the Martin Luther King, Jr. tradition." To CAM's claim that women's ordination would prompt a schism in the church over women's ordination, Murray responded:

> I am sure you cannot seriously expect one who is the descendent of slaveowning white (European) planter fathers and African-Amerindian bondwomen mothers, and who represents the American counterpart of the Old Testament Ishmaelite, to be persuaded by your statement.... The church...lived relatively comfortably with chattel slavery...for two centuries or more, and survived that "scandal" without splitting apart. I predict that it will survive the ordination of women.[35]

In addition to public attacks, Murray also caught wind of a whisper campaign about her sexuality. In an unsent letter from her personal files, she wrote to the Reverend John Walker because "I hear you have been making 'tut' 'tut' remarks about my sexuality. 'It's unfortunate that she's a 'so-and-so.'" Having gone through a series of responses she had planned, including "blacking both of your eyes," reminding him that such slander could make him vulnerable to a civil suit, praying God to forgive him, or ignoring him altogether, Murray recognized that since Walker was about to be named the first black Diocesan Bishop of Washington, DC, "it is in my racially identified group interest that you be a great Bishop." But, she warned him, "if you go around putting such words about fellow clergy in the 'street', you are going to fall flat on your face." She concluded her letter with a rhetorical question, "God made me as I am. Are you, a Bishop of the Church, questioning God's handiwork?"[36] While she did not elaborate on it publicly, Murray was developing a positive account of her sexuality, describing it as an intentional part of God's design.

Murray did not elaborate a theological account of sexuality, but her sermons and letters point to a place for sexuality in her theological considerations of identity. When in sermons from the late 1970s and early 1980s Murray listed identity categories, such as race, gender, or class, she often included sexuality as well. In a 1977 letter to friends, Murray talked about her vision for her ministry, that "we bring our total selves to God, our sexuality, our joyousness, our foolishness, etc. etc. I'm out to make Christianity a joyful thing."[37] Yet, as she wrote to friends that we must bring our total selves—including sexuality—to God, Murray did not include her own sexuality among her public, theological reflections.

Murray published a handful of theological articles, including her Masters thesis, but the force of her theological voice is expressed in her sermons.[38] She spent the final eight years of her professional life pastoring to churches in Baltimore and Washington and serving often as a guest pastor at various churches. Selections of her sermons have been published in two collections, but the majority remains in her papers, archived at the Schlesinger Library at Harvard University.[39]

Though Murray had turned her energies to the church, many of her sermons made arguments that would have been familiar to her legal, activist, and academic colleagues. There are risks in removing sermons from their primary context of spoken words within a congregational setting and receiving them in their written form. When sermons are deracinated and *read*, the crucial experience of how the congregation received the sermons is missing, whether "the people received that extra strength to go one more miles in their struggle to survive."[40] Yet Murray was careful also to preserve written copies of her sermons and to catalogue them in chronological order to be archived. She intended her sermons also to be received by an additional community, this time of *readers*.

In one of the first sermons she gave after ordination, Murray analogizes democratic and ecclesial transformation. Ministry provided Murray a homecoming. She had left her childhood home of Durham, NC, after high school and had returned to the South infrequently. After the pastor of Murray's grandmother and great aunt's church read about Murray's ordination, he invited her to administer her first Eucharist at Chapel Hill's Church of the Holy Cross.[41] On February 13, 1977, Murray preached to an integrated congregation about *two* American revolutions. She called the events from 1789 through 1976 efforts to complete the first American revolution and January 1, 1977, the date of the first woman's official ordination, as a signal for the visible beginning of the second American revolution. The second revolution should carry on the work of first, the healing and reconciliation of people alienated from each other by race, sex preference, political differences, and economic status.

Murray offered herself as a sign of these first and second revolutions—an African American woman with multiple ancestries who offered her first Eucharist at the church where her grandmother was baptized into freedom in Christ but recorded by church records as a slave. Presenting herself as evidence that reconciliation is possible, Murray preached:

> It was my destiny to be the descendent of slaveowners as well as slaves, to be of mixed ancestry, to be biologically and psychologically integrated in a world where the separation of the races was upheld by the Supreme Court of the United States as the fundamental law of the Southland. My entire life's quest has led me ultimately to Christ in whom there is not East or West, no North or South, no Black or White, no Red or Yellow, no Jew or Gentile, no Islam or Buddha, no Baptist, Methodist, Episcopalian, or Roman Catholic, no male or female. There is not Black Christ nor White Christ nor Red Christ—although these images may have transitory cultural value. There is only Christ, the Spirit of love and reconciliation, the Healer of deep pychic [sic] wounds, drawing us all closer to that Goal of perfection which links us to God our creator and to eternity.[42]

In the same way that her own deep psychic wounds had been healed, Murray believed that reconciliation on a national scale was a possibility. As she had used her own experiences in articulating Jane Crow and in her landmark legal contributions, so did she employ intensely personal experiences of overcoming rejection and discrimination to posit national prospects. In a relationship with God centered in Christ, Murray saw the possibility for a community of diverse people to be reconciled. Drawing from the baptismal formula in Paul's letter to the Galatians, Murray imagined a nonhierarchical community, but she does not advocate it be nondifferentiated.[43] In the benediction to her sermon, Murray called on a creation account which presented diversity as God's intention and a reflection of Godself, "God, who created all peoples in your image, we thank you for the wonderful diversity of races and cultures in this world."[44]

Murray's account of reconciliation was exemplary of how democratic and theological norms can inform each other. When she envisioned the second revolution—of women's ordination in the Episcopal Church—carrying on the work of the first—the democratic, American revolution—she suggested that the church can use democratic ideals as an important reminder of its own egalitarian tradition. In this case, Murray's characterization of a democratic revolution and a ecclesial revolution revealed that they share similar goals of making more justice available to more people. She believed that reconciliation may be possible in the United States, because in "places like Chapel Hill, North Carolina, where we are today, witnessing to the reconciliation of Isaac and Ishmael in the house of Abraham."[45] The biblical trope of the Ishmaelite indicated the challenges to develop democratic practices that can reconcile and integrate estranged members of the national family, but Murray had faith that reconciliation is possible.

As one of the first women to be ordained officially by the Episcopal Church, Murray's homiletic voice emerged out of the debates about whether or not to ordain women. These debates arose at the same time as a growing feminist theological movement, which considered the church, Christian tradition, and scripture in light of patriarchy. An early and enduring strategy of feminist theologies is historical investigation of women's roles in tradition, scripture, and history, thus memory and history have become important *leitmotifs* in black feminist, womanist, and white feminist theologies. Murray's sermons sustain an attention to history that was integral to her memoir and dissertation.

In a "Sermon on the Ordination of Women," Murray addressed the division in the Episcopal Church over the question of women's ordination. By 1976, bishops had voted twice and in an increasing majority agreed that women are spiritually fit for a priestly vocation. The theological question had been ecclesiologically settled. The remaining and looming question about women's ordination, according to Murray, was historical—what was the tradition of the church?[46] While there was not, Murray admitted, a lot of information about women's ministry in the church's history, there are, she insisted, biblical accounts of women being called to discipleship and to preach the Gospel. There was an important antecedent to the historical question: "Why is this particular issue at this particular time threaten[ing] to tear our church apart." The answer lay in the relationship between "the spirit of prophecy and the spirit of order that has been present in the church since . . . Christianity . . . became the established religion of the Roman Empire." Murray interpreted the contemporary debate in the church as one more rehearsal of the historical interplay between prophecy and order. In the tradition of Isaiah and Jeremiah, prophecy "sees the world as under judgment and seeks a radical transformation of the social order to bring it back to God." Order, meanwhile, "is content to seek more moderate reform, working more slowly within the existing social structures." Both impulses are necessary and natural in the church, insisted Murray, but when the tension between prophecy and order is disrupted, polarization follows. In response to particularly strident prophetic calls, the church can become too concerned with order and "too inflexible within its orthodoxy . . . too static to achieve self-reform and self-renewal."[47] In these moments, movements must "arise to call the church back to its prophetic mission," which Murray understood as calling the church back to its own role of calling for—and modeling—radical transformation of the social order. Murray's arguments in favor of women's ordination employed historical accounts of women acting as disciples and itinerant preachers, and in so doing she appealed to the past to point the church toward an egalitarian future.

Murray's sermons also employed democratic norms to challenge ecclesial practices. "Mary Has Chosen the Best Part" used Luke's story of Jesus' visit

with Mary and Martha to illustrate that Jesus took women seriously as theological students.[48] While Martha fussed around to tidy the house and prepared
food for her guest, Mary sat at Jesus' feet and listened to his teachings. In biblical times, Murray reminded her listeners, women were not allowed to study
Torah or to engage in theological conversation with a rabbi. "In this perspective," argued Murray, "we can see Mary as an unusual woman, one who was
unwilling to accept the role defined for her and was drawn to Jesus of Nazareth
because he treated her like a *person* with an intellect and a quest for knowledge
of God." In allowing Mary the privilege of sitting at his feet, Jesus was treating
her like a "young male divinity student" and defended his decision, by explaining "the part that Mary has chosen in the best; and it shall not be taken away
from her."[49] Here, Murray used a popular biblical text to preach that Jesus
intended for women to be theological students. In light of the recent division in
the Episcopal Church over the ordination of women, Murray reminded her congregation that Jesus had supported women's intention to study his teachings
since the earliest days of the Christian community. Murray's emphasis on personhood echoes her argument in the PCSW memo that sex was not necessarily
a reasonable basis for classification. Fifteen years earlier, Murray had emphasized women's personhood when she clarified that women who were mothers
had special needs, but they always already had needs and rights as persons. In
the same sermon, Murray compared Mary's choice of the "best part" with the
career of Alice Paul, a women's rights pioneer who had died the week before.
A Quaker and founder of the National Women's Party (NWP), Paul gained
national attention after her arrest in a suffragette protest in 1917. Having led a
successful campaign to ratify the Nineteenth Amendment, Paul worked steadily
through the second wave of feminist activism, particularly in support of the
Equal Rights Amendment (ERA).

Murray's use of Alice Paul's work as a lens through which to read the Luke
story is an example of how Murray used democratic ideals to examine religious
practices. Paul's democratic demand for universal suffrage acts as a hermeneutic
with which Christians can read the Luke story; it reminds Christian listeners of
their own endemic commitments to egalitarianism. Even though biblical stories
depict Jesus teaching women in his ministry and women preaching the Gospel,
Murray was faced with contemporary arguments that women were not fit to lead
congregations. Murray appealed to Paul's democratic efforts in order to remind
her listeners of egalitarianism that Jesus himself taught. With this sermon,
therefore, Murray offered a two-part critique. As historically situated institutions, Christian churches must engage in ongoing critical reflection about whether
and how they, as institutions, model the kind of egalitarianism Jesus taught.
And Christians themselves should bring their whole selves to their faith, for different aspects of their personality can bring to light important new ways of
understanding Christian scripture and tradition.

Students of history are aware, however, that Paul's democratic efforts were vitiated by her and the NWP's refusal to work explicitly toward securing the right to vote for black women. For example, in 1921 Paul refused NAACP field secretary Addie Hunton's request to address the NWP about black women's disfranchisement, because Paul considered this an issue for racial, rather than feminist, organizations.[50] The NWP was the leading national organization identified with the feminist cause. As a result, the NWP's support for the ERA, in the face of working-class women's concerns that it would overturn protective legislation and its refusal to advocate for the enfranchisement of African American women meant that many progressives equated feminism with classism and racism. Murray's willingness to celebrate Paul's work is surprising given Murray's long-standing devotion to the indivisibility of human rights. Yet Murray may have been making a strategic concession here: in the same way that she overlooked King's sexism in her sermons (though she claimed in her autobiography that she could never forgive King for not inviting Rosa Parks to his Nobel Prize acceptance ceremony, she lionized him in her sermons), so did she overlook Paul's racism.[51] While their emancipatory politics were limited, Murray nevertheless emphasized how King and Paul used religious convictions to interrogate American democratic practices.

Murray's sermons remembered women as crucial to the Christian story. In "Out of the Wilderness," Murray described Hagar as "a strong, proud, independent woman of the desert, conscious of her own worth who feels herself equal of her mistress, and as the innocent victim of Sarah's jealousy." Murray encouraged African American women to be conscious of their self-worth as children of God. God's promise to Hagar confirmed that "the God of the wealthy patriarch is also the God who hears the cry of the afflicted and oppressed." Murray depicted Hagar as worthy of receiving God's word and of bearing God's promise: "Through her faith and determination, this heroic woman found her way out of the wilderness and led her son to freedom and dignity."[52] Murray compared Hagar's story to the situation of many enslaved women who were sexually exploited by white slave owning men and white women.

The sermon connected Hagar's story with examples of African American women, who—like Hagar—found a way out of the wilderness, women like Harriet Tubman, Sojourner Truth, and Dr. Mary McLeod Bethune. While Murray developed a genealogy of African American women that reached back to Hagar, she recognized at the same time that American history is incomplete, for there are many black women's stories that we will never know. This recognition was doubly feminist. On the one hand, she lamented that many women's stories will remain anonymous due to an incomplete historical record, and, on the other hand, she offered examples of black women's leadership of and participation in liberation movements as the rule, rather than an exception. Murray's appeal to African American women's history in her sermons anticipated womanist ethicist Katie

Cannon's hermeneutic of "remembering what we never knew," which brings questions to biblical stories and theological texts that remind us of who often gets unremembered, such as "where are the women in the story? Where are the children? Are you in the story? Why or why not?" Cannon argues that "remembering is no less than incarnation. In other words, re-membering is no less than the words of our bygone days re-embodying themselves in our present flesh."[53] When she connected African American women to models of biblical leadership, Murray re-membered African American women's histories and contemporary understandings of black women. Her sermons created black feminist-centered theological and democratic memories.

These three sermons underscore Murray's continued commitment to women's, particularly African American women's, liberation. By reading through the breadth of Murray's sermons, a reader can also glean a broad systematics, including accounts of God, Jesus Christ, human being, salvation, suffering, and the kingdom of God. Throughout Murray described God as acting in history and inviting human beings to participate with God in working for justice. In the "Inaugural Sermon" she preached as a first-year seminarian, Murray described God as "active in the affairs of humankind to bring us redemption, salvation, and reconciliation with Him, the source of our being."[54] In one of the final sermons she delivered before retirement, she insisted that "as Christians, we must continually remind ourselves that God is eternally working in history to bring all creation to perfection, and that we are God's creatures and part of God's divine plan."[55] Throughout her ministry, therefore, Murray described God as interested and active in human affairs, as wanting human beings to participate in God's work of leading creation toward its fulfillment. God's relationship to Jesus Christ provides the model of this kind of participation.

Murray agreed with Paul Tillich that the universal significance of the Christ event is the potential for reconciliation between human beings and God. Tillich was a German-born Protestant theologian who had moved to the United States after the rise of the Third Reich. Tillich secured a post at Union Theological Seminary and became a leading theologian in the US. Tillich's theology sought to put Christian doctrines in conversation with culture, particularly with developments in existentialism. Murray agreed with Tillich that the Gospel tells the story of one person's "quest for the 'New Being,' in which man's estrangement will be overcome and reunion with God can be achieved." Drawing from Tillich, Murray described the human condition as resulting in a fragmentary fellowship with God, yet "it is not a fixed status but a dynamic process of continuous struggle to overcome evil and sin which separate us from God." As King had, Murray embraced Tillich's commitment to and faith in the possibility of people overcoming existential alienation. The new life and new person in Christ that baptism inaugurates are not finished or complete, rather "we are constantly *becoming*, as we experience the tension between the 'now' and the 'not yet.'"[56] God wants human beings to be reconciled to God and grants them this potential. Murray had employed "becoming" in her family memoir and JSD dissertation to describe American democracy as partially present, but not yet fully realized. In each case, "becoming" indicated a dynamic process fueled by hope that reconciliation is possible.

Murray also engaged with the work of Scottish theologian John Macquarrie, who, like Tillich, sought to be in conversation with existential philosophy. A number of Murray's sermons referred to Macquarrie's emerging Christology, the idea that Christ became aware of his special status over the course of his life *and* that his status emerged along with his growing awareness. Murray followed Macquarrie in suggesting that Jesus progressively recognized his Christhood through the submission of his life to God, chronicled in biblical stories through the moments of his baptism, temptation, ministry, passion, and death. Murray suggested that "through God's action in him, Christhood finally emerged when his life reached its climax and fulfillment—at the point of death."[57] Jesus became fully incarnate when he completely and absolutely accepted the Cross. At this moment, selfhood passed into Christhood and, according to Macquarrie, the Jesus of history became the Christ of faith.

On Macquarrie's reading, the incarnation remained thoroughly a work of God, but it included the cooperation of Jesus as a human being. Murray concluded "because of what God wrought in Jesus Christ, we are called to participate in the human struggle against suffering, injustice, and evil, confidently entrusting ourselves and the future of humankind to God's all-embracing and saving love."[58] The Gospels tell the story of Jesus participating in God's will; "Jesus made it clear that in the totality of human existence we are all bound together inseparably in our relationship to God, to our own selves and to one another."[59] Murray emphasized repeatedly that the reconciliation of Christ with God, which made possible human beings' reconciliation with each other, resulted from an ongoing process. Murray's references to Tillich and MacQuarrie demonstrate how her theological vision was influenced importantly by white male thinkers. Her employment of their arguments may be one reason why her sermons did not emphasize Jesus' historical identity as marginalized and rejected, nor did they specify the historical and material realities of those human beings whom she hoped would be reconciled.

Murray's theological anthropology drew from Tillich's discussion of the dialectical relationship between freedom and destiny. According to Tillich, an individual bears freedom within the larger social structures to which she belongs; destiny is the term to describe these structures, the situations that make up the larger world. Destiny is not some strange power that determines what will happen to a person; it is not fate. Rather, destiny is better described as a series of givens, for example nature, history, and a person's self. Murray described destiny as "one's biological heritage, one's history, one's environment, and the interaction between one's self (personal center) and all of these factors—this is what balances with a person's freedom." Murray embraced Tillich's focus on the individual and on the social structures that affect and often limit her freedom. To accept Tillich's analysis about the relationship between freedom and destiny was, Murray argued, "a very liberating experience."[60]

Murray offered herself as an example of Tillich's reasoning: "The historical and environmental restrictions of race and sex do not constitute wholly my destiny. They are the 'given,' but the 'given' also includes *myself*. And myself includes the freedom to deliberate, make decisions, and be responsible for those decisions. How I exercise this freedom will share the destiny which contains restrictions of race and sex."[61] Murray found in Tillich's theology, therefore, a familiar emphasis on the integrity of the individual in the midst of social structures. It is this point that Murray brought critically to bear on black and white feminist theologies when she called on each to consider the experiences of African American women. The reconciliation she imagined was not an assimilation of personalities or identities into a corporate sameness, rather reconciliation means integration into a whole in which the integrity of each part is upheld in unity.

Throughout her writing, Murray had steadfastly avoided narrowly interpreting her own or other's experiences. Anthony Pinn characterizes Murray as "comfortable with paradox, with thickness, with tension And that battles she fought involved a desire to maintain a sense of life's ambiguity, the complexity of life that white supremacy and racism sought to destroy."[62] Like her arguments in support of Title VII that had used the historical particularity of her own identity in order that equal protection of the laws have, de facto, a more universal purview, her sermons reflected on African American women of the recent past and women of the Gospel stories to point toward universal salvation. An example is the sermon she preached in Chapel Hill, in which she presented herself as a sign of two American revolutions, because she was a contradiction to legal (or ideological or theological) prescriptions that classify her in the singular.

Her existential condition—of multiplicity and so of not fitting neatly into prescribed categories—led her to an understanding of Christ who is not readily identifiable with any particular location, group, or even religious tradition. That is, although Murray's theological anthropology embraced physiological and ontological specificity, her Christology eschewed it. James Cone had argued that Jesus' identity as a poor Palestinian Jew living under Roman occupation points toward Jesus' identity as the black Christ in the context of late twentieth-century United States. Similarly, in advocating for the Black Messiah, Roberts had specified that as "the universal Christ, he speaks to the oppressed everywhere in their own language and in their situation."[63] Murray's Christology was not rooted in the particularity of black experiences, nor did she emphasize Jesus' identity as among the most rejected and marginalized. Unlike her legal theory that championed equal protection for all as it focused on the particularity of African American women's experiences, Murray's Christology emphasizes reconciliation without addressing historical aspects of Jesus' identity. As his student, Murray had challenged Roberts on the limited value of a male Christ figure, yet her sermons neglected feminist or other particularized interpretations of Jesus or Christ in favor of Tillich's and MacQuarrie's existentialist readings. Murray had asked Roberts if he could imagine a female Christ; a reader of Murray's sermons might ask her the same.

If the human being, Jesus, and God were the protagonists in Murray's theological drama, then her stage was the kingdom of God. Throughout her sermons, Murray returned again and again to what she characterized as the central message of the Gospel—the kingdom of God is drawing near. According to Murray, "when we hear Jesus' timeless message and open our hearts to the power of God's boundless love and compassion, the Kingdom of Heaven draws near."[64] Discernment and love are hallmarks for the coming of the kingdom. When people are able to hear and enact God's commandment to love, they become able to discern signs of the kingdom here on earth.

In a sermon entitled "Are you He Who Is To Come?" Murray compared Jesus' ministry to that of John the Baptist. Jesus and John shared "the belief that God would soon bring the world to an end and would establish a new heaven and a new earth, but where John thundered about the fires of judgment Jesus brought a message of joy." The good news that Jesus brought was that "the world would be transformed through self-giving love rather than violent judgment, and the signs of God's kingdom were already present." Despite Jesus' revolutionary message, John asked Jesus "Are you he who is to come?" Murray reminded her audience that we do not know whether Jesus ever convinced John that he was, and she admitted that John's question reflects the fear and doubts of people in every age who long for certainty and security amid contradictions and ambiguities. Murray suggested that John's question compels Christians to ask a second, "Who is Jesus Christ for us?" Murray answered: "In our co-humanity with Jesus we share the promise of participating with him in the new creation, the new humanity, the consummation of God's kingdom of love." Jesus is exemplary because "his entire cause was God's cause, and he insisted that the kingdom of God must be sought first above all else, after which those things which humanity longed for would be added."[65] Elsewhere Murray described the kingdom of God as "a community of love, peacefulness and productivity under God's rule shared in by all peoples and all nations."[66] According to Murray, the kingdom did not arrive at some apocalyptic end-time in the future but was partially present in the here and now. Indeed, the kingdom for Murray was a call to action. She described Jesus' call to participate in the kingdom as "more than merely offering refuge and comfort in a troubled society. It is a call to alertness, watchfulness, action and risk."[67]

Risk is a familiar watchword in Murray's sermons, where it often alludes to suffering. In "The Second Great Commandment" (1976), she described how loving one's neighbor necessarily involves risk, "the risk of pain and unpopularity, the risk of being wrong, the risk of sacrifice and defeat, the risk of distrust and even abuse from those whom we want to serve." Risk was a sign for Murray that working toward reconciliation likely will involve suffering, for "living in accordance with God's will does not spare use from the pain of suffering ourselves or seeing others suffer; it makes us an instrument of God's power working to bring all Creation into harmony and perfection in the fullness of time."[68] In another sermon, she accepted the apparent inevitability of suffering, "yes, we must suffer with and for one another before we will be healed of the sickness of our common history, before we will be free to face one another and walk together toward a brighter future."[69]

In 1943, Murray had characterized African American suffering as redemptive, providing a political way forward with nonviolent resistance.[70] In her sermons, Murray focused on the vocation of minority Christians to take on the role of Suffering Servant. In 1974, "The Dilemma of a Minority Christian" described minority Christians as "God's Suffering Servants in the salvation history of the world." The Suffering Servant is a person who "could call the people back from their sins, someone who could intervene on their behalf, and bring about atonement for their alienation from God." The Suffering Servant arrives as a person "loathed and shunned by the community and looked upon with contempt."[71] She suffers not for her own sins but for the sins of others.

Murray concluded that to be a Suffering Servant requires a person to acknowledge that "all I am and all I have belongs to my Creator, that I am not here for my own purpose, my own glory, but for the purpose and glory of God."[72] She recognized a dilemma for a minority Christian, who strives against all odds for self-respect, to give her back to smiters. But Murray privileged the role of the Suffering Servant as one who works not only for survival but for liberation of humankind.

In a "Palm Sunday Sermon" Murray offered Martin Luther King as a paradigm of the minority Christian as Suffering Servant,

> Do you recall as we approached Easter season six years ago, our own Dr. Martin Luther King made a triumphal march in Memphis, TN?... That on the day of his death he had planned to eat a meal of special delight with his disciple, colleague, and successor, the Reverend Abernathy? That with his death by an assassin's bullet, the dream of justice with reconciliation seemed to die and throughout our nation cities went up in flames?[73]

Devastation at King's assassination can leave us discouraged if we understand it as pointing "to a reversal of our march toward freedom." Murray reminded her congregation that the Crucifixion was not the end of King's efforts, for "Christian faith reaffirms constantly that Crucifixion and Resurrection are part of one continuous Event, that humiliation, degradation and death are followed by victory, the overcoming of death by rebirth and the making of all things new."[74] King was an instrument of God's participation in liberation struggles. Murray believed that "when humans act in the world based upon acceptance of this relationship... their actions help to establish the beloved community promised by God to those who persevere."[75] God would transform the suffering of the oppressed, the devastation of Good Friday, into salvation on Easter Sunday. Murray did not characterize minority suffering as deserved or want minority Christians to invite suffering, but nor did she acknowledge risks in making theological use of suffering.

Murray was among the first to outline a black feminist theological agenda, but she did not anticipate what have become prominent black feminist and womanist critiques of suffering. Many contemporary womanist and African American feminist theologians refuse to give theological credence to suffering. Instead, black feminist and womanist theologians and ethicists have emphasized Jesus' ministry and posed critical questions about whether Jesus' death on the Cross is salvific for black women. Emilie Townes, Jacquelyn Grant, and Delores Williams have made representative arguments.

Womanist ethicist Emilie Townes declares that "suffering is outrageous. Suffering does not ennoble, enable or equip this generation or future generations of Black people." Townes recognizes that the Black Church makes frequent use of the Suffering Servant motif, but she insists nevertheless that "the inevitability and desirability of suffering needs to be challenged."[76] Townes adopts Audre Lorde's distinction between suffering and pain to argue that if Christians take the Resurrection seriously, then they recognize that suffering has been removed through the redemptive event of the Crucifixion. According to Townes, "the oppressed are set free to struggle against injustice, not out of their suffering, but out of their pain that can be recognized and named as injustice and brokenness."[77] Townes wants womanists and other Christian ethicists to move from the reactive posture of suffering to the transformative power of pain. Townes' interrogation of the inevitability and desirability of suffering addresses critical questions to Murray's theology. Even as Murray cautioned that people should not seek out suffering, she nevertheless valued suffering as potentially pedagogical and redemptive and insisted on the centrality of the Cross in Jesus' redemptive work. Murray did not challenge the inevitability of suffering, rather her sermons continued a theme from her earlier writing that African Americanes' experiences of suffering grant them a special role in God's reconciling work.

Womanist theologian Jacquelyn Grant rules out servanthood, particularly the Suffering Servant motif, as an appropriate theological metaphor for black women. Grant argues that the "Christian notion of servanthood has been fused and confused with the oppressive, unjust, social and political designation of servanthood—what in fact means servitude." Grant describes the conditions under which black women have been forced to live as a prime example of servanthood. She argues that "recognizing this can help free up our thinking and language from getting too imbricated in social structures, those that could prevent us from creating the reigndom of God."[78]

Grant's criticism of the Suffering Servant motif is at the heart of her constructive Christology. Grant describes Jesus' solidarity with the least of the people as an "implied universality, which made him identify with others—the poor, the woman, the stranger." She argues that black women experience a similar universality, for black women's tridimensional reality of racism, sexism, and classism is "an implied universality which connects them to others." Theorizing critically about this tridimensional reality should be a primary focus of womanist Christology, but Grant cautions against reading into the Gospel stories a "romanticized contentment with one's oppressed status in life."[79] Instead, Grant argues that the Gospels describe the context in which particular people struggle for hope and liberation. Theorizing about the tridimensional reality of black women's lives is an effort to name a context for struggle, hope, and liberation. Grant's critical engagement with the Suffering Servant motif indicates how Murray's theological perspective on suffering did not address experiences of African American women specifically. She did not acknowledge or analyze how an understanding of redemptive suffering might be particularly harmful to African American women.

In *Sisters in the Wilderness*, Delores Williams elaborates a womanist theology that "challenges all oppressive forces impeding black women's struggle for survival and for the development of a positive, productive quality of life conducive to women's and the family's freedom and well-being." Toward that end, Williams rejects a substitutionary account of atonement, or how Jesus covers over sin. She argues that a model of atonement that requires Jesus to suffer on behalf of human beings is not beneficial for African American women who have been compelled to be sexual and labor surrogates for white women during slavery and after emancipation. Williams rejects surrogacy as a significant aspect of atonement and rejects the Cross as the central symbol of Jesus' redemptive work. Williams asserts, "humankind is, then, redeemed through Jesus' ministerial vision of life and not through his death. There is nothing divine in the blood of the Cross." Rejecting a traditional explanation that Jesus came as a substitute for humanity, Williams insists, "Jesus did not come to be a surrogate. Jesus came for life." Williams recognizes that suffering is a central aspect of African American women's existential experience and that "as Christians, black women cannot forget the Cross, but neither can they glorify it."[80]

When Murray accepted the vocation of Suffering Servant, she allowed that there is value in Jesus' suffering and, by extension, that there might be value in African American women's and men's suffering. By ascribing African American suffering to others' sins, she rejected any justification of suffering as punitive or deserved, yet she allowed that African American women and men serve as surrogates for the community when the Suffering Servant intervenes on people's behalf in order to attenuate their alienation from God. While Murray did not counsel African Americans to seek out pain or affliction, she nevertheless points to the suffering that results from white racism as equipping African Americans with certain skills and authority to bring about reconciliation. Williams, on the other hand, refuses to accept that pain and humiliation are necessary to God's atoning work; Williams presents the Cross instead as the "evil of humankind trying to kill the *ministerial* vision of life in relation that Jesus brought to humanity."[81] Murray's sermons considered both Jesus' ministry and his death on the Cross as aspects of his redemptive work. Central to Murray's account of salvation was Jesus' proclamation that the kingdom is at hand and people's attendant obligation to work toward making the kingdom more present. But Murray retained the Cross as a central feature of her own theology when she spoke of the pain, humiliation, and death that haunt the Cross as part of one continuous event with the Resurrection, rebirth, and making all things new.

Shawn Copeland's work exemplifies how a theologian committed to liberation might employ suffering as part of a theological program. A Roman Catholic systematic "theologian, who is black and a woman," Copeland does not categorically deny value in suffering.[82] She explains, "evil is the negation and deprivation of good; suffering, while never identical with evil, is inseparable from it. Thus, and quite paradoxically, the suffering caused by evil can result in interior development and perfection as well as in social and cultural good." Focusing particularly on the lives of enslaved African American women, Copeland argues that a theology of suffering can be redemptive because it remembers and retells "the lives and sufferings of those who 'came through' and those who have 'gone to the glory land' ... in their narratives black women invite God to partner with them in the redemption of Black people. They make meaning of their suffering."[83] Copeland is careful to point out that a theology of suffering should not spiritualize suffering, rather it must take suffering seriously as an important aspect of black women's lives. Copeland grounds her argument in concrete data of African American women's experiences during enslavement and employs these witnesses as resources for a theology of suffering that is characterized by resistance. Copeland models how "black women remember and draw strength in their own anguish from hearing and imitating strategies adopted by their mothers, grandmothers, great-grandmothers, and great-great-grandmothers to handle their suffering. These stories evoke growth and change, proper outrage and dissatisfaction, and enlarge black women's moral horizons and choices."[84] In light of Copeland's appeals to specific stories of African American women, a reader notices that Murray's discussion of minority Christians lacks historical particularity and risks spiritualizing African American suffering. While Murray's sermons considered historical experiences of African American women in order to remember women as crucial to the Christian story, she did not employ these directly in her evaluation of suffering, nor did she explicitly challenge the fact of suffering. Townes, Williams, Grant and Copeland, leading scholars of the generation following Murray, demand that Christian theologians and ethicists transform the outrageousness of African American suffering. But Murray insisted that suffering is an opportunity to identify with the humanity of Jesus Christ, for whom after "the powers of evil had done all that they could do to him, death did not have the last word. God raised him to new life."[85]

God's desire that humanity be God's coworkers and the paradigm of Jesus becoming the Christ point toward Murray's preeminent theological concern—reconciliation. Reconciliation entails reconciliation between human beings and between human beings and God. For Murray reconciliation is intimately connected with salvation. Salvation is not simply a private event because it cannot be removed from our commitment to the well-being of our neighbor. She agreed with Tillich's insistence that the universal significance of the Christ event is salvation in the form of overcoming the rift between God and human being, between human beings and the world, and between a human being and herself. Murray worried that despite clear teaching to the contrary, many people assume that their religious faith offers private salvation, because many Christians do not understand the second great commandment with the same urgency as the first. Murray reminded her congregation that "Jesus taught us, wholeness of being and salvation depend upon continual awareness of and response to the inseparability of love of God and love of neighbor." But once people understand that we have a responsibility to individuals, they must accept perhaps an even more difficult responsibility, that we have an ongoing responsibility to "whole communities of people victimized by an uncaring social system, beaten down by oppression, poverty, and neglect, victimized of their chance to share in the benefits of the richest nation on earth."[86] Murray maintained an attention to the individual, but also underscored how attention to entire communities can reveal details about individual experiences, for instance how poverty, oppression, and neglect often grow as corporate ills. When we see the individual divorced from her community and the social and economic variables of her particular situation, we cannot take responsibility for our part in our neighbor's social situation.

Salvation is necessarily social, because "we cannot be whole human beings when we are alienated from our neighbors." Calling it the greatest theme of Christian ethics, "the command to overcome hostilities and conflicts and to find a sense of community in spite of differences," Murray equated "redemption or salvation" with unity with God. Here Murray offered a theological reading of identity, "Jesus treated each person as a unique individual, not on the basis of categories of race, sex, or social status, but on the basis of their common humanity."[87] But Murray does not acknowledge the kinds of individuals with whom Jesus associated, including sinners, tax collectors, and the poor. In her work for the PCSW and in lobbying around Title VII, Murray called on African

American women's experiences in order to point to a universal standard of equal protection. In an effort to emphasize common humanity, Murray passed over Jesus' preference for the marginalized and rejected and missed an opportunity to ground her Christology in the particularities of identity.

A sermon preached in 1977 at Wake Forest University, "Our Highest Selves" referred to Black Power (without calling it by name) as a source of alienation. "In trying to destroy the heritage of enforced inferiority," Murray cautioned, "we find ourselves struggling with new phases of alienation." Black Power carried theological risks because it rejected a sense of community in spite of differences, was an impediment to reconciliation, and therefore an impediment also to salvation. She reminded her college-age listeners that "wholeness does not imply the eradication of differences," rather it is the hard-won recognition of differences and of the integrity of each individual. Only when we come to appreciate and affirm these differences, can "we find the common humanity which binds us together." Recognition of this common humanity allows us to live up to the great ethical demand to love our neighbor. And this, according to Murray, is the message of two great theologians, King and Paul, who "sought to bring the Gospel of reconciliation to a world seething with deep human passions and divisions.... This vision of oneness of humanity in Christ, even in the midst of strife, is our hope of a new era and we ... are called upon to carry forward the task of healing in our world of broken relationships."[88] By juxtaposing what she characterized as the alienation promoted by Black Power with King's ethic of reconciliation, she ignored what many of her listeners knew—that King himself had wondered if perhaps separation was a necessary step before integration. Her appeal to a "common" humanity also obscured pressing economic, political, and social differences between people that meant that people of particular economic classes, races, and gender identities tended to be objects of economic exploitation and political disfranchisement. Murray had spent the better part of her life making the case that her own particularized identity be considered by the great social movements of the century who professed to speak on her behalf. She knew all too well, therefore, the rhetorical and political dangers of presuming a universal or common humanity.

In a subsequent sermon, "What Shall I Do To Inherit Eternal Life?" Murray again connected salvation to a Christian ethic of love, but this time on a global scale. Murray preached, "I believe that we have reached a stage in human civilization where Christ's command to love our neighbor is not merely a spiritual and moral principle governing our ultimate salvation but a present necessity of human survival on this earth."[89] Murray underscored the political importance of a theological category as our "national boundaries become progressively irrelevant" as a result of advancements in technology and transportation, such that the call to love our neighbor requires a sophisticated recognition of the interdependence of all life on earth. In a prescient explanation of the current migration crisis in the Americas, she compared the plight of migrant workers with African Americans who fled slavery:

> The risks endured by tens of thousands who have...perished of thirst in the Arizona desert should recall us to our own racial history of little more than a century ago—the history of runaway black slaves in the United States seeking freedom in Canada. Human need and the urge for freedom know no national boundaries.

She concluded simply, "we are all involved with one another, and salvation is more than an individual matter; it involves the whole world."[90] In previous sermons, she related salvation to a recognition of a common humanity in spite of differences; here she preached that salvation does not refer simply to the afterlife, rather it starts in the here and now.

For Murray, salvation entailed the power and possibility of transforming the world and of restoring creation. She emphasized that it is *now* that we must risk in our work toward liberation and freedom, so that God's will be done on earth as it is in heaven. She equated this work with the content of Jesus' ministry, "it seems to me that this is what Jesus meant when he proclaimed, 'The Kingdom of heaven is at hand.' And again, 'The Kingdom of Heaven is within you.'" Murray imagined the kingdom as a partial reality that can be discerned and worked toward by loving our neighbor. She concluded that "while we cannot fully experience in the here and now this future God is bringing, in faith we can follow Jesus Christ, working to transform the world in accordance with God's promise, 'Behold I make all things new.'"[91] Human beings undertake eschatological labors with God to build the kingdom on earth, as it is in heaven. For Murray then, people's participation with God in building the kingdom involves concretely welcoming those who need work, providing social services, and working toward racial reconciliation, among other tasks.

Murray's contributions to building the kingdom on earth ended on July 1, 1985 when she died of pancreatic cancer. She spent the last eight years of her life ministering to churches in Washington and Baltimore and serving as a visiting minister when she was often called to do so. Near what would be the end of her life, she moved to Pittsburgh and bought a house next door to her lifelong friend Maida Springer Kemp and Springer's husband. Obituaries in the *New York Times* and *Washington Post* cataloged her notable accomplishments and inventoried her number of careers. What these straightforward notices missed was Murray's prophetic democratic vision. In the late 1930s and early 1940s, Murray's writing repeatedly appealed to eschatological categories like contradiction, risk, and suffering to evaluate American democracy. After the 1943 Harlem riots, a young Murray despaired that she and her compatriots would not gain the gates of the city. In her sermons of the late 1970s and early 1980s, a mature Murray was confident that salvation and redemption are available through justice-building work. Risk and suffering remained important to Murray's theological and democratic vision, but they were contextualized within profound democratic faith and hopeful anticipation of the coming kingdom.

Murray was careful never to equate simply the kingdom with American politics and, at times, expressed profound doubt about American democracy. In a 1976 interview, she compared the United States to biblical Israel and wondered whether American democracy could live up to its promise. She said that America

> is constantly falling down from these high ideals which we have set, that racism and sexism are actually sins, the sickness of sin, that human beings are not really in harmony in relationship to their Creator, and since they are not, they are not able to be in harmony and relationship to love and respect their neighbor. So, I'm not sure that I—I'm not even sure, for example, that America will win this. I'm not even sure that America isn't like the Israel of the Old Testament, that she is not standing under the judgment of God.[92]

At first glance, it seems that Murray issued a jeremiad. Deriving its name from the prophet Jeremiah who warned of Israel's downfall because its rulers have broken the covenant with God, a jeremiad is "rhetoric of indignation, expressing deep dissatisfaction and urgently challenging the nation to reform."[93] Historians of religion have outlined American versions of the jeremiad. Sacvan Bercovitch traces the jeremiad to Puritan roots and discerns a three-part rhetorical structure that includes a citing of the promise, criticism of present declension from this promise, and a prophecy that society can complete its mission and redeem the promise. Bercovitch argues that the Puritan jeremiad became central to American rhetorical tradition.[94]

A uniquely African American jeremiad developed in which, according to Theophus Smith, "African American writers eventually adapted the genre to their own rhetorical strategies, principally as a means for provoking their countrymen to fulfill the egalitarian ideals of the young republic."[95] The jeremiad is inherently conservative, for "the deep structural intent was not to repudiate or diverge from the covenantal heritage or the democratic ideals of the republic."[96] The jeremiad functions, then, to sustain social control and affirm normative social and political beliefs.[97] In the aforementioned passage from an oral history interview, Murray rehearsed at least the first two parts of the jeremiad's rhetorical structure. She cited high ideals and lamented Americans' continued failure to meet them because of sin and alienation from God. (Murray's subject slipped back and forth between "America" and, seemingly, "American Christians.")

In this instance, she did not articulate the third part, a prophecy that the United States can redeem itself and attempt to live up to its ideals. But, elsewhere we have seen her apparently articulate a version of the jeremiad's third part, faith in both democratic and Christian ideals and calling for Americans to live up to these ideals. But Murray's theological and political vision exceeded the rhetorical structure of the jeremiad, because Murray did not merely affirm extant democratic or theological ideals. Instead, she sought to transform democratic and theological traditions.

Murray's legal, activist, academic, and theological work rejected a nostalgic account of American beginnings. Murray's work on the PCSW and on legal briefs about women's right to serve on juries broadened the legal interpretation of the Fourteenth Amendment. In so doing, Murray changed what legal protection means for Americans today. Repeatedly she insisted on the interrelatedness of all human rights when she demonstrated how a particular attention to African American women's experiences expands moral imagination. In *Proud Shoes* and in her law school dissertation, Murray presented a past that, as George Shulman characterizes Toni Morrison's sense of past in *Beloved*, "must be confronted but not repeated in the way it is retold."[98] Murray's democratic and theological vision exceeded the structure of the jeremiad, because Murray focused on transformation, rather than redemption, in advocating that American democracy live up to its promise.

Murray's eschatological hope and her faith in democratic ideals were not utopian or romantic, rather they demanded consistently critical evaluation of democratic and theological norms. Even so, as Murray remained committed to a vision of beloved community, we are compelled to ask if it was viable. In 1984, Murray's former colleague James Baldwin would say that "we are behind the gates of a kingdom that is determined to destroy us."[99] Could Murray's democratic eschatology meet the challenge of Baldwin's claim? Was Murray's vision anachronistic, aspiring as it did for reconciliation and integration? Was it also incomplete, claiming to organize itself around an ethic of wholeness, yet deferring explicit attention to sexuality and heterosexism? Chapter 5 addresses these questions and examines whether Murray's project is relevant to our own era.

5

The Gates of the City

An Eschatological Vision of American Democracy

The primary aim of this book has been to demonstrate that Pauli Murray was an innovative, if often overlooked, democratic thinker. The preceding chapters have demonstrated how Murray was on vanguard of civil rights and feminist movements, was a groundbreaking legal theorist, an important literary voice who argued that African American experiences were paradigmatically American experiences, and a prescient theological critic who underscored the importance of feminist reflection on African American women's experiences. The preceding chapters have also argued that a straightforward catalog of Murray's achievements in diverse capacities—as lawyer, author, activist, and priest—overlooks rhetorical threads that bind Murray's manifold achievements, including attentions to identity, history, and what I have identified as a democratic eschatology. Woven together, these threads provide a material account of American identity enlivened with historical consciousness of multiplicity and model a disposition of critical hope that strategically addresses current inequalities in order to point to justice that is come.

Murray characterized identity as unstable and complex, yet she employed identity strategically in her legal and religious writing. A lifetime of theorizing about identity culminated in a theological account of reconciliation, through which people estranged from one another might be reconciled in their differences. Murray's faith in the possibility of reconciliation grew from her own experiences in overcoming existential estrangement and coming to terms with herself. Her attention to the integrity of the individual developed importantly out of Murray's sense of herself as an exemplar of the kind of process of reconciliation that the nation must undergo. By investigating the character and meaning of identity categories, Murray demonstrated the limitations of a single category to describe a multiplicity of experiences. She witnessed how meaning is produced at the intersection of identities, an observation that was often overlooked by Murray's activist colleagues. Murray's own racial, gender, and sexual identities did not fit normative standards. In the midst of Jim Crow apartheid, she grew up learning a family history, which charted enslaved and free, African, Native American, Irish, and French ancestries. As a young woman, she sought explanations for her habits of dressing in men's clothes and her love for women. Decades before the term transgender was widely known, Murray's "little boy–girl personality," as she called it, defied classification.

Murray's self-conscious reflections about her own identity became central to her democratic thought. In the 1940s, she used the term Jane Crow to describe how she experienced discrimination at the intersection of race and gender. In the 1960s, she appealed to male leaders of the civil rights movement and white leaders of the women's movement to recognize the intersectional nature of oppression. The two great social movements of the 1960s would only fulfill their ambitions, Murray argued, if they were able to respond to the specific experiences of African American women who suffered discrimination because of race *and* sex. By appealing to her experiences of identity categories, Murray placed herself at the center of democratic reflection. In order to gage American democracy's success at protecting people's rights and providing opportunities to pursue life, liberty, and happiness, Murray insisted that we look to concrete historical experiences of African American women as a kind of bellwether of democracy's achievements.

Murray noted the contradiction between the nation's founding ideals and the history of Americans of African descent. Her family memoir witnessed her grandfather's service to the Union at the same time that he was politically disenfranchised. She noted that the history of many black Americans went unrecorded and continued to go unrecognized. *Proud Shoes* also documented the conflict in her family about its enslaved and free past. Reflecting Robert Bellah's call for Americans to recognize "dangerous memories that would unsettle our self-regard" Murray's portrayal of her family as Ishmaelite produced a dangerous memory of sexual violence and coercion that has shaped relationships between blacks and whites in the United States.[1]

History is important to Murray's democratic thought, because she believed that our historiographical attentions shape how we understand ourselves and this, in turn, has consequences for American democracy. In the mid-1950s when Murray wrote her family memoir, mainstream history largely ignored the complicated family history of black and white Americans. Only when these connections were considered, argued Murray, would a sense of relatedness as a precursor to reconciliation be possible among contemporary Americans. Murray recognized that some people's stories would remain untold, so that our sense of ourselves is necessarily partial and incomplete. The intimate connections between identity and history were nurtured in Murray's democratic eschatology.

From the contradiction between founding promises and historical realities, Murray elaborated a democratic model of promise and fulfillment. The Declaration of Independence foretells "we the people" and the Bill of Rights ensures our liberty, but American democracy has failed to fulfill these promises. Yet there is implicit hope in Murray's formulation. She understood American democracy eschatologically, which means that democracy is always in the process of becoming as it looks toward its completion in the future and demands people's participation in making it more present. Just as she forwarded a vision of American democracy as beset by contradiction and not yet fully present, Murray developed a theological vision preoccupied with the kingdom of God. Positing a God who works in history and the possibility of human beings being reconciled with God and one another as they work together to build the kingdom, Murray articulated an eschatological hope that recognized individual and structural sins. Murray's sense of identity rests on the uniqueness of the individual as a child of God and is steeped in history. To be an American Christian, according to Murray, is to live in a situation of already and not yet. Whereas God has promised the kingdom, it is not yet fully present. Whereas the Constitution has enshrined democratic promises, these promises have yet to be enjoyed by all Americans.

Previous chapters have emphasized limitations of Murray's democratic vision, including her reluctance to address publicly her own sexuality. Murray did not speak publicly about her sexuality when contemporaries, like Audre Lorde and James Baldwin, did. Does Murray's refusal to address this aspect of her identity undermine her contention that her existential journey was exemplary of the possibility for reconciliation on a national level? Does Murray's reluctance affect her theological legacy of an ethic of wholeness? Womanist ethicist Kelly Brown Douglas might answer yes. She argues, "if the task of the theologian is not simply to reflect its community's thinking but also to be prophetic in relation to it, then Black and womanist theologians cannot abandon their prophetic role. They, especially womanists, are compelled to break the silence concerning Black sexuality."[2] While Murray may not have found the means or vocabulary in her homeletic or other public voices to break the silence, she included among files that she herself organized for archival preservation discussions with doctors about her sexuality, letters to family and friends in which she addressed frankly her sexuality and gender presentation, as well as romantic photos with women, and journal entries in which she expressed love for her female partner. While Murray did not reflect specifically on how this aspect of her identity shaped her understanding of herself as exemplary of an American identity, she did leave her readers with important witnesses to this part of herself.

Another notable limitation is Murray's defense of American principles in the face of white racist government policies and practices. From Ghana in 1960, Murray prioritized the capacity of the American Constitution to address growing state violence in the United States and in place of pan-African identities and solidarities. Later in the decade, Murray was hostile to Black Power and continued to insist on the possibility of reconciliation between black and white

Americans. Murray's faithfulness to American democratic principles during these (and previous) decades can seem naïve, or at the very least remarkably stubborn. But her faith in American democratic principles was motivated importantly by what she saw as their strategic potential to provide philosophical, historical, and legal resources to witness the interrelatedness of all human rights.

This book has consistently contextualized Pauli Murray's accomplishments in particular historical moments. As I look to assess the legacy of her political and religious contributions, I am faced with questions of if and how Murray's project can speak to another historical moment, our own. In order to gage this possibility, I put Murray's project in conversation with two contemporary approaches to religion and politics that aim to inform democratic theory with Christian theological imagination and commitments. Jean Bethke Elshtain and Cornel West share Murray's commitment to a democratic *and* theological vision and each proffer specific, contemporary diagnoses about the condition of American democracy. Both Elshtain and West are public intellectuals. They are academics who have translated their disciplinary concerns—political theory for Elshtain, philosophy of religion for West—into a publically accessible argument about the role of religion in public life and the character of contemporary American democracy. Like Murray did, both Elshtain and West use Christian categories to interpret and critique democratic practices. Placing Murray in conversation with two leading contemporary voices will help readers to gage if and how Murray's writing of the mid-twentieth century can advance an account of American democracy that is relevant today. In order to do so, I offer a brief overview of each scholar's work and consider how Murray's project contests or strengthens it.

Elshtain examines American democracy by focusing on how boundaries are drawn between public and private life, the importance of civil society to a flourishing democracy, and how religious institutions offer moral critiques of democratic practices. Most recently, these attentions have culminated in her Gifford Lectures in which she explores the notion of sovereignty in contemporary (American) politics. Elshtain's work is characterized by a critique of the isolated self that liberalism puts forward. Insisting that religious language and institutions offer a more realistic anthropology, Elshtain believes that American Christians can make important contributions to democratic renewal.

Elshtain's initial appraisal of American democracy came in *Public Man Private Woman* (1981), in which she advocates a feminist model of citizenship. Her first step is to affirm what is axiomatic about human being: human beings are distinguished by a drive to understand and create meaning and are part of ongoing traditions that give parameters to meaning making. Elshtain's individual is necessarily entangled in webs of community and tradition. The individual is not, against the assumption of much of liberal political theory, independent or self-actualized. In her constructive vision of an alternative to the ancient divide between public and private, Elshtain affirms that the familiar sphere has its own dignity and that it informs the public sphere. Or, put another way, Elshtain argues that the public sphere is not—and, contra the Greeks has never been— impervious to the concerns of everyday life, including what is often relegated to the private. In her discussions of the public, Elshtain is careful not to assign the public to a "sphere" or a "space," and thereby designate it as something separate or uninterested in private concerns. Instead, she developed what she called "a constructive vision" of the public that is "very much *in* and *of* the world." Elshtain's comparable appraisals of the individual and the public—that both are implicated in other social structures—led her to critique second wave (white) feminist political and theoretical projects, which according to Elshtain put forward an anemic, selfish, and unrealistic model of the individual as citizen. Elshtain regrets that "strangely few feminists have couched their political vision in terms of what it means to be an 'American' or a 'citizen' save in a thin instrumentalist sense ('How to get yours'). Where is a feminist analogue to Dr. King's 'I Have a Dream'? In whose behalf is the feminist dream being dreamt?"[3]

In the next decade, Elshtain worried that American democracy is faltering because of deep cynicism that results, in part, from a kind of acquisitive individualism that translates wants into rights. In *Democracy on Trial* (1995), Elshtain argues that a significant reason for the erosion of our democratic dispositions is a transition from an understanding of a rights-bearing individual as a civic creature to a rights-bearing individual who stands alone, as if rights were something she possessed. Elshtain worries that as "rights were construed increasingly in individualistic terms...their civic dimensions withered on the vine." Contemporary appeals to rights devolve into a demand for affirmation of a person's particular identity. Elshtain dismisses identity politics as misguided "politicized ontology" in which "persons are to be judged not by what they do or say but by what they *are*." She proposes a renewal of the concept of the political as "that which is, in principle, held in common and what is, in principle, open to public scrutiny and judgment."[4] She wants citizens to organize around a set of concrete, common concerns, instead of merely proclaiming who they are and demanding special recognition.

A coincident concern is for Americans to recognize the value of civil society organizations. Elshtain fears that American civil society is losing its vibrancy and thus American democracy is imperiled. She warns that "our democracy is growing weaker because we are using up, but not replenishing, the civic and moral resources that make our democracy possible."[5] Elshtain specifies that civil society refers to those aspects of associational life, including neighborhood life, religious, economic, civic, and educational associations; civil society fosters "competence and character in individuals, build[s] social trust, and help[s] children become good people and good citizens."[6] Countering what she charges is a kind of triumphant progressivism that assumes that the federal government can and should fix what ails democracy, Elshtain indicates that not all problems are potentially solvable. Elshtain is careful to specify that her commitment to civil society stems not from a conviction that civil society will solve democracy's problems, rather she believes that a thriving civil society creates citizens who are equipped to address in a realistic way social, economic, and political challenges.

Elshtain argues that it is in civil society that religion and politics have most often met in American history and she emphasizes the importance of religious institutions to provide the "moral understandings that are essential to liberal democratic institutions."[7] In response to a Rawlsian caveat that only public reasons should be used in political discussions, Elshtain insists that "in the real world of religion and politics as they actually coexist in America, citizens resort to 'god talk' at least as much as they use 'rights talk.'"[8] She rejects calls for institutions in democratic society to conform to a single authority principle or a single vocabulary, for example to the standard of public reason. Elshtain argues that secularists, whom she characterizes as assuming that religion is either irrationalism or a claim to epistemological privilege, want a separation of religion and politics not only on the level of the state but also within civil society.[9] But Elshtain champions religious language and institutions as crucial for a vibrant civil society and so too for a healthy democracy.

Elshtain locates the possibility of "democratic renewal" in a "new social covenant," which "rests on the presumption that one's fellow citizens are people of goodwill who yearn for the opportunity to work together, rather than to continue to glare at one another across racial, class, and ideological divides."[10] As the metaphor of renewal implies, Elshtain wants to return to the well of democratic hope. In *Who Are We?* (2000), Elshtain specifies that Christian churches and Christian citizens have special roles to play in this democratic renewal. "Enjoined to live in hope," according to Elshtain, Christian citizens can model a democratic stance "aware of human sin and shortcoming but aware also of our capacities for stewardship and decency in our openness to grace." Similarly, churches are called to "play a critical role as interpreters of culture to the culture."[11]

In her Gifford lectures, published as *Sovereignty: God, State, and Self* (2008), Elshtain investigates the development of the concept of sovereignty from early Christianity to the modern West. While sovereignty had originally been applied exclusively to God, the term shifted to descriptions of state and political power, and today makes it home among descriptions of the self. In contemporary terms, to be sovereign, argues Elshtain, means a person can exercise absolute power over her self and her fate. Sovereignty means, in short, that she is not answerable to anyone. A sovereign self that seeks to overcome nature particularly worries Elshtain. Referring to eugenics projects of the early twentieth century as well as what she identifies as radical feminism's connection between reproductive health issues, particularly abortion, and political equality, Elshtain argues that visions of a sovereign self present "a mixed picture to the world, for it is an odd combination of excarnation—the bodies we are now in are demeaned—with a type of biological, or better, genetic obsession." Elshtain responds to what she sees as unrealistic and dangerous liberal and radical feminist anthropologies with a model of a contingent self, who discovers her inherent dignity and makes meaning "in growing to become a full person according to our human natures."[12]

Murray's political and theological vision offers many resources to contest and contextualize Elshtain's diagnosis of cynicism and its chief symptom, right-grubbing individualism. It is a pity that Elshtain likely did not know about Murray's work, because Murray presented a democratic vision of the interrelatedness of all human rights. Murray did not offer a mere analog to King's dream; her feminist commitments were intimately and, according to Murray, necessarily tied to her civil rights commitments. Just as Elshtain's anthropology depicts the political subject as historically situated, Murray demonstrates how history and memory are constituent to democratic identity. While Elshtain's breaks down divisions between public and private, by demonstrating the public life is concerned everyday life, including family life, Murray employed her family's history as emblematic of the nation. In so doing, Murray demonstrated what Elshtain theorized, that the so-called private story of racial violence in one family had critical public implications for democratic practices and participation. Murray's repeated characterization of American democracy as partially present and yet to come and requiring people's participation to make it present resonates with Elshtain's insistence that "citizenship, like a robust social gospel, must dirty its hands in the present."[13]

Murray's feminist and egalitarian politics demanded rights and protections so that, in particular, African American women would be included in equal protection. But, Murray's arguments for equal protection always returned to a vision of what it means to be American, even as they relied on particular theorizing about identity. Murray paid special attention to the situation of African American women as a matter of democratic integrity. Murray's greatest contributions toward broadening the possibility of women and African American women's democratic participation came in the 1950s and 1960s, when, according to Elshtain, the "confusion" over rights sowed the seeds of democratic cynicism and despair. Murray's activism and legal achievements call into question Elshtain's odd sense of history, in which the weakening of democratic civil society coincides with gains in civil rights such as the right to vote, the right to serve on juries, and the right of farm workers to organize.

Murray's project does not entirely disabuse Elshtain's cynicism. Murray herself contested a nascent identity politics she saw at work in Black Power. She felt that narrow nationalisms and identification with others' democratic efforts evaded important democratic work that needed to be done in the United States. But Murray was sympathetic to what motivated this kind of identification. As much as she decried what she saw as the misogyny of Black Power among Brandeis students, for example, Murray recognized the importance of African American students creating a positive account of their identity. But Murray wanted this identity to be provisional enough that it might recognize multiple aspects of identity, such as African American women's experiences. While Murray would likely have agreed with Elshtain's model of a contingent self, Murray's *Proud Shoes* offers an implicit challenge to Elsthain's criticism of sovereignty. Even as Elshtain discusses eugenics projects, she neglects to consider America's history of racial slavery. That black bodies were once treated as property, Murray would argue, ought to be part of any contemporary discussion of autonomy or self-determination in light of claims to political equality. Elshtain's positions regarding abortion and genetic engineering notwithstanding, Americans have a vested interest in strong articulations of the self's autonomy and sovereignty.

Murray affirmed that citizens who are Christians should play a role in the realization of American democracy, but she cautioned against assuming that Christians have special skills as interpreters of culture. On the contrary, Murray called on Christians to apply the same vigor of interpretation to their own institutions and norms as Elshtain would have them apply to cultural and political institutions. Murray demonstrated how democratic norms remind Christians of an egalitarianism that characterized aspects of the earliest Christian communities. Christians are always already historically situated subjects as they appeal to Christian ideals and that their situatedness circumscribes the extent to which they can enact these ideals.

Murray's consistent attention to history problematizes Elshtain's call for democratic renewal. While Elshtain characterizes American democracy as "faltering" and calls for a "new social covenant," Murray rejected any myth of pristine democratic beginnings. Where Elshtain complains that democratic cynics are convinced that "the entire history of American democracy is one of hegemonic imposition, 'nothing but' a story of inegalitarianism," Murray's new kind of American history takes seriously past and continued suffering and inegalitarianism as it finds within its own tradition resources for how to make contemporary and future relationships between citizens more just.[14] Murray did not call for democracy to be *renewed*; she called for democracy to be *realized*.

To contemporary discussions about Christianity and democracy, Cornel West contributes a democratic hope fueled by a prophetic Christianity that has faith in the possibility of a nonracist society, despite material and historical realities of American racism. West's project is outlined in fifteen books, countless essays, interviews, and public lectures. His voluminous production is nearly matched by his intellectual allegiances. West situates himself within a genealogy of American pragmatism, identifies as a Chekhovian Christian, insists on the importance of Marxist theory for historical and material critiques of American racism, and puts forward his own brand of prophetic Christianity. In the past quarter century of his intellectual production, West has employed these allegiances in order to offer a moral vision of American democracy that is hopeful that America can be transformed from a racist to a nonracist society, while at the same time he recognizes that "the decline and decay in American life *appears*, at the moment, to be irreversible."[15] How does West's approach allow for such a seemingly logical inconsistency? How does he hold conclusions about death-dealing historical and material structures of white racism in tension with faith in people's ability to transform said structures? Three major streams of West's intellectual development indicate answers: These are Marxist theory, pragmatism, and a prophetic Christianity.

West affirms the potential for Marxist theory to examine historical and material conditions through which African American oppression emerged and to reveal how social, economic, and political practices continue to shape oppression. Yet he sees limits in how Marxist theory views race in solely economic and class terms and worries, that as a European intellectual product, it is susceptible to Western racist logics. But West nevertheless heralds Marxist theory's emphasis on materialism and employs this as the starting point for his own "genealogical materialist analysis" which allows him to look beyond economics to social, political, and psychic spheres and to the cultural traditions of civilizations in order to investigate African American oppression.[16] West's critics interpret in his recent work a lapse in commitments to Marxist theory, and specifically to a radical reorganization of capitalist structures. While writing from the early 1980s, such as *Prophesy Deliverance!*, called for a reorganization of American society so that it was no longer dependent on capitalist logics, more recent reflections, for example West's work with Sylvia Ann Hewlett on parenting in the United States, call for reform, rather than overthrow, of capitalist systems.[17] West's pragmatism may explain a perceived shift in his Marxist orientation. A pragmatist might recognize, for example, that revolution and reform are not necessarily at odds. Rather, each is a different, but strategic way, to call for the transformation of society.

West's philosophical disposition is consistently pragmatic. Pragmatism is a way of doing philosophy that rejects philosophy's traditional concern with finding the Truth. Instead, pragmatism posits that there are multiple truths that may arise from human experiences and some truths may be better than others. It values the capacity of the individual to engage in public discussions that construct and revise democratic commitments. Pragmatism presumes, therefore, that truths depend on a particular set of circumstances *and* that truths can be clarified, cultivated, and improved. Rather than explaining reality and determining truth, the goal of philosophy, from a pragmatic perspective, is to provide ameliorating descriptions of current realities in order to improve experiences.

West allows that pragmatism has been limited by its refusal to take class struggle seriously, yet he affirms its potential to destabilize modern thought's focus on epistemology in favor of a crucial emphasis on ethics.[18] West embraces pragmatism for its flexibility and potential to challenge hegemonic notions of truth.

In *The American Evasion of Philosophy* (1989), West promotes a specifically American philosophical tradition that can speak from the standpoint of and so witness to America's existential uniqueness. The title refers to a principal pragmatic method—the evasion of abstract claims to truth and reality in favor of an experimental approach—but also the source of this kind of philosophy as quintessentially American. In order to address white racism and African American oppression, West employs a philosophical tradition that emerges from the American condition and that allows for the transformation of self and society.[19]

West connects his pragmatic disposition to his own Christian faith and the possibility that prophetic Christianity can serve as a trenchant social critique of contemporary American democratic practices. Christian faith fuels West's hope in the possibility of multiracial American democracy, despite overwhelming evidence to the contrary. In 1993, West wrote that "the decline and decay in American life *appears*, at the moment, to be irreversible; yet it may not be. This slight possibility—the historic chance that a window of opportunity can be opened by our prophetic thought and action—is, in part, what keeping faith is all about."[20] For West, "Jesus of Nazareth has something to do with" this keeping faith, and motivates a "courage to fight for justice in the midst of such intolerable and overwhelming circumstances and conditions."[21] West's Christocentric perspective is pragmatic insofar as, according to West, his "acceptance of the prophetic Christian tradition is rational in that it rests upon good reasons." He allows that if another tradition were to provide "more acceptable and enabling moral visions," then he would be persuaded of its usefulness and would think with its moral standards and worldview.[22] West's association of pragmatism and Christianity may seem logically inconsistent, because West adheres to a Christian view of human beings and dignified and depraved while at the same time he affirms a pragmatic understanding of human nature and history as transformable.[23] While West's attention to sin does indeed temper an idealized understanding of human being, he remains committed to the idea that the human condition and human realities can be improved, if not perfected.

An outline of West's intellectual commitments must not ignore what he aspires to be the public implications of his theoretical work. West recognizes a number of different ways that intellectuals (he tends to discuss academics particularly in this regard) can intervene in public discussions and democratic critique. He is well known for his support of Bill Bradley's and Al Sharpton's presidential campaigns and long-standing involvement with the Democratic Socialists of America. Throughout his writing, West promotes multiracial coalitions as a way for the Left to make democratic inroads. His belief in the potential of coalitions mirrors the multidisciplinary approach of his democratic reflections. West insists that the Left's political potency lies neither in becoming "a vanguard party nor purist ideology, but rather [in] a coming together to pursue the common goals of radical democratic and libertarian projects that overlap."[24] Although West repeatedly employs Jesse Jackson's Rainbow Coalition as an object lesson, he cautions that coming together must not be limited to electoral politics. The only way to address chronic racism, sexism, and jingoism in American society, he argues, is with a broad-based coming together of people who are deeply committed to democratic ideals and forward a kind of moral reasoning that results in wise politics.

In *Democracy Matters* (2004), West conceives of American democracy as a tradition that includes reason giving, creation of new political vocabularies, and an attitude of striving and longing. Our conception of what democracy is should not be limited to electoral politics, he insists, for "such a focus fails to appreciate the crucial role of the underlying moral commitments and visions and fortifications of the soul that empower and inspire a democratic way of living in the world."[25] Three traditions that fuel democratic commitment in the American context are a Socratic commitment to questioning, an inheritance of the Jewish invention of a prophetic commitment to justice, and a tragicomic commitment to hope. Picking up on a theme he articulated in *Race Matters* (1993), West focuses on nihilism as a primary reason that American democracy is ailing.[26] To understand current American nihilism, West looks to "deeply racist and imperial roots of our democratic project."[27] Just as American democracy has wavered between democratic and imperial impulses, American Christianity has charted a path between its Constantinian and prophetic expressions. Previous centuries' dogmatic justifications of slavery and women's inequality and contemporary violence wrought in the name of "pro-life" and "pro-family" agendas are indications of how "strains of Constantinianism were woven into the fabric America's Christian identity from the start."[28] But another kind of nascent American Christianity was evident in the democratic practices of Christian groups that escaped British persecution and found their national voices in grand social movements of the nineteenth and twentieth centuries to end slavery, treat workers fairly, ensure universal suffrage, and guarantee civil rights for all Americans. Renewal of prophetic Christianity, West insists, is essential for democratic impulses to win out over imperial ones.

West's account of prophetic Christianity is drawn from his earlier work in *Prophesy Deliverance!* (1982), where he describes a prophetic Christianity "that has been guided by a profound conception of human nature and human history, a persuasive picture of what one is as a person, what one should hope for and how one ought to act." It also proposes "two fundamental norms of individuality and democracy as the center of Afro-American thought."[29] West's black prophetic Christianity shares many important similarities to Murray's project, such as an emphasis on the individual, an attention to history, and a sense of pro-found hope. But an important difference between Murray's project and West's contemporary criticism of American democracy in *Democracy Matters* reflects a difference between West's earlier and later use of prophetic Christianity.

In *Prophesy Deliverance!*, West revealed how prophetic Christianity could be an important source of democratic criticism. With its commitment to both the dignity *and* depravity of persons, West's early exposition of prophetic Christianity recognized that "contradiction and transformation are at the heart of the Christian gospel."[30] In *Democracy Matters*, West appeals to prophetic Christianity as a righteous political solution. Against Constantinian Christians' imperial desires, prophetic Christians must assert their own desires for justice, in order to "transform corrupted forms of elite rule into more democratic ways of life."[31] In *Democracy Matters* there is little concern that human depravity will under-mine movements toward democratization.

Murray advised against such prophetic certainty.[32] Her consistent efforts, and often failures, to have white feminists recognize racism and to have male civil rights leaders recognize women's leadership indicate how, even in prophetic social justice movements, human depravity undermines justice seeking. Murray's experiences of marginalization and rejection from movements to which she gave so much taught her the importance of humility when claiming to have the right answer. When she became a priest, a moment she understood as a culmination of her lifelong dedica-tion to social justice work, Murray admitted that she had doubts about whether women should be ordained: "Having been on the losing side for so much of my life, I take very seriously the pain of those who cling to an article of faith which appears to be overtaken by history."[33] Murray recalled West's earlier attention to how a pro-phetic Christianity "recognizes the depravity of person in that it acknowledges human disabilities," in all Christians, not merely the Constantinians.[34]

Just as Murray's project reminds West of his earlier attention to depravity, Murray's appeal to concrete data of experience and her deep sense of history complement West's three traditions of democratic commitment. West offers attitudinal and methodological strategies; he counsels to draw on the Socratic in the face of manipulation and lies; to call on the prophetic in the face of indiffer-ence to suffering; and to draw on the tragicomic in the face of disillusioned acquiescence to the status quo. Murray, meanwhile, offers a new kind of American history developed out her family's enslaved and free past, innovative legal strat-egies that grew out of her own experiences of Jane Crow, and a black feminist biblical hermeneutics that recognizes that there is some history we can never know. Murray's project shares West's "democratic longings" and it insists that justice-building efforts in the here and now can help us to reach the gates of the city.[35] Murray's experiences in coalition building—for example her successful lobbying to have "sex" included among Title VII standards—confirms West's assertion of the importance of alliances for leftist politics.

Similar to the connections Elshtain and West draw between religion and politics, Murray's rhetorical habit of describing American democracy in terms of promise and fulfillment indicates a role for religion in American public life. Pauli Murray is part of an American tradition of calling on Scripture and theological norms to evaluate American democracy's failings. Whether it was the contradiction between concrete historical realities of Jim Crow and the ideals of Christianity and democracy, America's Ishmaelite character, or questions about how African Americans would reach the "gates of the city," Murray used theological language to evaluate American democratic realities. Murray demonstrated, then, a Christian witness to injustice that called on democracy to be more fully present. Her eschatological understanding of American democracy provided a way to name contradictions between present realities and future promises of freedom, while at the same time it called for people to participate in making freedom available to more people in the here and now.

At the same time, Murray did not presume that any appeal to Christian norms is either transparent or absolute, for Murray also used democratic norms to critique religious practices and institutions. When she answered the Bishop's call for donations to the Church—the majority of whose members were not (yet) permitted to be ordained—with the democratic rallying cry that "taxation without representation is wrong," Murray employed a democratic ideal of fair representation to remind the church of historical examples of its own egalitarianism. When she compared Alice Paul's political organizing with Mary of Bethany's choice to learn from Jesus, Murray likened the reform efforts of a leading first wave feminist with Mary's bold choice, which Jesus later confirmed as the right one. Murray used Alice Paul's democratic organizing to remind her congregation of the egalitarianism Jesus affirmed. Murray used democratic ideals to critique religious practices, but also to show how religious ideals are always already mediated through human institutions that can and often do distort them.

Murray did not self-consciously articulate a theory of American democracy, but the three themes that appear repeatedly in her writing provide one. Murray proposed an American identity grounded in plurality and commitment to human rights, as the primary democratic identity. Who we are presently is also shaped by our past relationships and Murray's attention to history insists that reconciliation depends on an awareness of our relatedness, especially when relationships have historically been characterized by violence and exploitation. Murray's democratic thought aspires for the United States to be a multiracial polity in which everyone's rights are protected. This vision of American democracy becomes possible, argued Murray, when we reflect critically on our own identities and continually uncover and publicize histories that broaden understandings of our Americanness. Although Murray hoped for reconciliation between black and white Americans, she did not call for transcendence of racial or gender (or any other) categories. Instead, Murray appealed to the interrelation of human rights specifically from the standpoint of an American African woman. Similarly, when she made claims about what is at the heart of the American history, she offered her own family's Ishmaelite story to reveal how white racism has and continues to shape contemporary relationships. In other words, Murray situates herself, an African American woman of multiple ancestries, as a primary democratic subject, rather than as a problem or an exception.[36] The Americanness that Murray promotes does not, then, require assimilation to an ideal imposed by the dominant white culture. Instead, it calls for many different voices to express American democratic vistas. As someone who lived at the intersection of what were commonly recognized to be different identities, Murray insisted that coalition politics should be standard democratic practice.

In referring to her own experiences and her family's story, Murray focused on Jim Crow, the Great Migration, and the Black Freedom movement. Yet the conclusions Murray drew about identity and history from these mid-twentieth century phenomena can help us to respond to current realities, for example of a "new Jim Crow" and of "Juan Crow."[37] When racial disparities in drug convictions and sentences result in the mass incarceration—and thus typically disfranchisement—of hundreds of thousands of African American men, Murray's attention to identity recognizes that human rights are universal and belong to everyone, but they can only be effectively protected if the law is responsive to concrete historical realities, in this case to the reality that certain communities are targeted by the "War on Drugs." When border, foreign, and economic policies engender a group of people who live and work with few legal protections, who have few opportunities to participate in public life, and who are often considered to be illegal, Murray's attention to history recalls when people living in the United States have been denied citizenship, in part because they were not recognized as ontological equals with those in the ruling class.

Murray's eschatological disposition rejects deceptive characterizations of our current epoch as "post-racial." Regardless that a black American has been elected president, Murray would counsel that contradiction between democratic realities and democratic promises demands that we work in the here and now for justice that is to come. Murray's democratic eschatology points to an existential quandary of living between two epochs and advances a hope that moors itself in the spaces between "already" and "not yet."[38] Her sense of American democracy as being in the process of becoming infuses her democratic vision with a sense of purpose, but do not posit a teleological certainty.[39] This democratic eschatology builds momentum, direction, and energy to undertake justice-building projects, at the same time that it refuses to view any particular social policy or political achievement as the proper goal of democratic efforts. Murray's democratic eschatology is enlivened by the ambition of democratic ideals, but also grounded in concrete realities of experience, history, and social and economic policies. In a

1969 poem entitled "Prophecy," Murray concluded that her vision of American democracy was a hopeful paean tempered by historical realities:

> I sing of a new American
> Separate from all others,
> Yet enlarged and diminished by all others.
> I am the child of kings and serfs, freemen and slaves,
> Having neither superiors nor inferiors,
> Progeny of all colors, all cultures, all systems, all beliefs.
> I have been enslaved, yet my spirit is unbound.
> I have been cast aside, but I sparkle in the darkness.
> I have been slain but live on in the rivers of history.
> I seek no conquest, no wealth, no power, no revenge;
> I seek only discovery
> Of the illimitable heights and depths of my own being.[40]

NOTES

Introduction

1. Robert Martin, "A Transcript of a Tape-Recorded Interview with Pauli Murray," The Ralph J. Bunche Oral History Collection, Moorland–Spingarn Research Center, Howard University (August 15 and 17, 1968), 63. Cited hereafter as Martin, "Interview with Pauli Murray."

2. Scholarly attention has been paid to Murray's groundbreaking legal arguments by historians and legal scholars, but much of this work focuses solely on Murray's work in the 1960s on the PCSW or on the ACLU's national board. For example, see Mary Becker, "The Sixties Shift to Formal Equality and the Courts: An Argument for Pragmatism and Politics," *William and Mary Law Review* 40, no. 1 (October 1998): 209–77; Linda Kerber, *No Constitutional Right to be Ladies: Women and the Obligations of Citizenship* (New York: Hill & Wang, 1998), 185–204; Susan Mallon Ross, "Dialogic Rhetoric: Dorothy Kenyon and Pauli Murray's Rhetorical Moves in *White v. Crook*," *International Journal of the Diversity* 6, no. 5 (2007): 89–100; Serena Mayeri, "A Common Fate of Discrimination: Race-Gender Analogies in Legal and Historical Perspective," *Yale Law Journal* 110, no. 6 (April 2001): 1045–87.

   Historians have emphasized Murray's groundbreaking activism in the 1930s and 1940s as well as her family's notable contributions to Durham's development, see Glenda Gilmore, *Defying Dixie: The Radical Roots of Civil Rights, 1919–1950* (New York: W.W. Norton & Company, 2008) and Leslie Brown, *The Upbuilding of Black Durham: Gender, Class, and Black Community Development in the Jim Crow South* (Chapel Hill: The University of North Carolina Press, 2008).

   Three articles have appeared focusing on Murray's writing life. See, Elaine Caldbeck, "The Poetry of Pauli Murray: African American Civil Rights Lawyer and Priest," in *Gender, Ethnicity, and Religion*, ed. Rosemary Radford Ruether (Minneapolis: Fortress Press, 2002); Jean M. Humez, "Pauli Murray's Histories of Loyalty and Revolt," *Black American Literature Forum* 24, no. 2 (1990): 315–55; and Christiana Z. Peppard, "Poetry, Ethics, and the Legacy of Pauli Murray" *Journal of the Society of Christian Ethics* 30, no. 1 (Spring/Summer 2010): 21–44.

   Anthony Pinn has paid the most attention to the breadth of Murray's religious thought; he has focused on Murray's contribution to what he characterizes as a tradition in African American religious thought of redemptive suffering; Pinn has also edited a volume of Murray's sermons and speeches, making available many documents which had been previously available only in archives and written a volume on Murray's religious thought. See, Anthony Pinn, ed., *Pauli Murray: Selected Sermons and Writings* (Maryknoll, NY: Orbis Books, 2006); Pinn, ed., *Moral Evil and Redemptive Suffering: A History of Theodicy in African-American Religious Thought* (Miami: University Press of Florida, 2002); "Religion and 'America's Problem Child:' Notes on Pauli's Murray Theological Development," *Journal of Feminist*

Studies in Religion 15, no. 2 (1999): 21–39; and *Becoming America's Problem Child: An Outline of Pauli Murray's Religious Life and Theology* (Eugene: Pickwick Publications, 2008).

3. Murray, *Song in a Weary Throat: An American Pilgrimage* (New York: Harper & Row, 1987), 36.
4. Ibid., 20.

Chapter 1: The Crusader: The Political Education of a Young Radical (1930s and 1940s)

1. Judith Weisenfeld, *African American Women and Christian Activism: New York's Black YWCA, 1905–1945* (Cambridge: Harvard University Press, 1997), 169.
2. Barbara Ransby, *Ella Baker and the Black Freedom Movement: A Radical Democratic Vision* (Chapel Hill: University of North Carolina Press, 2003), 71.
3. Murray, *Song in a Weary Throat: An American Pilgrimage* (New York: Harper & Row, 1987), 75.
4. Murray, *Song in a Weary Throat*, 74. See also Jon Mcihael Spencer, "The Black Church and the Harlem Renaissance," *African American Review* 30, no. 3 (Autumn 1996): 458.
5. Murray, *Song in a Weary Throat*, 76; 82.
6. Ibid., 94.
7. Murray, Diary from April 27, 1935–May 24, 1935, Pauli Murray Papers (Box 1; Folder 25), MC 412 on file at the Schlesinger Library of the Radcliffe Institute for Advanced Study, Harvard University; hereafter cited as "PM Papers."
8. Pauli Murray, "Three Thousand Miles on a Dime in Ten Days," in *Negro Anthology: 1931–1934*, ed. Nancy Cunard (London: Wishart and Co., 1934), 90–93.
9. Murray, *Song in a Weary Throat*, 79–82.
10. The photo seems to be of Murray and Peg Holmes. Murray met Holmes during a stay at a WPA camp in 1934; Murray and Holmes visited Holmes' family in Newport, Rhode Island, in 1937 where the photos were taken, in Murray, "The Life and Times of an American Called Pauli Murray," PM Papers (Box 1; Folder 29).
11. Michelle Stephens, "Black Transnationalism and the Politics of National Identity: West Indian Intellectuals in Harlem in the Age of War and Revolution," *American Quarterly* 50, no. 3 (September 1998): 598.
12. Hughes includes two of Murray's poems in a special issue of *Voice: A Quarterly of Poetry* on Negro Poets, which he guest-edited, see PM Papers (Box 97: Folder 1730); Pauli Murray, "Tongues," in *Dark Testament and Other Poems* (Norwalk, CT: Silvermine, 1970), 61.
13. Murray, "Color Trouble," in *Dark Testament and Other Poems*, 30.
14. Murray, "Mulatto's Dilemma," in *Dark Testament and Other Poems*, 32–33.
15. Kathleen Pfeiffer, "Individualism, Success, and American Identity in *The Autobiography of an Ex-Colored Man*" *African American Review* 30, no. 3 (Autumn 1996): 416.
16. Werner Sollors, *Neither Black nor White Yet Both: Thematic Explorations of Interracial Literature* (New York: Oxford University Press, 1997), 242.
17. Murray, *Song in a Weary Throat*, 32; 31.
18. Yevette Richards, *Maida Springer: Pan-Africanist and International Labor Leader* (Pittsburg: University of Pittsburg Press, 2000), 32.
19. Gregory Stephens, *On Racial Frontiers: In the* New *Culture of Frederick Douglass, Ralph Ellison, and Bob Marley* (New York: Cambridge University Press, 1999), 30–32. See also Naomi Zack, *Race and Mixed Race* (Philadelphia: Temple University Press, 1993), 96.
20. Genna Rae McNeill, "Interview with Pauli Murray," February 13, 1976, Southern Oral History Program University of North Carolina at Chapel Hill, 41–42. Hereafter cited as McNeill, "Interview with Pauli Murray."
21. Gerald Horne, *Black Liberation/Red Scare: Ben Davis and the Communist Party* (Newark: University of Delaware Press, 1994), 68–71.
22. Murray, *Song in a Weary Throat*, 103. Ted Morgan, *A Covert Life: Jay Lovestone, Communist, Anti-Communist, and Spymaster* (New York: Random House, 1999), 124–33; John P. Diggins, *Up From Communism: Conservative Odysseys in American Intellectual Development*

(New York: Columbia University Press, 1994), 140–41. Murray's affiliation with the Lovestonites in the 1930s prompted an FBI investigation in 1967 when she applied for a position with the US Civil Service Commission. On her application to a question that asked, "Are you now, or have you ever been, a member of the Communist Party, United States of America, the Communist Political Association, the Young Communist League, or any other communist organization?" Murray answered no, but offered a qualification in an appendix. In an appendix to her application, she wrote "During 1936–1938, I was associated with the Lovestonite group in New York City. I joined this group because I was informed I could get an understanding of and critical appraisal of Communism, which I did. While the leaders of this group were former members of the Communist Party in the 1920s, they were the most knowledgeable critics of the Communist methods and tactics, and for that reason I have never regretted my exposure to them. My own philosophy has been one of creative non-violent direct action which I have studied and espoused since my law student days in the early 1940s," from Report, "Pauli Murray, Applicant Federal Administrative and Management Examination, Civil Service Commission, Washington DC" 1/10/67, New York, NY, Bureau File 140–16717, p. 2.

23. Report, "Pauli Murray, Applicant Federal Administrative and Management Examination, Civil Service Commission, Washington DC" 1/10/67, New York, NY, Bureau File 140–16717, p. 43.

24. Murray, *Song in a Weary Throat*, 9.

25. "Roosevelt's Address at Chapel Hill," *New York Times*, December 6, 1938, A16.

26. Murray, "Dear Mr. President," December 8, 1938, PM Papers (Box 15; Folder 380), 1.

27. Graham quoted in John Egerton, *Speak Now Against the Day: The Generation Before the Civil Rights Movement in the South* (New York: Alfred A. Knopf, 1994), 188.

28. Glenda Gilmore characterizes Graham as "sounding for all the world like Pauli Murray" and also notes the irony of Graham, in Murray's case, being "powerless to pass his own test," in Gilmore, *Defying Dixie*, 271.

29. Murray, *Song in a Weary Throat*, 123; 116

30. Murray, *Song in a Weary Throat*, 15.

31. Eleanor Roosevelt, "Dear Miss Murray," December 19, 1938, PM Papers (Box 15; Folder 380), 1.

32. Murray, *Song in a Weary Throat*, 128.

33. Ibid., 142, 143, 144.

34. Mark V. Tushnet, *Making Civil Rights Law: Thurgood Marshall and the Supreme Court, 1936–1961* (Oxford: Oxford University Press, 1994), 73.

35. Murray, *Song in a Weary Throat*, 149.

36. Scott H. Bennett, *Radical Pacifism: The War Resisters League and Gandhian Nonviolence in America, 1915–1963* (Syracuse: Syracuse University Press, 2003), 155–158.

37. Murray, Notebook entry, Monday, March 25, 1940, PM Papers (Box 4; Folder 85), 3.

38. Evelyn Brooks Higginbotham, *Righteous Discontent: The Women's Movement in the Black Baptist Church, 1880–1920* (Cambridge: Harvard University Press, 1993), 187.

39. Gilmore, *Defying Dixie*, 323, 324.

40. In her autobiography, she recounts a brief marriage to a man she calls simply "Billy." She describes herself and Billy as "sexually inexperienced" and she implies that they were not able to consummate the marriage because they could find "no place where we could meet in privacy. After several months of mounting frustration, we gave up in despair. Billy left the city, and some years later we had the marriage annulled," in Murray, *Song in a Weary Throat*, 77. The 1967 FBI investigation into Murray's background indicates that the marriage was never annulled: "Miss Murray indicated that she and [blank] had never lived together and that [blank] has moved to another state. Miss Murray indicated that she had intended to get an annulment of her marriage, but had never had the means to do so," in Report, "Pauli Murray, Applicant Federal Administrative and Management Examiniation, Civil Service Commission, Washington DC" 1/10/67, New York, NY, Bureau File 140–16717, p. 41.

41. Murray, "Dear Bill," February 9, 1939, PM Papers (Box 10; Folder 238), 1.

42. In 1968 she explained that "my name doesn't always disclose my sex," in Martin, "An Interview with Pauli Murray," 71.

43. Murray, "Dear Mother," June 2, 1943, PM Papers (Box 10; Folder 253), 3.

44. Henry L. Minton, "Femininity in Men and Masculinity in Women: American Psychiatry and Psychology Portray Homosexuality in the 1930s," *Journal of Homosexuality* 13, no. 1 (1986): 7; Joanne Meyerowitz, "Sex Change and the Popular Press: Historical Notes on Transsexuality in the United States, 1930–1955," *GLQ* 4, no. 2 (1998): 164.

45. In a letter to a doctor who treated her sister during a psychiatric hospital stay, Murray asks the doctor to reflect on her sister's condition and father's medical history and asks him if he thinks that insanity in congenital. She insists that she needs information in order to "protect her family," in Murray, "Letter to Dr. Meng" PM Papers (Box 10; Folder 231), 1.

46. Doreen Marie Drury, "Experimentation on the Male Side: Race, Class, and Gender, and Sexuality in Pauli Murray's Quest for Love and Identity" (PhD diss., Boston College, 2000), 164.

47. During a 1937 hospital stay, Murray outlined a number of questions she planned to ask the doctor and, to some, offered her own provisional answers, "14. Why the inverted sex instinct—wearing pants, wanting to be one of the men, doing things that fellows do, hating to be dominated by women unless I like them?—Answer—glandular;...25. Why do many other Homosexuals irritate me instead of causing me a bond of sympathy, particularly when I think it is acquired? (Don't know)" in Murray, "Interview with Dr. ____" Tuesday, December 16, 1937, PM Papers (Box 4; Folder 71), 1–2; see also Murray, "Memorandum on PM," July 13, 1942, PM Papers (Box 4; Folder 71), 1.

48. Nancy Ordover, *American Eugenics: Race, Queer Anatomy, and the Science of Nationalism* (Minneapolis: University of Minnesota Press, 2003), 107.

49. Murray, "Note to Peg," PM Papers (Box 96; Folder 1688), 1. The addressee is likely the "Peggie" of the series of photos in which Murray appears in drag.

50. Leila J. Rupp and Verta Taylor, "Lesbian Existence and the Women's Movement: Researching the 'Lavender Herring,'" in *Feminism and Social Change: Bridging Theory and Practice*, ed. Heidi Gottfried (Chicago: University of Illinois Press, 1996), 147.

51. Ibid., 145.

52. Jennifer Terry, "Theorizing Deviant Historiography," *Differences: A Journal of Feminist Cultural Studies* 3, no. 2 (1991): 55.

53. Murray, "Summary of Symptoms," March 8, 1940, PM Papers (Box 10; Folder 238), 1; Murray, *Proud Shoes: The Story of an American Family* (New York: Harper Collins, 1978), xvi; Murray, *Song in a Weary Throat*, 271; Reflecting on the difficulties she had at Howard Law School as one of the few women students, Murray wrote "the harsh reality was that I was a minority within a minority, with all the built-in disadvantages that such status entailed," in Murray, *Song in a Weary Throat*, 240.

54. A. MacBean, "Dear Sir," November 9, 1939, PM Papers (Box 4; Folder 71), 1.

55. Marjorie Garber, *Vested Interests: Cross-Dressing and Cultural Anxiety* (New York: Harper Perennial, 1993), 17.

56. Patricia Hill Collins, correspondence with the author, December 1, 2006.

57. Richard B. Sherman, *The Case of Odell Waller and Virginia Justice, 1940–1942* (Knoxville: The University of Tennessee Press, 1992), 33.

58. Murray, *Song in a Weary Throat*, 167, 170; Martin, "Interview with Pauli Murray," 43.

59. Murray, *Song in a Weary Throat*, 107; see also CLR James et al., *Fighting Racism in World War II: A Week by Week Account of the Struggle to End Racism and Discrimination in the United States During 1939–1945* (New York: Pathfinder, 1980); and Lee Finkle, "The Conservative Aims of Militant Rhetoric: Black Protest During World War II," *Journal of American History* 60, no. 3 (1973): 692–713.

60. Murray, *Song in a Weary Throat*, 174, 175.

61. Pauli Murray and Henry Babcock, "An Alternative Weapon," *South Today* (Winter 1942–43), 53–57; 54; 54; 57.

62. Anthony B. Pinn, ed., *Moral Evil and Redemptive Suffering: A History of Theodicy in African-American Religious Thought* (Miami: University Press of Florida, 2002), 8.

63. Ibid., 11.
64. Murray and Babcock, "An Alternative Weapon," 56.
65. Ibid., 55; 56; 56.
66. Anthony Pinn, "Becoming America's Problem Child," 97.
67. Pauli Murray, "A Blueprint for First Class Citizenship," *The Crisis* 51 (1944): 358. Murray felt implicated in her classmates' conscriptions: "Just because I was exempt, as a woman, this feeling fell upon me with a great sense of responsibility as to what should I do. And I came to the conclusion that I had a responsibility to fight for those guys in their absence. If they were on the military front, I would be on the domestic front. And this was the beginning of my militance in terms of Washington segregation," in Martin, "Interview with Pauli Murray," 47.
68. Murray, "A Blueprint for First Class Citizenship," 358.
69. Civil Rights Committee, NAACP Chapter, Howard University, "Memo, RE: What took place on 11th and Pennsylvania, April 22, 1944," April 23, 1944, PM Papers (Box 18; Folder 385), 1.

   The pledge is reproduced in *Black Protest Thought in the Twentieth Century*; the editors note that the pledge of how protesters should behave "contains the first use of words 'sitting in' which the editors found," in August Meier, Elliot Rudwich, and Francis L. Broderick, eds., *Black Protest Thought in the Twentieth Century*, Second ed. (New York: The Bobbs-Merrill Company, 1971), 246. See also, "The Civil Rights Committee," in PM Papers (Box 18; Folder 395) and Martin, "Interview with Pauli Murray," 59–62. In the months preceding the direct action campaign, the Committee sent out hundreds of questionnaires to Howard Students in order to gage students' attitudes about such a campaign. In what reads like Murray's humor, the Questionnaire opens with "Am I a 'screwball,' or am I a pioneer?" in PM Papers (Box 18; Folder 395).
70. Murray, "A Blueprint for First Class Citizenship," 359.
71. Martin, "Interview with Pauli Murray," 69.
72. Sean Chabot, "A Culture of Peace in Motion: Transnational Diffusion of the Gandhian Repertoire from India to the US Civil Rights Movement," *International Journal of Humanities and Peace.*
73. Murray, *Song in a Weary Throat*, 228.
74. Mark Chapman, 'Of One Blood': Mays and the Theology of Race Relations," in *Walking Integrity: Benjamin Elijah Mays, Mentor to Martin Luther King Jr.*, ed. Lawrence Edward Carter Sr. (Macon, GA: Mercer University Press, 1998), 235, 243; Henry Young, *Major Black Religious Leaders Since 1940* (Nashville: Abingdon, 1979), 28; Zachery Williams, "Prophets of Black Progress: Benjamin E. Mays and Howard W. Thurman, Pioneering Black Religious Intellectuals," *Journal of African American Men* 5, no. 4 (March 2001): 29.
75. Finkle, "The Conservative Aims of Militant Rhetoric: Black Protest During World War II," 668. See also Timothy B. Tyson, *Radio Free Dixie: Robert F. Williams & The Roots of Black Power* (Chapel Hill: University of North Carolina Press, 1999), 34–35; 37.
76. Pauli Murray, "Negro Youth's Dilemma," *Threshold* (April 1942): 8.
77. Ibid.
78. Pauli Murray, "Negroes are Fed Up," *Common Sense* (August 1943): 274; 275.
79. Pauli Murray, "And the Riots Came..." *The Call* Friday (August 13, 1943): 1.
80. Ibid.
81. Murray, "Harlem Riot, 1943," in *Dark Testament and Other Poems*, 35.
82. Murray, "Dear Mother," June 2, 1943, PM Papers (Box 10; Folder 253), 2; 3.
83. Murray, *Song in a Weary Throat*, 214.
84. A journal of southern writing co-edited by Lillian Smith and Paula Snelling, *South Today* was notable for publishing works of black authors and white authors side by side, without identifying the author racially, an exceptional practice in the 1940s and 1950s. Smith and Murray carried on a friendship through correspondence throughout the 1940s and into the 1950s; Murray credits Smith with being instrumental in encouraging her to write her family memoir, *Proud Shoes*, see PM Papers (Box 80; Folder 1402).
85. Murray, "Dark Testament," in *Dark Testament and Other Poems*, 13; 21; 21; 17.

86. Toni Morrison, *Beloved* (New York: Vintage Books, 2004), 324. Critics have asserted different readings of Morrison's epitaph; Anita Durkin argues that the line is purposefully multivocal, in Anita Durkin, "Object Written, Written Object: Slavery, Scarring, and Complications of Authorship in Beloved," *African American Review* (Fall 2007): 553–54.

87. Cornel West, "The Moral Obligations of Living in a Democratic Society," in *The Good Citizen*, eds. David Batstone and Eduardo Mendieta (New York: Routledge, 1999), 12.

88. Murray, "Dark Testament," in *Dark Testament and Other Poems*, 12; 25.

89. Murray, *Song in a Weary Throat*, 184.

90. Ibid., 240.

91. Pauli Murray, "Why Negro Girls Stay Single," *Negro Digest* 5, no. 9 (1947): 5. Murray's use of the term "sex" to describe her experience of discrimination would likely be rendered in terms of "gender" in today's vernacular. For an historical account of the development of the term "gender" in feminist theory, see Joan W. Scott, "Gender: A Useful Category of Historical Analysis," *The American Historical Review* 91, no. 5 (December 1986): 1053–75.

Chapter 2: Descendents of Hagar (1950s)

1. Pauli Murray, "The Right to Equal Opportunity in Employment," *California Law Review* 33 (1945): 388.

2. Murray, *Song in a Weary Throat*, 280.

3. Susan M. Hartmann, *The Other Feminists: Activists in the Liberal Establishment* (New Haven: Yale University Press, 1998), 193–94.

4. Murray, *Song in a Weary Throat*, 289.

5. Davison M. Douglas, "Foreward," to *States' Laws on Race and Color*, Compiled and edited by Pauli Murray (Athens: University of Georgia Press, 1997), xxii–xxiii.

6. Murray, *States' Laws on Race and Color*, 5.

7. Memorandum to Milton R. Konvitz, Re: Application in re Codification of Liberian Laws," April 15, 1952, PM Papers (Box, 72, Folder, 1283), 1. Among the organized targeted by HUAC with which Murray had been affiliated were the League for Mutual Aid and the National Negro Congress.

8. Murray, *Song in a Weary Throat*, 297.

9. Anne Firor Scott, ed., *Forty Years of Letters in Black and White*, 75.

10. Murray, *Song in a Weary Throat*, 298.

11. Clarence Taylor, *Black Religious Intellectuals: The Fight for Equality from Jim Crow to the 21st Century* (New York: Routledge, 2002), 102. Historians have focused Murray's family memoir as a witness to how American racial identities were shaped by racial slavery and later Jim Crow. See Darlene O'Dell, *Sights of Southern Memory: The Autobiographies of Katherine Du Pre Lumpkin, Lillian Smith, and Pauli Murray* (Charlottesville: University of Virginia Press, 2001) for how Murray develops a countermemory to official memorializing of the Confederate past and Leslie Brown, *Upbuilding Black Durham: Gender, Class, and Black Community in the Jim Crow South* (Chapel Hill: University of North Carolina Press, 2008) for the history of Murray's family in Durham, including the Fitzgeralds, Dames, and Smalls.

12. Penny M. Von Eschen, *Race Against Empire: Black Americans and Anticolonialism, 1937–1957* (Ithaca: Cornell University Press, 1997), 100.

13. Murray, *Proud Shoes*, xiii.

14. Gary Gerstle, *American Crucible: Race and Nation in the Twentieth Century* (Princeton: Princeton University Press, 2001), 246–48.

15. Murray, *Proud Shoes*, xiii.

16. Toni Morrison, "The Site of Memory," in *What Moves at the Margin: Selected Nonfiction* (Jackson: University of Mississippi Press, 2008), 66.

17. Murray, *Song in a Weary Throat*, 103.

18. Ibid., 152.

19. Following her arrest in Petersburg for integrating an interstate bus, Murray reflected her diary that in the Petersburg in June 1863, her grandfather "was fighting to free his colored brothers. His grandchild has been arrested and imprisoned in the same town nearly 80

years later for standing up for Negro rights," see Murray, Notebook, March 1940–June 1941, PM Papers (Box 84, Folder 146), 2.

20. Murray, *Proud Shoes*, 152.
21. Ibid., 111.
22. Since its founding in 1858, Liberia offered freedom and contradiction: Liberia offered Americans of African descent opportunities for freedom and self-determination unavailable in the United States, but the republic was sponsored by white Americans, whom many black Americans interpreted as trying to repatriate formerly enslaved people, see James Fairhead, Tim Geyseek, Svend E. Holsoe and Melissa Leach, *African-American Exploration in West Africa: Four Nineteen Century Diaries* (Bloomington: Indiana University Press, 2003): 1.
23. Murray, *Proud Shoes*, 24; 104.
24. Ibid., 46; 49.
25. Rev. Peter James Lee, "Servant Children," February 13, 1977, PM Papers (Box 94; Folder 1637), 1.
26. Murray, *Proud Shoes*, 50; 33.
27. Ibid., 33.
28. Patricia J. Williams, *The Alchemy of Race and Rights: Diary of a Law Professor* (Cambridge: Harvard University Press, 1991), 154.
29. Patricia J. Williams, "On Being the Object of Property," *Signs* 14, no. 1 (Autumn 1988): 6.
30. Murray, *Proud Shoes*, 50.
31. James H. Cone, *The Spirituals and the Blues: An Interpretation* (Maryknoll, NY: Orbis Books, 2008), 33.
32. Allen Dwight Callahan, *The Talking Book: African Americans and the Bible* (New Haven: Yale University Press, 2006), 82.
33. In a sermon she would deliver in 1978, Murray recalled reading this passage with her grandmother. Murray explained that Ezekiel "had a vision of hope, of rebirth, and the eventual restoration of the exiles to their homeland" and she claims that "symbolically, I am a returning exile to the American South after an absence of more than fifty years," in Murray, "Can These Bones Live Again?" March 12, 1978, PM Papers (Box 64; Folder 1095), 5, 14.
34. Murray, *Proud Shoes*, 32; 32; 34.
35. Ibid., 34; 43; 34.
36. Catherine Clinton, "With a Whip in His Hand: Rape, Memory and African-American Women," in *History and Memory in African-American Culture*, eds. Genevieve Fabre and Robert O'Meally (New York: Oxford University Press, 1994), 207.
37. Trinh T. Minh-Ha, *Woman Native Other: Writing Postcolonialism and Feminism* (Bloomington: Indiana University Press, 1989), 119.
38. Jacquelyn Dowd Hall recognized a similar tendency in a much different context. In a discussion of the role of white Southern women in creating and disseminating a record of Confederate history and the Lost Cause, Dowd explains how male historians newly trained in "scientific" and archive-based history soon took over efforts at recording southern history; "women found themselves identified with imprecise, dilettantish, nostalgic 'memory'; the new professional history belonged to men," in Jacquelyn Dowd Hall, "'You Must Remember This': Autobiography as Social Critique," *The Journal of American History* 85, no. 2 (1998): 453. Julie Des Jardins offers a number of similar historiographical accounts in Julie Des Jardins, *Women and the Historical Enterprise in America: Gender, Race, and the Politics of Memory, 1880–1945* (Chapel Hill: University of North Carolina Press, 2003).
39. Trinh, *Woman, Native, Other*, 134.
40. Murray, *Proud Shoes*, 51.
41. Ibid., xvii; xvi, emphasis in the original. Ralph Ellison's protagonist in *Invisible Man* makes draws a similar conclusion about his grandparents: "And yet I am no freak of nature, nor of history. I was in the cards, other things having been equal (or unequal) eighty-five years ago. I am not ashamed of my grandparents for having been slaves. I am only ashamed of myself for having been ashamed," in Ralph Ellison, *Invisible Man* (New York: Vintage Books, 1947), 15.

42. Murray, *Proud Shoes*, 66; 66; 88.

43. Ibid., 88; 89; xvi; xvi.

44. Murray, *Proud Shoes*, xvi. For the relationship between American history and biblical typology, see L. DeAne Lagerquist, "Women and the American Religious Pilgrimage: Vida Scudder, Dorothy Day, and Pauli Murray," in *New Dimensions in American Religious History: Essays in Honor of Martin E. Marty*, eds. Jay P. Dolan and James P. Wind (Grand Rapids, MI: William B. Eerdmans, 1993), 208.

45. See Pauline Hopkins, *The Magazine Novels of Pauline Hopkins*, ed. Hazel Carby (New York: Oxford University Press, 1988); Langston Hughes, *Not Without Laughter* (New York: Simon and Schuster, 1969); and Toni Morrison, *Song of Solomon* (New York: Knopf, 1995).

46. Delores Williams, *Sisters in the Wilderness: The Challenge of Womanist God-Talk* (Maryknoll, NY: Orbis Books, 1993), 109.

47. Ashraf Rushdy, *Remembering Generations: Race and Family in Contemporary African American Fiction* (Chapel Hill: University of North Carolina Press, 2001), 106.

48. Pauli Murray, "Black Strategies," in *Rebels in Law: Voices in History of Black Women Lawyers*, ed. J. Clay Smith, Jr. (Ann Arbor: The University of Michigan Press, 1998), 164.

49. Emilie M. Townes, *Womanist Ethics and the Cultural Production of Evil* (New York: Palgrave MacMillan, 2006), 23.

50. Ibid.

51. Murray, *Song in a Weary Throat*, 318.

52. Williams quoted in Tyson, *Radio Free Dixie*, 149.

53. Tyson, *Radio Free Dixie*, 152.

54. Murray quoted in Tyson, *Radio Free Dixie*, 160.
    In a memo to Daisy Bates about Williams' case, Murray elaborated: "In my opinion, he was a man speaking out of understandable desperation, not knowing where else to turn, since his organization had no program designed to meet the problems with which he was faced...the Board must take into account this constant atmosphere of violence, implicit and explicit, under which Negroes live, when they are considering the statements of Williams," in Pauli Murray, "Memorandum to Mrs. Daisy Bates Re: Facts on Robert F. Williams," June 5, 1959 in PM Papers (Box 127; Folder 2312), 3.

55. Murray, "Collect for Poplarville," in *Dark Testament*, 38; Murray dates the poem "May, 1959."

56. Caldbeck, "The Poetry of Pauli Murray, African American Civil Rights Lawyer and Priest," 61.

57. Murray quoted in Casey Miller and Kate Swift, "Pauli Murray: The Life Story That Asks the Question: 'Can a Girl from a Little Town in North Carolina Find Happiness as a Priest/Poet/Lawyer/Teacher/Revolutionary/Civil Rights Activist?'" in *Ms.* (March 1980), 64.

58. Yevette Richards, *Conversations with Maida Springer: A Personal History of Labor, Race, and International Relations* (Pittsburg: University of Pittsburg Press, 2004), 207.

59. Pauli Murray and Leslie Rubin, *The Constitution and Government of Ghana* (London: Sweet and Maxwell, 1964).

60. S.A. Smith, "Review of *The Constitution and Government of Ghana*," *The Modern Law Review* 25, no. 4 (1962): 508–10; and Ekow Daniels, "Review of *The Constitution and Government of Ghana*," *Journal of African Law* 6, no. 1 (Spring, 1962): 63–64.

61. Joseph Appiah, *Joe Appiah: The Autobiography of an African Patriot* (New York: Praeger, 1990), 257. Appiah is the father of philosopher Kwame Anthony Appiah.

62. Murray, *Song in a Weary Throat*, 332. In a 1976 interview, Murray remembered, "it soon became clear to me that Kwame Nkrumrah had dictatorial instincts and was suppressing freedom of speech, was deliberately suppressing the freedom of trade unions, of women's organizations, of youth organizations, was permitting and in a sense encouraging and almost demanding a personality cult," in McNeill, "Interview with Pauli Murray," 81.

63. Murray, *Song in a Weary Throat*, 328.

64. Murray sent a copy of the essay to Harold Isaacs, who encouraged Murray to work toward getting the essay published as a book. In a letter to Murray, he revealed that he has heard that the Little Brown publishing house had commissioned James Baldwin to write a book about a Negro going "home"; "it will be important writing and good writing, no mistake about it; Baldwin is good... hence I write to say, Pauli, *get on it*, Take that piece down off the shelf and fatten it with vignettes and begin to put together the Pauli Murray book on precisely that theme. You ought to be writing it and finishing it, and it ought to be circulating here to get published before Baldwin gets back. This may sound competitive, but I think all's fair in love and writing.... So get on it Pauli—I don't care how hard the pull is at the Law School. In the longer run this will be the more important thing for you. Believe me," in Harold Isaacs, "Dear Pauli," March 2, 1961, PM Papers (Box 85; Folder 1482), 1. Murray never did publish the essay or write the book, but Isaacs' letter demonstrates Murray's standing among intellectuals in her era.

    Baldwin visited Liberia, Sierra Leone, and Senegal with his sister in the summer of 1962, but it seems that Baldwin never did write the essay to which Isaacs refers. Baldwin does write about the difficulty of black Americans identifying as Africans in an essay where he describes a conference he attended in Paris which included African writers, in James Baldwin, "Encounter on the Seine: Black Meets Brown," *Notes of Native Son* (Boston: Beacon Press, 1955), 123.

65. Murray, "A Question of Identity," Accra Ghana, November 14, 1960, PM Papers (Box 85; Folder 1478), 11. As a child, Murray had rejected the idea that race was biologically fixed: "I dimly perceived then, that skin color and race were two different things, since if skin color were a true test of anything there would have been a dozen races within my own family," in Murray, "Legacy of the South," in PM Papers (Box 84; Folder 1456), 15.

66. Murray "A Question of Identity," 7; 7; 13.

67. James Baldwin also wrote an essay entitled "A Question of Identity." Included in his *Notes of a Native Son*, the essay describes black American students studying in Paris under the GI Bill. Baldwin portrays the experiences of an archetypical young African American veteran: "From the vantage point of Europe he discovers his own country. And this is a discovery which not only brings to an end the alienation of the American from himself, but which also makes clear to him, for the first time, the extent of his involvement in the life of Europe," in James Baldwin, "A Question of Identity," in *Notes of a Native Son*, 137.

68. Horace Mann Bond, "Howe and Isaacs in the Bush: The Ram in the Thicket," *Apropos of Africa*, eds. Adelaide Cromwell Hill and Martin Kilson (London: Frank Cass & Co., Ltd, 1968), 287.

69. Richard Wright, *Black Power: A Record of Reactions in a Land of Pathos* (New York: Harper and Brothers, 1954).

70. For an analysis of Wright's reflections, see Kevin Gaines, "Revisiting Richard Wright in Ghana: Black Radicalism and the Dialectics of the Diaspora," *Social Text* 19, no. 2 (Summer 2001): 75–101.

71. Murray was not alone in questioning Nkrumrah's decisions. According to David Levering Lewis, Du Bois had misgivings about Nkrumrah's autocratic rule, but kept them private, see David Levering Lewis, *W.E.B. Du Bois: The Fight for Equality and the American Century, 1919–1963* (New York: Henry Holt and Company, 2000), 568.

72. Kevin Gaines, *American Africans in Ghana: Black Expatriates and the Civil Rights Era* (Chapel Hill: University of North Carolina Press, 2006), 111.

73. Ibid., 111, 113.

74. Murray, "A Question of Identity," 18.

75. Richards, *Conversations with Maida Springer*, 228.

76. Murray, Journal entry dated Sunday, June 5, 1960, 4:30 pm, PM Papers (Box 41; Folder 710), no page number.

77. Murray, Journal entry dated Saturday, July 2, 1960, 7:30 pm, PM Papers (Box 41; Folder 710), no page number.

Chapter 3: Jane Crow (1960s)

1. Cynthia Harrison, *On Account of Sex: The Politics of Women's Issues, 1945–1968* (Berkeley: University of California Press, 1988), 35–41.
2. Harrison, *On Account of Sex*, 151–52; Susan M. Harmann, *The Other Feminists: Activists in the Liberal Establishment* (New Haven: Yale University Press, 1998), 62–63.
3. Pauli Murray, "A Proposal to Reexamine the Applicability of the Fourteenth Amendment to State Laws and Practices Which Discriminate on the Basis of Sex Per Se," December 1962, PM Papers (Box 50; Folder 887).
4. Murray, "A Proposal to Reexamine," 9.
5. Ibid.
6. Mary Becker, "The Sixties Shift to Formal Equality and the Courts: An Argument for Pragmatism and Politics," *Williams and Mary Law Review* 40 (209): 210.
7. Ibid., 227.
8. Murray quoted in Lynn Olson, *Freedom's Daughters: The Unsung Heroines of the Civil Rights Movement from 1830–1970* (New York: Scribner, 2001), 289.
9. Martin, "Interview with Pauli Murray," 63.
10. Richards, *Maida Springer*, 263.
11. Dorothy I. Height, "'We Wanted the Voice of a Woman to Be Heard': Black Woman and the 1963 March on Washington," in *Sisters in the Struggle: African American Women in the Civil Rights-Black Power Movement*, eds. Bettye Collier-Thomas and V.P. Franklin (New York: New York University Press, 2001), 89.
12. James H. Cone, *Malcolm and Martin and America: A Dream or a Nightmare* (Maryknoll, NY: Orbis Books, 1991), 309.
13. Cornel West, "WEB Du Bois: An Interpretation," in *Africana: The Encyclopedia of the African and African American Experience*, eds. Kwame Anthony Appiah and Henry Louis Gates (New York: Basic Civitas Books, 1999), 1971.
14. See Jo Freeman, "How 'Sex' Got Into Title VII: Persistent Opportunism as a Maker of Public Policy," *Law and Inequality* 9 (1991): 163–64; and Becker, "The Sixties Shift to Formal Equality and the Courts," 232–33.
15. Becker, "The Sixties Shift to Formal Equality," 234.
16. Pauli Murray, "Memorandum in Support of Retaining the Amendment to H.R. 7152, Title VII (Equal Employment Opportunity) to Prohibit Discrimination in Employment Because of Sex," April 14, 1964, PM Papers, 9.
17. Murray, *Song in a Weary Throat*, 357.
18. Murray, "Memorandum in Support of Retaining the Amendment to HR 7152," 6; 12; 13.
19. Ibid., 20; 21.
20. Mayeri, "A Common Fate of Discrimination," 1067.
21. Pauli Murray and Mary O. Eastwood, "Jane Crow and the Law: Sex Discrimination and Title VII," in *The George Washington Law Review* 34, no. 2 (December 1965): 243.
22. Edith Evans Asbury, "Protest Proposed on Women's Rights," in *The New York Times*, October 13, 1965, A32.
23. Maryann Barakso, *Governing NOW: Grassroots Activism in the National Organization for Women* (Ithaca: Cornell University Press, 2004), 43, 22.
24. Serena Mayeri, "Constitutional Choices: Legal Feminism and the Historical Dynamics of Change," *California Law Review* 92, no. 3 (May 2004): 772; 791.
25. Murray, "Dear Al," November 24, 1971, PM Papers (Box 2; Folder 30), 1; 2.
26. Hartmann, *The Other Feminists*, 189.
27. Mayeri, "A Common Fate of Discrimination" 1057.
28. Becker, "The Sixties Shift to Formal Equality," 225.
29. See *White v. Crook* (1966); the case dealt with the acquittal of three white men accused of the murder of Viola Liuzzo, a white woman, who was killed days after participating in the Selma to Montgomery March. The ACLU and the Department of Justice sought to have the acquittal overturned because African American women and white women were not allowed to serve on juries in Alabama (African American men were permitted by law, but

were rarely chosen). Kenyon traveled to Alabama to argue the case. While the three judge panel of the US Court of Appeals, 5th Circuit had been disposed to hear an argument on the basis of racial segregation (Frank Johnson was on the panel), they were less enthused by arguments about sex discrimination. The panel did, however, rule that race and sex discrimination were at issue: "jury service is a form of participation in the process of government, a responsibility and a right that should be shared by all citizens, regardless of sex," quoted in Kerber, *No Constitutional Right To Be Ladies*, 199.

30. Samuel Walker, *In Defense of American Liberties: A History of the ACLU* (Carbondale, IL: Southern Illinois University Press, 1999), 305.

31. Kerber, *No Constitutional Right to Be Ladies*, 199.

32. Kimberlé Crenshaw, "Demarginalizing the Intersection of Race and Sex: A Black Feminist Critique of Antidiscrimination Doctrine, Feminist Theory, and Antiracist Politics," *University of Chicago Legal Forum* (1989): 140.

33. The statute specifies that employers may not discriminate according to an "individual's race, color, religion, sex or national origin," *Unlawful Employment Practices, US Code* 42 (2009), § 2000e-2.

34. *DeGraffenreid v. General Motors*, 413 F.412 (8th Cir., 1977).

35. Bradley Allen Areheart, "Intersectionality and Identity: Revising a Wrinkle in Title VII," *Civil Rights Law Journal* 17, no. 1 (2006): 208.

36. Ibid., 234.

37. Tracy E. Higgins, "Democracy and Feminism," *Harvard Law Review* 110, no. 8 (June 1997): 1675; 1664.

38. Pauli Murray, "Roots of the Racial Crisis: Prologue to Policy" (JSD diss., Yale University, 1965), 8.

39. Murray's dissertation reflects the influence of Gunnar Myrdhal's work. Swedish economist Myrdhal wrote *An American Dilemma: The Negro Problem and American Democracy* about the hurdles for African Americans to participate fully in American democracy in the 1940s. The "dilemma" refers to the contradiction between a liberal promise of human rights and horrific treatment of black Americans. Regardless of political conditions contemporary to him, Myrdhal took the positive view that democracy could triumph over racism, see Gunnar Myrdhal, *An American Dilemma: The Negro Problem and American Democracy* (New York: Harper and Row, 1944).

40. Murray, "Roots of the Racial Crisis," 10; 10; 10, emphasis in original.
   In a sermon more than a decade later, Murray will make a similar claim that the new life and new person in Christ that baptism inaugurates is not finished or complete, rather "we are constantly *becoming*, as we experience the tension between the 'now' and the 'not yet,'" in Murray, "What Shall I Do To Inherit Eternal Life?" in PM Papers (Box 64; Folder 1101), 5. This sermon and its eschatological implications will be discussed in the next chapter.

41. Murray, "Roots of the Racial Crisis," 12; 12.

42. Ibid., 433.

43. For a concise account about the debate surrounding Elkins' books, see Jennifer Fleischner, *Mastering Slavery: Memory, Family, and Identity in Women's Slave Narratives* (New York: New York University Press, 1996), 11–13.

44. Murray, "Roots of the Racial Crisis," 223; 997.

45. Office of Policy Planning and Research, United States Department of Labor. *The Negro Family: The Case for National Action* (Washington, DC: GPO), 1965.

46. Robert L. Harris, "Coming of Age: The Transformation of Afro-American Historiography," *Journal of Negro History* 67, no. 2 (1982): 113. For responses to the Moynihan report, see Lee Rainwater and William L. Yancey, *The Moynihan Report and the Politics of Controversy* (Cambridge: MIT Press, 1967); James Berger, "Ghosts of Liberalism: Morrison's *Beloved* and the Moynihan Report," *PMLA* 111, no. 3 (1996): 408–20; and Ashraf H.A. Rushdy, *Remembering Generations: Race and Family in Contemporary American Fiction* (Chapel Hill: University of North Carolina Press, 2001), 12–14, 31.

47. Murray, "Roots of the Racial Crisis," 54–55; 54.

48. Ibid., 45.

49. Sandra Harding, "Comment on Hekman's 'Truth and Method: Feminist Standpoint Theory Revisited:' Whose Standpoint Needs the Regimes of Truth and Reality," *Signs* 23 (1997): 384. A definitive version of African American feminist standpoint theory has been developed by Patricia Hill Collins, who was an undergraduate student of Murray's at Brandeis University; see Patricia Hill Collins, *Black Feminist Thought: Knowledge, Consciousness, and the Politics of Empowerment* (New York: Routledge, 1991), especially 24–25; 269–71.

50. Thomas Holt characterizes the four generations as follows: the first is inaugurated by George Washington Williams' *History of the Negro Race in America* (1882); the second by the work of Carter G. Woodson and his contemporaries; the third by the work of W.E.B. Du Bois, particularly the publication of *Black Reconstruction* (1935); and the fourth by a generation of scholars in the late 1960s and early 1970s, in Thomas Holt, "*From Slavery to Freedom* and the Conceptualization of African-American History," *Journal of Negro History* 85, no. 1/2 (2000): 22.

51. Harris, "Coming of Age," 144. It should be noted that even as African American scholars were committed to studying the lived experiences of enslaved African Americans, few historians expressly considered women. An important example of historical scholarship to focus on slave women in the plantation South first appeared in 1985, see Deborah Gray White, *Ar'n't I A Woman? Female Slaves in the Plantation South*, Revised ed. (New York: Norton, 1999).

52. John McMillian, "'History Makes Its Demands': Identity Politics, Slavery Scholarship and the Narrative of Robert Starobin'," *Rethinking History* 6, no. 2 (2002): 154.

53. Holt, "*From Slavery to Freedom* and the Conceptualization of African-American History," 23.

54. Murray, "Roots of the Racial Crisis," 742.

55. Ibid., 47.

56. Ibid., 712, emphasis in original; 736; 738; 739.

57. Ibid., 742; 749; 738–9.

58. Murray and Baldwin were the first African American writers invited to the colony. Murray described Baldwin as "sensitive, soft spoken and delicately put together; moves in quick, hesitant glides, tears himself to pieces over his typewriter until he forgets the dinner bell and has to be rescued by a yell from Pauli as she starts homeward swinging her dinner basket," in Murray, Journal entry, undated, in PM Papers (Box 97; Folder 1731), 2.

59. Raymond A. Mazurek, "Writer on the Left: Class and Race in Ellison's Early Fiction," *College Literature* 29, no. 4 (2002): 110; 126.

60. James Baldwin, "Notes of a Native Son," in *Notes of a Native Son* (Boston: Beacon Press, 1955), 85; 88–89.

61. James Baldwin, "Encounter on the Seine: Black Meets Brown," in *Notes of a Native Son*, 123; 123.

62. Lawrie Balfour, *The Evidence of Things Not Said: James Baldwin and the Promise of American Democracy* (Ithaca: Cornell University Press, 2001), 44–45.

63. James Baldwin, "Many Thousands Gone," *Notes of a Native Son*, 24; 24; 25.

64. James Baldwin, "As Much Truth as One Can Bear," *New York Times Book Review*, January 14, 1962, 1; 38.

65. Baldwin, "Stranger in a Village," *Notes of a Native Son*, 162–63.

66. Ellison, "Blues People," *The Collected Essays of Ralph Ellison*, 280.

67. Ellison, "The Little Man at Chehaw Station: The American Artist and His Audience," *The Collected Essays of Ralph Ellison*, 501.

68. Ellison, "Perspective of Literature," *The Collected Essays of Ralph Ellison*, 83.

69. Murray, *Proud Shoes*, vxi, emphasis added.

70. Ellison, "The Little Man at Chehaw Station," *The Collected Essays of Ralph Ellison*, 500.

71. Ellison, "Twentieth Century Fiction and the Black Mask of Humanity," *The Collected Essays of Ralph Ellison*, 82.

72. Baker writes, "post-Civil Rights era black public intellectuals have been far more interested in serving as self-promoters than as thinkers committed to black majority interests," in Houston A. Baker Jr., *Betrayal: How Black Intellectuals Have Abandoned the Ideals of the Civil*

Rights Era (New York: Columbia University Press, 2008), 15. For Baker's criticism of then candidate Obama's speech on race, see Houston A. Baker Jr., "What Should Obama Do About Rev. Wright," in *Salon* (April 29, 2008), available at http://www.salon.com/opinion/feature/2008/04/29/obama_wright/index1.html

73. Houston A. Baker Jr., *Critical Memory: Public Spheres, African American Writing, and Black Fathers and Sons in America* (Athens: The University of Georgia Press, 2001), 19.

74. Ibid., 15.

75. Ibid., 30; 31; 31, 36.

76. Ibid., 10; 20.

77. Minutes, ACLU Equality Committee, Thursday, December 28, 1967, PM Papers (Box 54; Folder 943), 2.

78. Murray, "Draft Manuscript—Jane Crow: Black Power for Whom?" August 26, 1968, PM Papers (Box 2; Folder 30), 3.

79. Peniel Joseph, *Waiting 'Til the Midnight Hour: A Narrative History of Black Power in America* (New York: Henry Holt & Company), 99; 59–61.
    In November 1966, a number of Murray's generation, including A Philip Randolph, Dorothy Height, and Bayard Rustin, published a statement, "Crisis and Commitment," which repudiated black separatism, but also recognized "the signs of a retreat by white America from the national commitment to racial justice," in *The New York Times*, October 14, 1966, 35. Signatories included Rustin, Randolph, Height, Whitney Young, Roy Wilkins, among others, see John D'Emilio, *Lost Prophet: The Life and Times of Bayard Rustin* (New York: Free Press, 2003), 456; and Theda Skocpol, Ariane Liazos, Marshall Ganz, *What a Mighty Power We Can Be: African American Fraternal Groups and the Struggle for Racial Equality* (Princeton: Princeton University Press, 2006), 215–18.

80. Murray, "Black Power for Whom?" 1.

81. Ibid., 3.

82. Susan M. Hartmann, "Pauli Murray and 'Juncture of Women's Liberation and Black Liberation'," *Journal of Women's History* 14, no. 2 (2002): 77.

83. Murray, *Song in a Weary Throat*, 390; 390.

84. Ibid., 389.

85. "The Ten Demands," http://lts.brandeis.edu/research/archives-speccoll/events/ford/occupation/tendemands.html, opened March 10, 2009.

86. Ibram Rogers, "The Marginalization of the Black Campus Movement," *Journal of Social History* 42, no. 1 (Fall 2008): 176.

87. Murray, Journal entry, January 1, 1969, 11:30 pm, Friday in PM Papers (Box 2; Folder 30), no page number.

88. Murray, *Song in a Weary Throat*, 413.

89. Murray's frustrations at Brandeis were not limited to the black students' campaign. Murray also found herself fighting for employment rights and benefits for female staff and faculty. As one of the few women faculty members and only African American woman, Murray organized women staff, students, and faculty to fight "deficiencies in hiring, promotion and salary patterns" and lay the groundwork for the school's Women's Studies program, see Joyce Antler, "Pauli Murray: The Brandeis Years," *Journal of Women's History* 14, no. 2 (2002): 80. During these years, her journals reveal the real personal toll these events took. She is hurt that Brandeis' president, who had personally recruited her, does not seek her counsel, as the only lawyer on faculty, in how to best settle the black students' grievances, see Murray, Journal entry, Friday, January 1, 1969, 11:30 pm, PM Papers (Box 2; Folder 30), no page number.

90. Peniel Joseph, "Black Liberation Without Apology: Reconceptualizing the Black Power Movement," in *The Black Scholar* 31, nos. 3–4 (2001): 2. For a genealogy of five distinct phases of black nationality formation in the United States, see Komozi Woodard, *A Nation Within A Nation: Amiri Baraka (LeRoi Jones) & Black Power Politics* (Chapel Hill: UNC Press, 1999), 12–25.

91. Peniel Joseph, "Black Studies, Student Activism, and the Black Power Movement," in *The Black Power Movement: Rethinking the Civil Rights-Black Power Era*, ed. Peniel Joseph

(New York: Routledge, 2006), 265. Timothy Tyson understands black radical politics during World War II as among the roots of Black Power in Tyson, *Radio Free Dixie*, 26–48.

92. Steven Ward, "The Third World Women's Alliance: Black Feminist Radicalism and Black Power Politics," in *The Black Power Movement*, 120.

93. Jean M. Humez, "Pauli Murray's Histories of Loyalty and Revolt," *Black American Literature Forum* 24, no. 2 (1990): 324.

94. McNeill, "Interview with Pauli Murray," 89.

95. Frances Young, "Dear Mike," December 19, 1969, PM Papers (Box 121; Folder 2181), 1.

96. A fellow student complains about notes that Murray leaves on seminary bulletin boards calling for GTS to diversify its enrollment and syllabi, he instructs Murray "it is about time that you realized that you are not only receiving a deaf ear from seminarians, especially me, but you are hurting your cause as a woman and a Negro," Earnest C. Pollock, "Dear Miss Murray," March 19, 1974, PM Papers (Box 23; Folder 466), 1–2.

Ever the letter writer, Murray responds to what she reads as Pollack's anger: "If you have to live with anger, I have to live with pain. I'll trade you both my pain, my sex, my race and my age—and see how you deport yourself in such circumstances. Barring that, try to imagine for 24 hours what it must be like to be a Negro in a predominantly white seminary, a woman in an institution dominated by men and for the convenience of men, some of whom radiate hostility even though they do not say a word, who are patronizing and kindly as long as I do not get out of my place, but who feel threatened by my intellect, my achievements, and my refusal to be suppressed.... If I can't take your judgmental statements and your anger I am in the wrong place. If you cannot take my methods of fighting for survival, then you have chosen the wrong vocation. In both instances we are called upon to be Suffering Servants, but nobody said a Suffering Servant couldn't scream when it hurts. And, brother, it hurts!" in Murray, "Dear Earnie," March 21, 1974, PM Papers (Box 23; Folder 466), 1.

97. Murray, "Dear Earnest" March 22, 1974, PM Papers (Box 23; Folder 466), 6.

98. Murray, *Song in a Weary Throat*, 424.

99. Murray, Journal entry, June 24, 1973, PM Papers (Box 2; Folder 30), no page number.

100. Murray, Journal entry, July 8, 1973, PM Papers (Box 2; Folder 30), no page number.

Chapter 4: Murray Among the Theologians (1970s and 1980s)

1. Murray, "Dear Bishop Stokes," October 19, 1969, PM Papers (Box 121; Folder 2184), 1.

2. Suzanne Hiatt, "How We Brought the Good News from Graymoor to Minneapolis: An Episcopal Paradigm," *Journal of Ecumenical Studies* 20, no. 4 (Fall 1983): 579. For another account of irregular ordination, see Carter Heyward, *A Priest Forever: One Woman's Controversial Ordination in the Episcopal Church* (Cleveland: Pilgrim Press, 1999).

3. See "The Acts of Convention 1976–2006: Resolution Number 1976-B005" *The Archives of the Episcopal Church*, http://www.episcopalarchives.org/cgi-bin/acts/acts_resolution.pl?resolution=1976-B005, opened, March 21, 2009.

4. Murray, "Black Theology: Heresy, Syncretism, or Prophecy?" April 16, 1975, PM Papers (Box 23; Folder 472), 7; emphasis in original.

5. James Cone, *Black Theology and Black Power*, 20th Anniversary ed. (San Francisco: Harper San Francisco, 1989), 38; 19; 52.

6. Ibid., 39; 136; 147.

7. James Cone, *A Black Theology of Liberation* (Maryknoll, NY: Orbis Books, 1986), 76; note 5, 32.

8. Ibid., 121; 215.

9. J. Deotis Roberts, *Liberation and Reconciliation: A Black Theology* (Maryknoll, NY: Orbis Books), 1; 5; 8.

10. Ibid., 25.

11. Ibid., 72; 39.

12. Murray "J. Deotis Roberts on Black Theology: A Comparative View," November 20, 1975, PM Papers (Box 23; Folder 474), 4.

13. Murray is not alone in this criticism, of course. Cone himself recognized his "complete blindness to the problem of sexism," in the twentieth anniversary edition of *Black Theology and Black Power*, x.

14. Cone, *Black Theology and Black Power*, 31, author's emphasis.

15. James H. Cone, "They Sought a City: Martin's Dream and Malcolm's Nightmare," in *Liberating Eschatology: Essays in Honor of Letty M. Russell*, eds. Margaret A. Farley and Serene Jones (Louisville: Westminster John Knox Press, 1999), 101.

16. Cone, *Black Theology and Black Power*, 4.

17. Murray, "Black Theology," 15.

18. Murray, "J. Deotis Roberts on Black Theology," 13.

19. Ibid., 19–20; 11.

20. Ibid., 21; 21; 22.
    In a note attached to her paper, Roberts responded to Murray's charge that he needed to take women's experiences more seriously, he argued that his recent work has shown concern for the black family. Roberts retained his criticism of the women's movement in general because "thus far [it] is fostered by and large by those women who have benefited most from being among the privileged in this society...I do not exactly question their sincerity, but I do raise a question regarding their ability to feel the hurt of a whole people who suffer from racism...I do feel that women have a just cause, but their cause can only have full meaning when poor as well as black women are given a means to expression" see Roberts' note to Murray's paper "J. Deotis Roberts on Black Theology," 2.

21. Murray "Black Theology and Feminist Theology: A Comparative Study," March 20, 1976, PM Papers (Box 23, Folder 475), 86.

22. Murray's master's thesis was later published as Pauli Murray, "Black Theology and Feminist Theology: A Comparative View," *Anglican Theological Review* 60 (January 1978): 3–24. I will refer to the version she wrote while in seminary.

23. Murray, "Black Theology and Feminist Theology," 94; 94; 88.

24. Alice Walker, *In Search of Our Mothers' Gardens* (New York: Harcourt Brace Jovanovich, 1983), xi.

25. Stephanie Y. Mitchem, *Introducing Womanist Theology* (Maryknoll, NY: Orbis Books, 2002), 72.

26. Joanne Terrell, *Power in the Blood? The Cross in the African American Experience* (Maryknoll, NY: Orbis Books, 1998), 5.

27. Jacquelyn Grant, *White Women's Christ and Black Women's Jesus: Feminist Christology and Womanist Response* (Atlanta: Scholars Press, 1989), 206.

28. Pinn, "Religion and 'America's Problem Child,'" 31.

29. Patricia Hill Collins, *Fighting Words: Black Women and the Search for Justice* (Minneapolis: University of Minnesota Press, 1998), 60.

30. Ibid., 65; 67; 70.

31. Traci C. West, "Is a Womanist a Black Feminist? Marking the Distinctions and Defying Them: A Black Feminist Response," in *Deeper Shades of Purple: Womanism in Religion and Society*, ed. Stacey Floyd Thomas (New York: New York University Press, 2006): 295; 293.

32. Murray, "Healing and Reconciliation," February 13, 1977, PM Papers (Box 64; Folder 1092), 4.

33. Marjorie Hyer, "Episcopal Priests Ordained" *Washington Post*, January 9, 1977, p. A3.

34. James C. Wattley, "Dear Mr. Secretary," January 13, 1977, PM Papers (Box 63; Folder 1078), 1.

35. Murray, "Dear Rev. Wattley," January 21, 1977, PM Papers (Box 63; Folder 1078), 1; 2.

36. Murray, "Dear Johnny Walker," March 14, 1977, PM Papers (Box 63; Folder 1078), 1.

37. Murray, "Dear Jim and Mary," February 4, 1977, PM Papers (Box 63; Folder 1078), 2. Murray kept herself apprised of gay and lesbian issues in the church; in her files, she had multiple issues of "Integrity: Gay Episcopal Forum," PM Papers (Box 121; Folder 2254).

38. See Pauli Murray, "Black theology and Feminist Theology: A Comparative View," in *Anglican Theological Review*. Murray's sermons were published in the Episcopal Journal *Witness* as well as in *Phoebe: A Theological and Religious Journal for Women*.

39. See Bettye Collier-Thomas, *Daughters of Thunder: Black Women Preachers and Their Sermons, 1850–1979* (San Francisco: Jossey-Bass, 1998), and Pauli Murray, *Pauli Murray: Selected Sermons and Writings.*

40. James Cone, *God of the Oppressed* Revised Edition (Maryknoll, NY: Orbis Books, 1997), 54–55. For a discussion of the challenge of reading and analyzing sermons, see Hortense J., "Moving on Down the Line," in *American Quarterly* vol. 40, no. 1 (March 1998): 83–109.

41. In the homily given on the day that Murray visited, Reverend James Peter Lee preached "tonight you stand among us as a priest, a pontiff, that Latin word that means 'bridge,' and in your priesthood, you recall to all of us our priesthood, our call to be bridge builders in a broken world," in James Peter Lee, "Servant Children," preached at the Chapel of the Cross, Chapel Hill, NC, on February 13, 1977, PM Papers (Box 64; Folder 1092), 1.

    In 2006, Lee was the bishop of the Episcopal Diocese of Virginia; his efforts to keep Virginia churches from seceding over the ordination of an openly gay bishop have been documented in Michael Massing, "Bishop Lee's Choice," *New York Times Magazine*, January 4, 2004, 34–37; and Laurie Goodstein, "Episcopal Rift Drawing Near Point of Revolt," *New York Times*, December 17, 2006, A1.

42. Murray, "Healing and Reconciliation," PM Papers (Box 64; Folder 1092), 26–27.

43. Daniel Boyarin develops this distinction in *A Radical Jew: Paul and the Politics of Identity* (Berkeley: University of California Press, 1994), 8–9.

44. Murray, "Healing and Reconciliation," 27.

45. Ibid., 24.

46. Pauli Murray, "Sermon on the Ordination of Women," in *Pauli Murray: Selected Sermons and Writings*, 60.

47. Ibid., 61.

48. Murray, "Mary Has Chosen the Best Part," July 14, 1977, PM Papers (Box 64; Folder 1094), 2.

49. Ibid., 4, emphasis in the original; 4.

50. Louise Michele Newman, *White Women's Rights: The Racial Origins of Feminism in the United States* (OUP, 1999), 6.

51. Murray, *Song in a Weary Throat*, 377.

52. Murray, "Out of the Wilderness," July 21, 1974, PM Papers (Box 64; Folder 1089), 3; 4; 4.

53. Katie Cannon, "Remembering What We Never Knew," *Journal of Women and Religion* 16 (1998): 169; 171.

54. Murray, "Inaugural Sermon," March 3, 1974, PM Papers (Box 64; Folder 1089), 4.

55. Murray, Untitled Sermon, August 5, 1984, PM Papers (Box 65; Folder 1106), 3.

56. Murray, "Tillich: On Freedom and Destiny (A Personal Reflection or a Commentary)" May 6, 1975, PM Papers (Box 23; Folder 472), 18; 4; 5, emphasis in original.

57. Murray, "Are You He Who Is To Come?," Undated, PM Papers (Box 64; Folder 1100), 11.

58. Ibid., 12.

59. Murray, "The Second Great Commandment," November 21, 1976, PM Papers (Box 64; Folder 1091), 2.

60. Murray, "Tillich: On Freedom and Destiny," 5; 6.

61. Ibid., emphasis in original.

62. Pinn, *Becoming America's Problem Child*, 28.

63. Roberts, *Liberation and Reconciliation*, 78.

64. Murray, "Epipany 4," January 21, 1982, PM Papers (Box 65; Folder 1105), 7.

65. Murray, "Are You He Who Is To Come?" 5; 6; 10; 8.

66. Murray, Untitled, August 10, 1980, PM Papers (Box 64; Folder 1101), 3.

67. Ibid., 3.

68. Murray, "The Second Great Commandment," 12; 10.

69. Murray, "Gifts of the Holy Spirit to Women I Have Known," May 14, 1978, PM Papers (Box 64; Folder 1095), 10.

70. Murray and Babcock, "An Alternative Weapon," 54.

Martin Luther King spoke also about suffering being redemptive, perhaps most
famously in his speech at the 1963 March on Washington, in which he counsels, "continue to work with the faith that unearned suffering is redemptive," in Martin Luther
King, Jr., "I Have A Dream," *Testament of Hope: The Essential Writings and Speeches of
Martin Luther King, Jr.*, ed. James M. Washington (San Francisco: HarperSanFrancisco,
1986), 219.

71. Murray, "Dilemma of a Minority Christian," May 19, 1974, PM Papers (Box 64; Folder
    1089), 6; 2; 6.
72. Ibid., 4.
73. Murray, "Palm Sunday Sermon," April 4, 1974, PM Papers (Box 64; Folder 1089), 2.
74. Ibid., 4; 3.
75. Pinn, "Religion and 'America's Problem Child,'" 33.
76. Emilie M. Townes, "Living in the New Jerusalem: The Rhetoric and Movement of Liberation
    in the House of Evil," in *A Troubling in My Soul: Womanist Perspectives on Evil and Suffering*,
    ed. Emilie M. Townes (Maryknoll, NY: Orbis Books, 1993), 90; 84.
77. Ibid., 84.
78. Jacquelyn Grant, "Servanthood Revisited: Womanist Explorations of Servanthood
    Theology," in *Black Faith and Public Talk: Critical Essays on James H. Cone's Black Theology
    and Black Power*, ed. Dwight N. Hopkins (Maryknoll, NY: Orbis Books, 1999), 126.
79. Grant, *While Women's Christ and Black Women's Jesus*, 217.
80. Williams, *Sisters in the Wilderness*, xiv; 167; 167; 167.
81. Ibid., 165.
82. M. Shawn Copeland, *Enfleshing Freedom: Body, Race, and Being* (Minneapolis: Fortress
    Press, 2010), 3.
83. M. Shawn Copeland, "'Wading through Many Sorrows': Toward a Theology of Suffering in
    Womanist Perspective," in *A Troubling in My Soul: Womanist Perspectives on Suffering*, ed.
    Emilie M. Townes (Maryknoll, NY: Orbis Books, 1993), 109; 123–4.
84. Ibid., 124. Copeland recognizes the risks in reproducing accounts of "torture, sexual
    assault, and lunching." But insists that "drawing back the veil is an obligation to memory:
    the subjects and the subject of my theologizing are the dead, the 'Many Thousands Gone,'"
    in M. Shawn Copeland, *Enfleshing Freedom: Body, Race, and Being* (Minneapolis: Fortress
    Press, 2010), 3.
85. Murray, "The Great Commandment," undated, PM Papers (Box 64; Folder 1096), 11.
86. Ibid., 1; 7.
87. Murray, "Our Highest Selves," September 7, 1978, PM Papers (Box 64; Folder 1101),
    5;1; 4.
88. Ibid., 9; 12; 15.
89. Pauli Murray, "What Shall I Do To Inherit Eternal Life?" undated (Box 64; Folder 1101),
    7–8. Though the sermon is undated, it is filed with other sermons that follow chronologi-
    cally from "Our Highest Selves," which was preached in 1978.
90. Murray, "What Shall I Do To Inherit Eternal Life?" 9; 8
91. Ibid., 11; 13.
92. McNeill, "Interview with Pauli Murray," 107.
93. David Howard-Pitney, *The African American Jeremiad: Appeals for Justice in America*
    (Philadelphia: Temple University Press, 2005), 5.
94. Sacvan Bercovitch, *The American Jeremiad* (Madison: University of Wisconsin Press, 1978),
    6–8.
95. Theophus H. Smith, *Conjuring Culture: Biblical Formations in Black America* (New York:
    Oxford University Press, 1994), 225.
96. Ibid.
97. Howard-Pitney, *The African American Jeremiad*, 218.
98. George Shulman, "American Political Culture, Prophetic Narration, and Toni Morrison's
    Beloved," *Political Theory* 24, no. 2 (1996): 304.
99. James Baldwin and Audre Lorde, "Revolutionary Hope: A Conversation Between James
    Baldwin and Audre Lorde," *Essence* 15, no. 8 (December 1984): 130.

Chapter 5: The Gates of the City: An Eschatological Vision of American Democracy

1. Robert Bellah, "Response to Charles Taylor," Kyoto Laureate Symposium, University of San Diego, March 20, 2009. Author's notes.

2. Kelly Brown Douglas, "Daring to Speak: Womanist Theology and Black Sexuality," in *Embracing the Spirit: Womanist Perspectives on Hope, Salvation, and Transformation*, ed. Emilie M. Townes (Maryknoll, NY: Orbis Books, 1997), 243.

3. Jean Bethke Elshtain, *Public Man and Private Woman: Women in Social and Political Thought* (Princeton: Princeton University Press, 1981), 347; 345.

4. Jean Bethke Elshtain, *Democracy on Trial* (New York: Basic Books, 1995), 15; 53, emphasis in original; 40.

5. Jean Bethke Elshtain, "A Call to Civil Society," *Society* (July/August 1999): 11.

6. Ibid., 13.

7. Ibid., 14.

8. Jean Bethke Elshtain, "Against Liberal Monism," *Daedalus* 132, no. 3 (Summer 2003): 79.

9. Jean Bethke Elshtain, "Religion and Democracy," in *Journal of Democracy* 20, no. 2 (April 2009): 8.

10. Jean Bethke Elshtain, *Democracy on Trial* (New York: Basic Books, 1995), 27, 35.

11. Jean Bethke Elshtain, *Who are We? Critical Reflections and Hopeful Possibilities* (Grand Rapids, MI: William B. Eerdmans, 2000), 127; 154.

12. Jean Bethke Elshtain, *Sovereignty: God, State, and the Self* (New York: Basic Books, 2008), 210; 229.

13. Elshtain, *Public Man and Private Woman*, 357.

14. Elshtain, *Democracy on Trial*, 49.

15. Cornel West, *Keeping Faith: Philosophy and Race in America* (New York: Routledge, 1993), xvi.

16. Ibid., 265.

17. Sylvia Ann, Hewlett and Cornel West, *The War Against Parents: What We Can Do for America's Beleaguered Moms and Dads* (Boston: Houghton Mifflin, 1998).

18. Cornel West, *Prophesy Deliverance! An Afro-American Revolutionary Christianity* (Philadelphia: Westminster, 1982), 21.

19. Rosemary Cowan, *Cornel West: The Politics of Redemption* (Malden, MA: Blackwell, 2003), 51.

20. West, *Keeping Faith*, xvi.

21. Cornel West, "Black Theology and Human Identity," in *Black Faith and Public Talk: Critical Essays on James H. Cone's Black Theology and Black Power*, ed. Dwight N. Hopkins (Maryknoll, NY: Orbis Books, 1999), 19.

22. West, *Keeping Faith*, 134.

23. Mark David Wood, *Cornel West and the Politics of Prophetic Pragmatism* (Chicago: University of Illinois Press, 2000), 36.

24. West, *Keeping Faith*, 247.

25. Cornel West, *Democracy Matters: Winning the Fight Against Imperialism* (New York: Penguin Books, 2004), 15.

26. In *Race Matters*, West clarified that "nihilism is to be understood here not as a philosophical doctrine that there are no rational grounds for legitimate standards or authority; it is, far more, the lived experience of coping with a life of horrifying meaninglessness, hopelessness, and (most important) lovelessness," in Cornel West, *Race Matters* (Boston: Beacon Press, 1993), 14.

27. West, *Democracy Matters*, 41.

28. Ibid., 149.

29. West, *Prophesy Deliverance!*, 16.

30. Ibid., 17.

31. West, *Democracy Matters*, 204.

32. Elshtain does as well; she warns us "I have long worried that, from time to time, those who embrace the powerful term *prophetic* for their work use it as a kind of ideological cover.

'Prophetic' too often seems to among to denunciatory rhetoric attached to a specific political agenda," in Elshtain, *Who Are We?*, xv.

33. Murray, "Healing and Reconciliation," 3.

34. West, *Prophesy Deliverance!*, 19.

35. West, *Democracy Matters*, 204.

36. Lawrie Balfour, "*Darkwater's* Democratic Vision," *Political Theory* 38, no. 4 (August 2010): 539.

37. Michelle Alexander, *The New Jim Crow: Mass Incarceration in the Age of Colorblindness* (New York: The New Press, 2010); Roberto Lovato, "Juan Crow in Georgia," *The Nation*, 286, no. 20 (May 8, 2008): 20–24.

38. Lane A. Burgland, "Eschatological Tension and Existential *Angst*: 'Now' and 'Not Yet' in Romans 7: 14–25 and 1QS11 (Community Rule, Manuel of Discipline)" *Concordia Theological Quarterly* 61, no. 3 (July 1997): 169.

39. I am borrowing the distinction between purpose and teleology from William Connolly's account of a politics of becoming, which he describes as "purposeful without being teleological," in Connolly, *Why I Am Not a Secularist* (Minneapolis: University of Minnesota Press, 1999), 58.

40. Murray, *Dark Testament and Other Poems*, 7.

SELECTED BIBLIOGRAPHY

Archives

Pauli Murray Papers. *The Arthur and Elizabeth Schlesinger Library on the History of Women in America*, Cambridge, MA: Harvard University.

Ralph, J. *Bunche Oral History Collection*, Washington, DC: Moorland-Spingarn Research Center, Howard University.

Southern Oral History Program, Wilson Library. Chapel Hill, NC: University of North Carolina.

Special Collections, Alderman Library. Charlottesville, VA: University of Virginia.

Books and Articles

Anderson, Victor. *Beyond Ontological Blackness: An Essay on African American Religious and Cultural Criticism*. New York: Continuum, 1995.

———. *Contour of an American Public Theology*. In http://livedtheology.org/wkgp_race_2.htm, 2001.

———. *Pragmatic Theology: Negotiating the Intersections of an American Philosophy of Religion and Public Theology*. Albany: State University of New York Press, 1998.

Antler, Joyce. "Pauli Murray: The Brandeis Years." *Journal of Women's History* 14, no. 2 (2002): 78–82.

Appiah, Kwame Anthony. *The Ethics of Identity*. Princeton: Princeton University Press, 2005.

Appiah, K. Anthony, and Amy Gutmann. *Color Conscious: The Political Morality of Race*. Princeton: Princeton University Press, 1996.

Baker Jr., Houston A. *Critical Memory: Public Spheres, African American Writing, and Black Fathers and Sons in America*. Athens: The University of Georgia Press, 2001.

Baldwin, James. *Notes of a Native Son*. Boston: Beacon Press, 1955.

Balfour, Lawrie. *The Evidence of Things Not Said: James Baldwin and the Promise of American Democracy*. Ithaca: Cornell University Press, 2001.

Becker, Mary. "The Sixties Shift to Formal Equality and the Courts: An Argument for Pragmatism and Politics." *William and Mary Law Review* 40, no. 1 (October 1998): 209–77.

Black, Alida M. *Casting Her Own Shadow: Eleanor Roosevelt and the Shaping of Postwar Liberalism*. New York: Columbia University Press, 1996.

Blight, David W. "WEB Du Bois and the Struggle for American Historical Memory." In *History and Memory in African-American Culture*, eds. Genevieve Fabre and Robert O'Meally, 45–71. New York: Oxford University Press, 1994.

Braxton, Joanne M. *Black Women Writing Autobiography: A Tradition within a Tradition*. Philadelphia: Temple University Press, 1989.

Brown, Flora Bryant. "NAACP Sponsored Sit-Ins by Howard University Students in Washington, D.C., 1943–1944." *The Journal of Negro History* 85, no. 4 (2000): 274–86.

Brown, Leslie. *The Upbuilding of Black Durham: Gender, Class, and Black Community Development in the Jim Crow South*. Chapel Hill: The University of North Carolina Press, 2008.

Butterfield, Stephen. *Black Autobiography in America*. Amherst: University of Massachusetts Press, 1974.

Caldbeck, Elaine. "The Poetry of Pauli Murray, African American Civil Rights Lawyer and Priest." In *Gender, Ethnicity, and Religion: Views from the Other Side*, ed. Rosemary Radford Ruether, 45–65. Minneapolis: Fortress Press, 2002.

———. "A Religious Life of Pauli Murray: Hope and Struggle." PhD diss., Northwestern University, 2000.

Callahan, Allen Dwight. *The Talking Book: African Americans and the Bible*. New Haven: Yale University Press, 2006.

Cannon, Katie. "Remembering What We Never Knew." *Journal of Women and Religion* 16 (1998): 167–78.

Carson, Clayborne. "Martin Luther King, Jr., and the African-American Social Gospel." In *African American Religious Thought: An Anthology*, eds. Cornel West and Eddie Glaude, 696–714. Louisville: Westminster John Knox Press, 2003.

Clinton, Catherine. "'With a Whip in His Hand': Rape, Memory, and African-American Women." In *History and Memory in African-American Culture*, eds. Genevieve Fabre and Robert O'Meally, 205–18. New York: Oxford University Press, 1994.

Collier-Thomas, Bettye. *Daughters of Thunder: Black Women Preachers and Their Sermons, 1850–1979*. San Francisco: Jossey-Bass, 1998.

Collins, Patricia Hill. *Black Feminist Thought: Knowledge, Consciousness, and the Politics of Empowerment*. Second ed. New York: Routledge, 2000.

———. *Fighting Words: Black Women and the Search for Justice*. Minneapolis: University of Minnesota Press, 1998.

———. "The Social Construction of Black Feminist Thought." *Signs* 14, no. 4 (1989): 745–73.

Cone, James H. "Black Theology in American Religion." *Theology Today* 43, no. 1 (1986): 6–21.

———. *Black Theology and Black Power*. 20th anniversary ed. San Francisco: Harper San Francisco, 1989.

———. *A Black Theology of Liberation*. Maryknoll, NY: Orbis Books, 1986.

———. *Malcolm and Martin and America: A Dream or a Nightmare*. Maryknoll, NY: Orbis Books, 1991.

———. *The Spirituals and the Blues: An Interpretation*. Maryknoll, NY: Orbis Books, 2004.

Copeland, M. Shawn. *Enfleshing Freedom: Body, Race, and Being*. Minneapolis: Fortress Press, 2010.

———. "Memory, Emancipation, and Hope: Political Theology in the 'Land of the Free.'" The Santa Clara Lectures, Santa Clara University, November 9, 1997.

Deneen, Patrick. *Democratic Faith*. Princeton: Princeton University Press, 2005.

DesJardins, Julie. *Women and the Historical Enterprise in America: Gender, Race, and the Politics of Memory, 1880–1945*. Chapel Hill: University of North Carolina Press, 2003.

Douglas, Kelly Brown. *The Black Christ*. Maryknoll, NY: Orbis Books, 1994.

Drury, Doreen Marie. "'Experimentation on the Male Side': Race, Class, Gender, and Sexuality in Pauli Murray's Quest for Love and Identity." PhD diss., Boston College, 2000.

Early, Gerald. "The Quest for a Black Humanism." *Daedalus* 135, no. 2 (2006): 91–104.

Egerton, John. *Speak Now Against the Day: The Generation Before the Civil Rights Movement in the South*. New York: Alfred A. Knopf, 1994.

Ellis, Marc. "WEB Du Bois and the Formation of Black Opinion in World War I: A Commentary on 'the Damnable Dilemma'." *The Journal of American History* 81, no. 4 (1995): 1584–90.

Ellison, Ralph. *The Collected Essays of Ralph Ellison*, ed. John F. Callahan. New York: The Modern Library, 1995.

Elshtain, Jean Bethke. "Against Liberal Monism," *Daedalus* 132, no. 3 (Summer 2003): 78–79.

———. *Augustine and the Limits of Politics*. Notre Dame, IN: University of Notre Dame Press, 1995.

———. "A Call to Civil Society." *Society* 36, no. 5 (July/August 1999): 11–19.

———. *Democracy on Trial*. New York: Basic Books, 1995.

———. "The National Prospect: Response to Conservatism and Social Decline." *Commentary* 100, no. 5 (1995): 48–49.

———. "Not a Cure-All: Civil Society Creates Citizens: It Does Not Solve Problems," *The Brookings Review* 15, no. 4 (Fall 1997): 13–15.

———. "Politics and Persons." *Journal of Religion* (2006): 402–11.

———. *Public Man, Private Woman: Women in Social and Political Thought*. Princeton: Princeton University Press, 1981.

———. *Sovereignty: God, State, and Self*. New York: Basic Books, 2008.

———. *Who Are We? Critical Reflections and Hopeful Possibilities*. Grand Rapids, MI: William B. Eerdmans Publishing Company, 2000.

Felder, Cain Hope, ed. *Stony The Road We Trod: African American Biblical Interpretation*. Minneapolis: Fortress Press, 1991.

Finkle, Lee. "The Conservative Aims of Militant Rhetoric: Black Protest During World War II." *The Journal of American History* 60, no. 3 (1973): 692–713.

Fiorenza, Elisabeth Schüssler. "Changing the Paradigms." *Christian Century* 107, no. 25 (1990): 796–800.

———. *In Memory of Her: A Feminist Theological Reconstruction of Christian Origins*. Tenth Anniversary ed. New York: Cross Road, 1994.

Fitzpatrick, Ellen. "Caroline F. Ware and the Cultural Approach to History." *American Quarterly* 43, no. 2 (1991): 173–98.

Fleischner, Jennifer. *Mastering Slavery: Memory, Family, and Identity in Women's Slave Narratives*. New York: New York University Press, 1996.

Foner, Philip S. *American Socialism and Black Americans: From the Age of Jackson to World War II*. Westport, CT: Greenwood Press, 1977.

Fox-Genovese, Elizabeth. "Slavery, Race, and the Figure of the Tragic Mulatta; or, the Ghost of Southern History in the Writing of African-American Women." In *Haunted Bodies: Gender and Southern Texts*, eds. Anne Goodwyn Jones and Susan V. Donaldson, 464–91. Charlottesville: University Press of Virginia, 1997.

Fraser, Nancy. "Rethinking the Public Sphere: A Contribution to the Critique of Actually Existing Democracy." *Social Text* 25/26 (1990): 56–80.

Gaines, Kevin K. *American Africans in Ghana: Black Expatriates and the Civil Rights Era*. Chapel Hill: University of North Carolina Press, 2006.

Gerstle, Gary. *American Crucible: Race and Nation in the Twentieth Century*. Princeton: Princeton University Press, 2001.

Gilkes, Cheryl Townsend. "Dual Heroisms and Double Burdens: Interpreting Afro-American Women's Experience and History." *Feminist Studies* 15, no. 3 (1989): 573–90.

Gilmore, Glenda. *Defying Dixie: The Radical Roots of Civil Rights, 1919–1950*. New York: W.W. Norton, 2008.

Grant, Jacquelyn. "Servanthood Revisited: Womanist Explorations of Servanthood Theology." In *Black Faith and Public Talk: Critical Essays on James H. Cone's Black Theology and Black Power*, ed. Dwight N. Hopkins, 126–37. Maryknoll, NY: Orbis Books, 1999.

———. *White Women's Christ and Black Women's Jesus: Feminist Christology and Womanist Response*. American Academy of Religion Academy Series, no. 64. Atlanta: Scholars Press, 1989.

Hall, Jacquelyn Dowd. "Partial Truths." *Signs* 14, no. 4 (1989): 902–11.

———. "'You Must Remember This': Autobiography as Social Critique." *The Journal of American History* 85, no. 2 (1998): 439–65.

Hardin, Michael. "Ralph Ellison's *Invisible Man*: Invisibility, Race, and Homoeroticism from Frederick Douglass to E. Lynn Harris." *The Southern Literary Journal* 37, no. 1 (2004): 96–121.

Harris, Paisely. "Gatekeeping and Remaking: The Politics of Respectability in African American Women's History and Black Feminism." *Journal of Women's History* 15, no. 1 (2003): 212–22.

Harris, Robert L. "Coming of Age: The Transformation of Afro-American Historiography." *Journal of Negro History* 67, no. 2 (1982): 107–21.

Harrison, Cynthia. *On Account of Sex: The Politics of Women's Issues, 1945–1968*. Berkeley: University of California Press, 1988.

————. "Pauli Murray and 'Juncture of Women's Liberation and Black Liberation'." *Journal of Women's History* 14, no. 2 (2002): 74–77.

Hartmann, Susan. *The Other Feminists: Activists in the Liberal Establishment.* New Haven: Yale University Press, 1998.

Height, Dorothy I. "'We Wanted the Voice of a Woman to Be Heard': Black Woman and the 1963 March on Washington." In *Sisters in the Struggle: African American Women in the Civil Rights-Black Power Movement,* eds. Bettye Collier-Thomas and V.P. Franklin, 83–91. New York: New York University Press, 2001.

Higginbotham, Evelyn Brooks. *Righteous Discontent: The Women's Movement in the Black Baptist Church, 1880–1920.* Cambridge: Harvard University Press, 1993.

Holt, Thomas. "*From Slavery to Freedom* and the Conceptualization of African-American History." *Journal of Negro History* 85, no. 1/2 (2000): 22–26.

Howard-Pitney, David. *The African American Jeremiad: Appeals for Justice in America.* Philadelphia: Temple University Press, 2005.

Humez, Jean M. "Pauli Murray's Histories of Loyalty and Revolt." *Black American Literature Forum* 24, no. 2 (1990): 315–55.

Joseph, Peniel. *Waiting 'Til the Midnight Hour: A Narrative History of Black Power in America.* New York: Henry Holt & Company, 2006.

Kerber, Linda K. *No Constitutional Right to Be Ladies: Women and the Obligations of Citizenship.* New York: Hill and Wang, 1998.

Lagerquist, L. DeAne. "Women and the American Religious Pilgrimage: Vida Scudder, Dorothy Day, and Pauli Murray." In *New Dimensions in American Religious History: Essays in Honor of Martin E. Marty,* eds. Jay P. Dolan and James P. Wind, 208–30. Grand Rapids, MI: William B. Eerdmans Publishing Company, 1993.

Mallon Ross, Susan. "Dialogic Rhetoric: Dorothy Kenyon and Pauli Murray's Rhetorical Moves in *White v. Crook*." *International Journal of the Diversity* 6, no. 5 (2007): 89–100.

Margalit, Avishai. *The Ethics of Memory.* Cambridge: Harvard University Press, 2002.

Mayeri, Serena. "A Common Fate of Discrimination: Race-Gender Analogies in Legal and Historical Perspective." *Yale Law Journal* 110, no. 6 (April 2001): 1045–87.

McCartney, John T. *Black Power Ideologies: An Essay in African-American Political Thought.* Philadelphia: Temple University Press, 1992.

McMillian, John. "'History Makes Its Demands': Identity Politics, Slavery Scholarship and the Narrative of Robert Starobin." *Rethinking History* 6, no. 2 (2002): 151–74.

Meier, August, Elliot Rudwich, and Francis L. Broderick, eds. *Black Protest Thought in the Twentieth Century.* Second ed. New York: The Bobbs-Merrill Company, 1971.

Meyerowitz, Joanne. "Sex Change and the Popular Press: Historical Notes on Transsexuality in the United States, 1930–1955." *GLQ* 4, no. 2 (1998): 159–87.

Miller, Casey and Kate Swift. "Pauli Murray: The Life Story That Asks the Question. 'Can a Girl from a Little Town in North Carolina Find Happiness as a Priest/Poet/Lawyer/Teacher/Revolutionary/Civil Rights Activist?'" *Ms.* (March 1980): 60–64.

Minton, Henry L. "Femininity in Men and Masculinity in Women: American Psychiatry and Psychology Portray Homosexuality in the 1930s." *Journal of Homosexuality* 13, no. 1 (1986): 1–21.

Minton, Henry L., and Scott R. Mattson. "Deconstructing Heterosexuality: Life Stories from Gay New York, 1931–1941." *Journal of Homosexuality* 36, no. 1 (1998): 43–61.

Mitchem, Stephanie. *Introducing Womanist Theology.* Maryknoll, NY: Orbis Books, 2002.

Moltmann, Jürgen. *Theology of Hope: On the Ground and the Implications of a Christian Eschatology.* New York: Harper & Row, 1975.

Morrison, Toni. "The Site of Memory." In *Out There: Marginalization and Contemporary Cultures,* eds. Russell Ferguson, Martha Gever, Trinh T. Minh-ha and Cornel West, 299–326. Cambridge: MIT Press, 1990.

Murray, Pauli. "An American Credo." *Common Ground* 5, no. 2 (1945): 22–24.

————. "And the Riots Came." *The Call,* Friday, August 13, 1943, 1; 4.

————. "A Blueprint for First Class Citizenship." *The Crisis* 51 (1944): 358–59.

———. "Black Strategies." In *Rebels in Law: Voices in History of Black Women Lawyers* ed. J. Clay Smith, Jr., 162–64. Ann Arbor: The University of Michigan Press, 1998.

———. *Dark Testament and Other Poems*. Norwalk, CT: Silvermine, 1970.

———. "Negroes Are Fed Up." *Common Sense*, August 1943, 274–76.

———. "Negro Youth's Dilemma." *Threshold*, April 1942, 8–11.

———. *Proud Shoes: The Story of an American Family*. New York: Harper & Row, 1978.

———. "The Right to Equal Opportunity in Employment." *California Law Review* 33 (1945): 388–433.

———. "Roots of the Racial Crisis: Prologue to Policy." JSD diss., Yale University, 1965.

———. *Song in a Weary Throat: An American Pilgrimage*. New York: Harper & Row, 1987.

———. *States' Laws on Race and Color*. Cincinnati: Women's Division of Christian Service, Board of Missions and Church Extension, Methodist Church, 1951.

———. "Three Thousand Miles on a Dime in Ten Days." In *Negro Anthology: 1931–1934*, ed. Nancy Cunard, 90–93. London: Wishart, 1934.

———. "Why Negro Girls Stay Single." *Negro Digest* 5, no. 9 (1947): 4–8.

——— and Henry Babcock. "An Alternative Weapon." *South Today*, Winter 1942–1943, 53–57.

——— and Leslie Rubin. *The Constitution and Government of Ghana*. London: Sweet and Maxwell, 1964.

——— and Mary O. Eastwood. "Jane Crow and the Law: Sex Discrimination and Title Vii." *George Washington Law Review* 43, no. 2 (1965): 232–56.

Niebuhr, H. Richard. *The Kingdom of God in America*. Middletown, CT: Wesleyan University Press, 1988.

Nora, Pierre. "Between Memory and History: *Les Lieux De Mémoire*." *Representations* 26, no. Special Issue: Memory and Counter-Memory (1989): 7–24.

O'Dell, Darlene. *Sites of Southern Memory: The Autobiographies of Katharine Du Pre Lumpkin, Lillian Smith, and Pauli Murray*. Charlottesville: University Press of Virginia, 2001.

Olson, Lynn. *Freedom's Daughters: The Unsung Heroines of the Civil Rights Movement from 1830–1970*. New York: Scribner, 2001.

Ordover, Nancy. *American Eugenics: Race, Queer Anatomy, and the Science of Nationalism*. Minneapolis: University of Minnesota Press, 2003.

Peppard, Christiana Z. "Poetry, Ethics, and the Legacy of Pauli Murray." *Journal of the Society of Christian Ethics* 30, no. 1 (Spring/Summer 2010): 21–44.

Pinn, Anthony *"Becoming America's Problem Child": An Outline of Pauli Murray's Religious Life and Theology*. Eugene, OR: Pickwick Publications, 2008.

———. "Religion and 'America's Problem Child:' Notes on Pauli's Murray Theological Development." *Journal of Feminist Studies in Religion* 15, no. 2 (1999): 21–39.

———. *Why, Lord? Suffering and Evil in Black Theology*. New York: Continuum, 1995.

———, ed. *Moral Evil and Redemptive Suffering: A History of Theodicy in African-American Religious Thought*. Miami: University Press of Florida, 2002.

———, ed. *Pauli Murray: Selected Sermons and Writings*. Maryknoll, NY: Orbis Books, 2006.

Ransby, Barbara. *Ella Baker and the Black Freedom Movement: A Radical Democratic Vision*. Chapel Hill: The University of North Carolina Press, 2003.

Richards, Yevette. *Conversations with Maida Springer: A Personal History of Labor, Race, and International Relations*. Pittsburg: University of Pittsburg Press, 2004.

———. *Maida Springer: Pan Africanist and International Labor Leader*. Pittsburg: University of Pittsburg Press, 2000.

Roberts, J. Deotis. *Liberation and Reconciliation: A Black Theology*. Philadelphia: Westminster Press, 1971.

Rosenberg, Rosalind. "The Conjunction of Race and Gender." *Journal of Women's History* 14, no. 2 (2002): 68–73.

Ross, Marlon B. "Pleasuring Identity, or the Delicious Politics of Belonging." *New Literary History* 31 (2000): 827–50.

Ruether, Rosemary Radford. *Sexism and God-Talk: Toward a Feminist Theology*. Boston: Beacon Press, 1983.

Rupp, Leila J., and Verta Taylor. "Lesbian Existence and the Women's Movement: Researching the 'Lavender Herring'." In *Feminism and Social Change: Bridging Theory and Practice*, ed. Heidi Gottfried, 143–59. Chicago: University of Illinois Press, 1996.

——— ———. "Pauli Murray: The Unasked Question." *Journal of Women's History* 14, no. 2 (2002): 83–87.

——— ———. *Survival in the Doldrums: The American Women's Rights Movement, 1945 to the 1960s*. New York: Oxford University Press, 1987.

Rushdy, Ashraf H.A. *Remembering Generations: Race and Family in Contemporary African American Fiction*. Chapel Hill: University of North Carolina Press, 2001.

Russell, Letty. *Human Liberation in a Feminist Perspective: A Theology*. Philadelphia: Westminster Press, 1974.

Scott, Anne Firor, ed. *Pauli Murray and Caroline Ware: Forty Years of Letters in Black and White*. Chapel Hill: University of North Carolina, 2006.

Sherman, Richard B. *The Case of Odell Waller and Virginia Justice, 1940–1942*. Knoxville: The University of Tennessee Press, 1992.

Shulman, George. "American Political Culture, Prophetic Narration, and Toni Morrison's *Beloved*." *Political Theory* 24, no. 2 (1996): 295–314.

Sitkoff, Harvard. "Racial Militancy and Interracial Violence in the Second World War." *The Journal of American History* 58, no. 3 (1971): 661–81.

Smith, Theophus H. *Conjuring Culture: Biblical Formations in Black America*. New York: Oxford University Press, 1994.

Springer, Kimberly. *Living for the Revolution: Black Feminist Organizations, 1968–1980*. Durham, NC: Duke University Press, 2005.

Taylor, Clarence. *Black Religious Intellectuals: The Fight for Equality from the Age of Jim Crow to the Dawn of the Twenty-First Century*. New York: Routledge, 2002.

Terrell, JoAnne. *Power in the Blood? The Cross in the African American Experience*. Maryknoll, NY: Orbis Books, 1998.

Terry, Jennifer. "Theorizing Deviant Historiography." *Differences: A Journal of Feminist Cultural Studies* 3, no. 2 (1991): 55–74.

Thomas, Linda E. "Womanist Theology, Epistemology, and a New Anthropological Paradigm." *Cross Currents* 48, no. 4 (1998/1999): 488–99.

Townes, Emilie. *Womanist Ethics and the Cultural Production of Evil*. New York: Palgrave MacMillan, 2006.

———. ed. *Embracing the Spirit: Womanist Perspectives on Hope, Salvation, and Transformation*. Maryknoll, NY: Orbis Books, 1997.

———. ed. *A Troubling in My Soul: Womanist Perspectives on Evil and Suffering*. Maryknoll, NY: Orbis Books, 1993.

Trinh, Minh-Ha T. *Woman, Native, Other: Writing Postcolonialism and Feminism*. Bloomington: Indiana University Press, 1989.

Tushnet, Mark V. *The NAACP's Legal Strategy against Segregated Education, 1925–1950*. Chapel Hill: The University of North Carolina Press, 1987.

Tyson, Timothy. *Robert F. Williams & The Roots of Black Power*. Chapel Hill: University of North Carolina Press, 1999.

Von Eschen, Penny. *Race Against Empire: Black Americans and Anticolonialism, 1937–1957*. Ithaca: Cornell University Press, 1997.

Warren, Kenneth W. "As White as Anybody': Race and the Politics of Counting as Black." *New Literary History* 31 (2000): 709–26.

Weisenfeld, Judith. *African American Women and Christian Activism: New York's Black YWCA, 1905–1945*. Cambridge: Harvard University Press, 1997.

West, Cornel. "Black Theology and Human Identity." In *Black Faith and Public Talk: Critical Essays on James H. Cone's Black Theology and Black Power*, ed. Dwight N. Hopkins, 11–19. Maryknoll, NY: Orbis Books, 1999.

———. *Democracy Matters: Winning the Fight against Imperialism*. New York: Penguin Books, 2004.

———. *Keeping Faith: Philosophy and Race in America*. New York: Routledge, 1993.

———. "The Moral Obligations of Living in a Democratic Society." In *The Good Citizen*, eds. David Batstone and Eduardo Mendieta, 11–19. New York: Routledge, 1999.

———. *Prophesy Deliverance! An Afro-American Revolutionary Christianity*. Philadelphia: Westminster Press, 1982.

———. *Race Matters*. Boston: Beacon Press, 1993.

West, Traci. "Is a Womanist a Black Feminist? Marking the Distinctions and Defying Them: A Black Feminist Response." In *Deeper Shades of Purple: Womanism in Religion and Society*, ed. Stacey Floyd Thomas, 291–96. New York: New York University Press, 2006.

White, E. Frances. *Dark Continent of Our Bodies: Black Feminism and the Politics of Respectability*. Philadelphia: Temple University Press, 2001.

White, Ronald C. *Liberty and Justice for All: Racial Reform and the Social Gospel (1877–1925)*. Louisville: John Knox Westminster Press, 2002.

Williams, Delores. *Sisters in the Wilderness: The Challenge of Womanist God-Talk*. Maryknoll, NY: Orbis Books, 1993.

Williams, Patricia J. *The Alchemy of Race and Rights: Diary of a Law Professor*. Cambridge: Harvard University Press, 1991.

Woodard Komozi. *A Nation Within A Nation: Amiri Baraka (LeRoi Jones) & Black Power Politics*. Chapel Hill: UNC Press, 1999.

Yancy, George, ed. *Cornel West: A Critical Reader*. Malden, MA: Blackwell, 2001.

INDEX